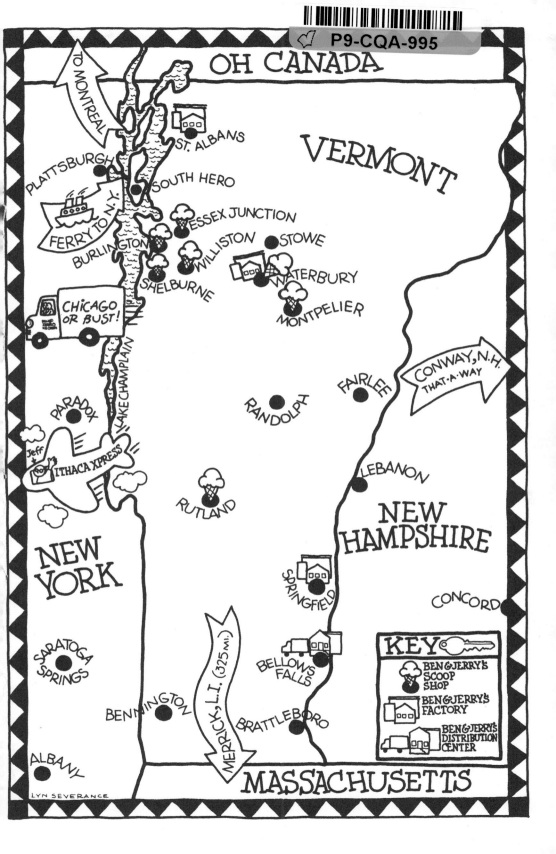

BEN &
JERRY'S:
THE INSIDE
SCOOP

BEN & JERRY'S: THE INSIDE SCOOP

How
Two Real Guys
Built a Business
with a
Social Conscience
and a
Sense of Humor

FRED "CHICO" LAGER

Crown Publishers, Inc.
New York

Published by Crown Publishers, Inc., 201 East 50th Street, New York, New York 10022. Member of the Crown Publishing Group.

Random House, Inc. New York, Toronto, London, Sydney, Auckland

CROWN is a trademark of Crown Publishers, Inc.

Manufactured in the United States of America

This book is printed on recycled paper.

Design by Jennifer Harper

Library of Congress Cataloging-in-Publication Data
Lager, Fred.
    Ben & Jerry's: the inside scoop : how two real guys built a
business with a social conscience and a sense of humor / by Fred
"Chico" Lager.
    1. Cohen, Ben (Ben R.).   2. Greenfield, Jerry.   3. Businessmen—
Vermont—Biography.   4. Ben & Jerry's (Firm)—History.   5. Ice
cream industry—Vermont.   6. Social responsibility of business—
Vermont.   I. Title.
HD9281.U53V558   1994
338.7′6374—dc20   93-39176
                                                              CIP

ISBN 0-517-59716-0

10 9 8 7 6 5 4 3 2 1

First Edition

For Yvette
Sine Qua Non

Contents

CONTENTS

Foreword

by Jerry Greenfield

From the moment Chico began voicing the idea of John Travolta playing him in the Ben & Jerry's movie, I knew there was going to be a problem. I'm sure there were earlier warning signals, but I guess I wasn't perceptive enough to catch them.

Ben and I have known Chico for years, and he's always had an innate sense about what elements make up a captivating story. The fact that he's been fascinated with several larger-than-life mythic figures, ranging from Mr. T to Mr. Clean, is something that I dismissed simply as Chico's quirkiness, rather than as a near total lack of judgment on his part.

So when Chico, soon after coming to work at Ben & Jerry's in 1982, started mentioning to Ben and me about his getting the movie rights to the Ben & Jerry's story, I didn't give it a second thought. Who, after all, would have the slightest interest in a movie about ice cream?

Little did I realize the master plan that was about to unfold. With Chico overseeing more and more operational areas within the company, he began making decisions based entirely on whether or not they would result in a good scene in the movie. He started to judge meetings not by what was accomplished, but by whether or not he got any good quotes for the screenplay.

So it's now clear to me that this book is all part of a calculated plan, and I, for one, refuse to be a part of it. I won't read it, nor will I be seeing the blockbuster movie, now breaking all records at theaters across the country, in which John Candy plays me, in a riveting and deeply moving portrayal of the brilliant yet troubled ice cream magnate.

Perhaps I'll catch it on video.

Enjoy.

Preface

In 1978, with a total investment of $12,000, Ben Cohen and Jerry Greenfield opened a homemade ice cream parlor in an abandoned gas station in Burlington, Vermont. From that humble beginning, Ben & Jerry's Homemade has grown into a $100 million publicly held company that is nationally recognized as one of the most innovative, progressive, and socially responsible businesses in the world. This book is the anecdotal story of how that happened.

In 1982, I was hired by Ben & Jerry's as the company's general manager, and became president and CEO in 1989. As both a member of the board of directors and the leader of the management group that was running the company day-to-day, I was in the unique position of participating in both sides of the debates that occurred as the company evolved from an entrepreneurial venture into a "professionally" managed business.

Other than its ice cream and yogurt, the company is perhaps best known for bringing "sixties values" to today's business world. The process of integrating those values into the organization during a period of rapid growth created conflict and setbacks with which the book attempts to deal openly. With hindsight, all of the participants agree that the tension, although frustrating and difficult at the time, contributed to an outcome of which all of us are extremely proud.

The idea that a company has obligations to stake-holding groups other than its shareholders is a relatively new one. As we grappled with the practical implications of that fundamental premise, there were few examples in the business world to follow and learn from. It's my hope that this book, by relating our company's experience, will be of assistance to the growing number of businesses that are now moving in that direction.

Although I talked extensively with many people in researching the book, the story is told through my eyes. As much as possible, I've attempted to give a broad perspective, but the reader is cautioned to recognize that the interpretation of the events can't help but be my own. As such, this book shouldn't taken as the company's definitive history, but only as one person's view of it.

Prologue
One from the Gipper

They arrived in Washington, D.C., on the morning of May 9, 1988, a beautiful warm and sunny day. A cab took them directly from the airport to the White House. After passing through security, they were escorted to the Rose Garden along with the winners from the other forty-nine states. The grounds were immaculate and the roses were in full bloom.

Jerry was wearing a dark blue suit, Ben an Italian waiter's jacket that he'd ordered out of a Banana Republic catalog for nineteen dollars. They both had ties on, exceptionally rare for two people who almost always wore T-shirts.

Their seats, they were told, were in the front row, which wasn't a complete surprise. Very early that morning, in their hotel room in Chicago, they'd received a phone call from someone at the Small Business Administration informing them that they were one of the four finalists for the national award. "Yeah, we'll be there," Ben reassured the nervous staffer. "We're flying in this morning." Both were more perturbed about being woken up prematurely than excited by the news the caller had conveyed.

When everyone was seated, President Reagan came out, followed by the Vice-President and some aides. "He had an incredible presence," Jerry recalls, "and he immediately took command of the situation."

"The record, quite simply, is incredible," the President said. "Small business provides well over two-thirds of all new jobs; about 40 percent of our aggregate national output; the bulk of new products and technologies; most of the jobs generated for younger, older and female workers; and over 66 percent of all 'first jobs.' " It was a very standard, small-business-is-the-backbone-of-the-economy stump speech, no different, they assumed, than the one he'd delivered the year before.

Toward the end of his prepared remarks, the President began to make references to the winner of the National Small Business Person of the Year Award. "Beginning with two employees in 1978, the company now employs two hundred, and the $8,000 in start-up money now generates annual sales of $30 million, selling to grocery stores in thirty-five states and in forty-five ice cream parlors around the country."

As the President spoke their names, Vice-President George Bush smiled at them, and Ben and Jerry looked at each other in astonished bemusement. Their company was about to introduce a product called "Peace Pops" as part of a campaign advocating massive reductions in the military budget. "Someone on the White House staff," they thought to themselves, "hasn't been doing his homework."

When Reagan finished speaking, he nodded in their direction, indicating that they should make their way up to the podium to receive their plaques. They hesitated slightly, stood up, and shuffled to the stage. On their way up, a man in a suit told them discreetly, "This is the President's show," making it clear that their role was to smile and shake hands, not make a speech. Maybe the White House staff had done their homework after all.

Up to this point, the entire ceremony had been completely choreographed and had come off without a hitch. The one unscripted part of the event was the actual presentation of the award. But the President, ever the Great Communicator, wasn't fazed in the least by having to improvise momentarily. "Which one is Jerry?" he asked with a smile.

CHAPTER ONE

The Quik Flick

Ben Cohen and Jerry Greenfield were the two slowest, chubbiest kids in their seventh-grade gym class, and they were lagging far behind the pack of runners up ahead on the gravelly oval track out behind Merrick Avenue Junior High School.

"Cohen, Greenfield," Coach Phelps yelled, "if you can't do the mile in under seven minutes, you're gonna have to do it again."

"But, Coach," Ben protested, "if we can't do it in less than seven minutes the first time, how are we gonna do it in under seven minutes the second time?"

It was then that Jerry realized this was someone he wanted to hang out with.

Merrick was part of the suburban sprawl on the south shore of Long Island, a mostly middle-class bedroom community filled with families whose breadwinners commuted to Manhattan on the Long Island Rail Road.

Ben lived in a ranch house on Millwood Lane, in what was considered North Merrick, with his dad, Irving, his mom, Frances, and his older sister, Alice.

Ben's father was an accountant, working at first for the State of New York, and then for a successful direct-mail business. His greatest contribution to Ben's future career occurred at conception, when he passed onto his son those genes that predispose an individual to eat copious amounts of ice cream at a single sitting. Irving, according to Ben, could polish off a half-gallon while sitting at the kitchen table after dinner.

Ben demonstrated his own fondness for eating at an early age, when he and his friend Fred Thaler created the Clean Plate Club for those kids at school who ate all their food. It got to the point where Ben and Fred, to demonstrate their commitment to the cause, were eating their straws and napkins.

Not surprisingly, Ben was fat as a kid and split his pants on more than one occasion in the school playground during recess. He wore dark-rimmed glasses, was lousy at sports, and didn't have a great deal of self-confidence. He took more than his share of abuse from bullies.

Ben was extremely bright, but he never applied himself to his schoolwork. Still, Ben had more than enough innate smarts to get by. He was valedictorian of his sixth-grade class at Old Mill Elementary School, and was also voted "most likely to succeed." Based on IQ testing, he was put into the advanced curriculum at junior high.

Jerry lived less than two miles from Ben, in a three-bedroom raised ranch house on West Loines Avenue, with his mom, Mildred, his dad, Malcolm, his older sister, Ronnie, and his younger brother, Geff.

Jerry went to what was unofficially known as Smith Street Elementary, three blocks from his house. Like Ben, Jerry was overweight enough to be called "Fatty," and relegated to shopping for clothes in the "husky" section at Robert Hall. Jerry wasn't an adventurous kid. He played a lot of sports in the schoolyard and hung out with a small circle of friends. He had a really good memory, and enough sense to pay attention in class and to study at home. He got really good grades, and he too was placed in the advanced curriculum for the seventh grade, where he would meet his future partner.

Jerry's first memory of Ben was the lesson in logic he gave the coach while running around the track. But in the eighth grade, Ben was transferred to a new junior high that had been built to relieve overcrowding at the Merrick Avenue school, and it wasn't until they both showed up at Calhoun High School, in the fall of 1966, that their friendship truly began.

Ben arrived at Calhoun relatively clean-cut, with short, blond, curly hair, thick glasses, and something of a baby face. He was still chubby, but at five feet ten inches he was relatively tall for his age, and his excess weight was not as noticeable as it had once been.

Ben had begun to run into problems academically in junior high, where, unlike elementary school, he could no longer get by without doing any homework. He was well-read, and he learned whatever caught his interest, but that rarely coincided with what was being taught in the classroom. He was perceived by some of his teachers as rebellious, but Ben preferred to think that he was simply intent on learning in his own way. While walking to school he would talk with his friends about having to turn over a new leaf and buckle down, but he never did.

Whatever enthusiasm Ben lacked for his schoolwork, he more than made up for in his interest in extracurricular activities. According to Fred Thaler, Ben had a tremendous amount of creativity and energy, and would focus so intensely on whatever project he was involved in that he was totally oblivious of what was going on around him. He excelled at debate, played the cello in the orchestra (great vibrato, lousy intonation), was on the student council, and edited the school's yearbook.

Ben was an independent spirit who was motivated only in the things he wanted to do. If it was something that he initiated or created, he was behind it one hundred percent. If it was imposed on him by others, he was totally uninterested.

When Jerry joined Ben at Calhoun, he had still not found the secret to losing weight. A self-described nerd, Jerry had short brown hair, wore glasses, and was of average height. According to Jeff Durstewitz, a close friend, "Socially, Jerry was a cipher. Academically, he was a wiz." Applying himself diligently to his schoolwork, he got ninety-eights, ninety-nines, and one hundreds on everything and emerged as one of the smartest kids at the school, ranking third in his class of over six hundred.

After school and on weekends, they hung out with a small, tight-knit group. They were typical suburban kids who cruised the neighborhood in their father's cars, went to Jones Beach, and sat around Sam & Tony's pizza parlor in the A&P shopping center. The summer prior to their senior year, they both worked for Ben's father's business, sorting direct-mail pieces by Zip Code.

For both boys, there was no question but that college would follow high school. Ben was not very interested in academics, but beyond parental expectations, there were two strong incentives—to get out of the house and out of the war. In 1969, with America deeply enmeshed in Vietnam, an eighteen-year-old male without a college deferment was all but assured of doing time in the paddies.

Ambivalent as he was about furthering his education, Ben applied to only one school, Colgate University, in Hamilton, New York. He chose the school not for its academic reputation, but after reading in the catalog that there were fireplaces in the dorms, which for some reason appealed to him. His father and his sister filled out the application and wrote the answers to the essay questions for him. He was shocked when he got in on early admissions.

Colgate was a very traditional school, and Ben's reaction to the highly structured collegiate atmosphere was predictable. He had no interest in what they were trying to teach him, or in the method they were using, which he found to be just like high school. His grades were poor.

During his freshman year, Ben worked for the college food service in the dish room at one of the dining halls. His primary job was to scrape the excess food off the plates into the "pig," the huge food-disposal unit, and to rack the dishes for the automatic washer. It was a natural position for the former founder of the Old Mill School Clean Plate Club.

Aside from a few errant plates going down the disposal ("It made a really great noise"), all was fine on the job site until Ben rankled the authorities by growing a beard, which put him at odds with Mrs. Castranova, the director of Colgate's food service. Concerned that some facial hair might fall into the pig, she ordered Ben to shave, but he refused, whereupon Mrs. Castranova fired him. Undaunted, Ben shaved a thin strip down the middle of his chin, turning the beard into two rather bushy sideburns. Mrs. Castranova was not amused, at least not publicly, and Ben remained unemployed. He appealed his dismissal to a board of administrators, faculty, and students, and Mrs. Castranova was forced to offer him his old job back. But having made his point, Ben had lost interest in shoving food scraps into the pig. In fact, he was losing interest in going through the motions at Colgate.

Meanwhile, Jerry was in Ohio, at Oberlin College. Despite having won a National Merit Scholarship, Jerry had been rejected at all the Ivy League schools he applied to, and had wound up at his "safe" school, Oberlin.

Oberlin had a reputation as a progressive school, and it attracted a lot of free thinkers, eccentrics, social misfits, and smart kids who didn't quite fit in during high school. The self-contained campus was a very friendly environment that didn't require advanced social skills, and Jerry felt very comfortable there. He made a smooth academic transition to college, coming home with a 3.8 grade-point average his first year.

In the summer between their freshman and sophomore years,

4

Jerry and Ben returned to Merrick. Ben took to the streets selling ice cream out of a Pied Piper truck with Fred Thaler, while Jerry parked cars at a local beach club.

The most notable event that summer was the day they got their draft numbers. Deferments were in the process of being phased out, and the draft lottery was intended to address the inequities of a selective service system that for the most part had excluded wealthy, smart kids who could afford to go to college. Jerry and Ben met with their cohorts that night, and consumed a watermelon that had been primed with a bottle of vodka. Everyone had agreed not to look up their numbers until they were all together. Jerry drew double digits, under 50, and was presented with a Vietnamese cookbook. Ben was in the high 300s. For Ben the lottery was a liberating experience. The high number meant that he was safe from the draft, and what made it even sweeter was that he no longer had to put up with the pretense of going to college to avoid military service.

While waiting for his ice cream truck to get loaded one morning, Ben talked with one of the mechanics at Pied Piper about the idea of dropping out of school.

"Why you wanna drop out of college? It'll be good for you," the mechanic said.

"I don't like it," Ben answered.

"Ahhh, you stick your hands in shit, you wash it off," the mechanic reasoned. Advice to live by. Ben was ready for the next pile of dung.

Ben returned to Colgate for the first semester of his sophomore year, and then left in January for a one-month independent study that was part of the 4–1–4 Colgate curriculum. He spent the month hitchhiking to and around California, and when the second semester started in February, Ben was still on the West Coast, with no intentions of going back to Hamilton.

Ben's stay in California was brief. His first thought was to get a job as an ice cream man, capitalizing on the only marketable skill he had. Undecided about which to find first, a job or a place to live, he put off making any decisions and quickly ran out of money. Feeling "the loneliest I had ever felt," he decided to hitchhike back to the closest person he knew. One week later he was camped out on the floor in Jerry's room at Oberlin.

After about a month on Jerry's floor, some of it gainfully employed selling subs in the dorms, Ben hitchhiked back to Long Island for another season with Pied Piper. Instead of driving the truck, he took a promotion and worked in the freezers as a box man, keeping track of the inventory, loading and unloading trucks.

In the fall of 1971, Ben went back to upstate New York, this time to Saratoga Springs, where he enrolled at Skidmore College as an exchange student from Colgate. Ben had a strong desire to work with his hands, dating back to the summer he had spent at Buck's Rock Work Camp when he was fifteen. The camp had been totally unstructured, and had allowed the kids to choose whatever activities they wanted to participate in. Ben had focused on crafts. He remembered Buck's Rock as the only educational environment that he had ever found nurturing. At Skidmore he took classes in film appreciation, jewelry, pottery, and three-dimensional design; this last class was an introductory course in sculpture, which he failed. "I was motivated to work really hard in the course," Ben recalls, "but in a different direction than the teacher."

Despite failing the one course, Ben thrived on his education for the first time since Buck's Rock. Unfortunately, since he had dropped out of Colgate, he couldn't really be an exchange student at Skidmore. When he went to sign up for a second set of courses, he was turned away.

His request to sit in on classes without registering (or paying) received a predictable response from his professors. Just when it looked as though he was out of options, a new program called the University Without Walls was created at Skidmore. It allowed him to take pottery courses at the school without being a fully registered student, and most important of all, it offered an easy payment plan.

While taking courses at Skidmore, Ben paid his bills by working at an assortment of jobs, including two as a night mopper, first at Jamesway, a local department store, and then at Friendly's, where he'd make ice cream sundaes for himself during his shifts. Night mopper was one of those positions that they never really tested you on to see if you could do the job before they hired you, which was too bad, because it was the one job that college had prepared Ben for. Mrs. Castranova knew how to mop, and she had taught Ben well. "You've got to wet-mop and then dry-mop," Ben explains. "First you put down the water, laying it on pretty liberally, about an eighth of an inch or so. You don't wring out the mop, you just swish it around. You want the dirt to bubble up by osmosis, and then you pick it up with the dry mop." Despite his flawless technique and, one would imagine, opportunity for advancement, he quit both jobs.

After a year at Skidmore, Ben came to the conclusion that, to further his pottery career, he needed to be exposed to different teachers and new influences. At the end of 1972 he moved to New York City, where he got an apartment on East Tenth Street in Greenwich Village.

Ben spent most of his time working a string of menial jobs to earn enough money to pay the rent. He worked the night shift at Bellevue hospital, admitting patients from 11:00 P.M. until 7:00 A.M., and worked an internship at the psychiatric ward of Jacobi Hospital in the Bronx. For a while he delivered pottery wheels to other potters, but he spent little time working on his own stuff. At one point he applied for a job working at a halfway house for emotionally disturbed kids in Staten Island, but they gave him the Minnesota Multiphasic Personality Inventory, and the test results indicated that he had "unresolved conflicts with authority." He eventually wound up driving a cab.

Compared to Ben's college career, Jerry's was reasonably uneventful. Jerry was a premed major, having concluded that was something you considered doing if you were good in math and science.

Although he had started out strong academically, his grades got progressively worse each semester as he began to take on more extracurricular activities. Jerry also began to get involved in sports, moving from intramural basketball to varsity lacrosse in his junior year. At five feet ten inches and 180 pounds, he was in great shape, and had finally shed the extra weight of his youth.

Jerry considered himself to be a good, if run-of-the-mill, candidate for medical school. He had finished up with a respectable 3.2 average, had done well on his medical boards, and had excellent recommendations. But there was really nothing to distinguish him from the field of other applicants, and he was rejected by every school he applied to.

Never having been fully committed to a career in medicine ("I didn't really want to be a doctor, I wanted to get into medical school"), it didn't take Jerry too long to overcome the initial sense of rejection. He graduated in May of 1973, moved into Ben's apartment in New York, and took a job as a lab technician at the city's Public Health Research Institute, where his job was to run experiments on mitochondria that he had extracted from ground-up beef hearts. At the same time, he took a biochemistry class at NYU Medical School, in hopes of improving his academic record. He reapplied to medical schools in the spring of 1974, but was once again turned down everywhere.

Shortly after Jerry moved in, two more friends from Merrick, Jeff Durstewitz and Vinny Vito, took up residence in the tiny, three-bedroom apartment. Between his assorted jobs, most of which were at night, and a girlfriend who lived in Brooklyn, Ben was rarely in the apartment at the same time as his roommates. The one way they would know Ben had been there was that he invariably left pieces of French bread and butter in various stages of preparation throughout the apartment. At the time, Ben was convinced that one could subsist on a diet of nothing but French bread and butter. He would often toast the bread, cutting off a hunk and shoving it in the apartment's two-slicer. Unfortunately, the toaster was quite old, and it no longer popped the toast or shut off automatically. Ben was doing so many things that it wasn't unusual for him to rush in, start to make himself some toast, forget about it, and run out again while the toast charred. It was the first hint Jerry had that Ben's sense of taste and smell was really deficient, an inexplicable handicap of birth. It was a discovery that would have major implications in the future.

By the summer of 1974, the pace of the city was taking its toll on Ben, and he was more often than not found with an aspirin bottle in hand. One day, while driving the cab, he reached under the seat and found something left by a previous driver—a club for fighting off would-be muggers. He decided that it was time to go. In the Sunday *New York Times*, he spotted a help-wanted ad for a crafts teacher at a private school in the Adirondacks. It seemed like a perfect opportunity. A chance to live in a rural setting, do crafts, and work with kids in an unstructured environment that was everything his own education hadn't been. Ben responded to the ad and was hired in the fall of 1974.

Highland Community was an alternative residential school for emotionally troubled teenagers. It was located on a six-hundred-acre working farm outside of Paradox, New York, which was about one hundred miles due north of Albany. The "campus" consisted of A-frames, geodesic domes, and an assortment of cabins that some of the staff had built for themselves in the woods. Most of the twenty-five students were under court order to be at the school. They covered the full range of incorrigibility. Some had drug problems, some were juvenile delinquents, and some were schizophrenic.

Ben started off teaching crafts and photography, and supervising the yearbook. He eventually set up a pottery studio, building the kiln, pottery wheels, tables, and benches himself.

The school was nontraditional, and its director, Naomi Tannen, was extremely open minded. There was some classroom learning, but within broad parameters, the staff was encouraged to engage the kids however they saw fit. This was perfect for Ben, who became an important creative presence at the school. According to Naomi, Ben had a wonderful sense of celebration, and he was always coming up with activities that helped the kids look at life a little differently. He organized the winter carnivals, which featured snow-sculpture contests and snow tug-of-wars, the school's baseball teams, and staff talent shows.

Ben also made a couple of films at Highland, utilizing an eight-millimeter camera that he had found lying around the school. Although he had never done a film before, he learned the basics from a "How to Shoot a Movie" paperback, and wrote out the screenplay with the ten kids who had signed up for the four-month project. The first film was "The Quik Flick," a whodunit that told the story of how everybody at the school had become addicted to Nestlé's Quik. They were using it for everything—brushing their teeth with it, using it for deodorant, showering with it, smoking it, and shooting it up. And then someone started stealing all the Quik. The kids were going into withdrawal, everyone had the shakes, and it was a horrible situation. Before long, someone was ringing the big bell on campus, and all the students and staff had come together for a marathon meeting that nobody could leave until they found out what was going on. The meeting went on day and night until finally the school dog, Panda, a huge black Newfoundland, walked into the meeting with an empty Quik container tied around her neck. When Panda took off, everyone followed in a wild chase across the campus that ended up at Ben's cabin. As the camera panned to the inside of the cabin, which was filled with empty cans, Ben emerged, covered with Quik. Lest any of the students get the idea that crime does indeed pay, or that drug addiction isn't the ruination of life, in the final scene, Ben was crucified. Filmmaking, religious studies, and morality lessons all rolled into one. Showing "The Quik Flick" became a regular event at Highland, until the night they ran it without the take-up reel into a just-emptied bowl of popcorn.

If there was one aspect of Highland that Ben didn't like, it was the large number of staff meetings. Ben was always better working one-on-one than in big groups, preferring to do things his own way without discussing it with everyone else.

It was at one of the staff meetings that the fate of Malcolm, Ben's dog, was decided. Reflecting his personal views on authority, Ben set no limits for Malcolm, and he was given free run of the campus. When the chickens on the farm started to disappear, Malcolm stood accused. In the face of what Ben maintains was "strictly circumstantial evidence," the staff voted that Malcolm should be chained up, but Ben didn't have the heart to do it, and instead shipped him to Fred Thaler's house in Maine.

At the end of 1976, Highland ran into legal problems with the State of New York after a bureaucrat determined that the buildings didn't meet code. They actually met the code for group homes, but because Highland was a school, it fell under stricter guidelines. As one staff member pointed out, that meant the buildings were unsafe, but only because they were teaching math in them. Although they eventually prevailed on appeal, the fight took the energy and heart out of the staff, and it became clear by January of 1977 that the current semester would be the last.

Ben had little interest in going back to work for somebody else. While he was at Highland, he had tried to sell some of his pottery at craft shows, but the results had been dismal, and it was pretty clear that he couldn't support himself that way. He started to think about opening up some other kind of business, and he decided to talk about the idea with Jerry.

Jerry had stayed in New York after Ben had gone up to Paradox, moving in with a friend on the Upper West Side. In January of 1975 he met his future wife, Elizabeth Skarie, a student at Cornell University's nursing school, which was based in the city. When Elizabeth graduated in the spring, she got a job and moved to Chapel Hill, North Carolina, and invited Jerry to come along. He moved into her apartment, and let Elizabeth support him for the next nine months. When he eventually got tired of hanging out on the University of North Carolina campus, he got another job as a lab technician, this time at the UNC Hospital. The research was gruesome enough to make him long for the days when he had ground up beef hearts. This time he worked with rats. After being subjected to some sort of stress, they were sacrificed by way of a guillotine. Their heads would fall off into a Thermos of liquid nitrogen, where they would freeze instantly.

Jerry would then take the heads into a cold room and chip out the brain with a chisel in order to run experiments on the tissue.

In January of 1977, Jerry got temporarily ditched by Elizabeth, which left him little incentive to stay in North Carolina. He was more than receptive to the idea of going into business with Ben, and in May he loaded up his car with all his possessions and headed north.

CHAPTER TWO

Jer & Benny's?

ith the exception of buying a big rig and becoming cross-country truck drivers, most of Jerry and Ben's ideas for a business involved food. They both liked to eat, so it seemed like a logical career move.

After carefully considering a full range of possibilities, they whittled the list down to a couple of options. Their first choice was a business they were going to name UBS, for United Bagel Service, which would deliver fresh bagels every Sunday morning, along with lox, cream cheese, and *The New York Times*. They hadn't figured out what to do the other six days of the week, but before they could resolve that issue, they went to a restaurant supply house, priced out the ovens and other equipment for making bagels at around forty grand, and realized they'd need to find a foodstuff that was a little less capital-intensive.

They never actually priced out the equipment for making ice cream, which was their second choice. They assumed it had to be cheaper than making bagels, and decided not to find out if that wasn't the case. They researched their new venture by visiting homemade ice cream shops, and split the tuition on a five-dollar correspondence course in ice cream making that was offered by Penn State University.

They were intent on finding a rural community with a large college population and a warm climate so they could sell a lot of ice cream. To identify the possibilities, they did what they've come to describe as a "manual cross-correlation analysis," putting a U.S. almanac on one side of the table and a guide to American colleges on the other. They generated a list of about ten towns that met the criteria, but quickly discovered that most of them already had a homemade ice cream shop.

They eventually decided on Saratoga Springs, the town Ben had lived in for about a year when he went to Skidmore College. It wasn't as warm as they had hoped for, but it had a race track and a strong summer tourist business. And it didn't have a homemade ice cream parlor. They moved to Saratoga in May of 1977, and found a great apartment right on Saratoga Lake.

Jerry and Ben had agreed that they would each invest $4,000 in their new venture. Jerry had accumulated his stake since graduating from college. Ben was quite a bit short. He decided to get a job in the local food-service industry, which would let him accumulate the cash he needed and garner some much-needed firsthand business experience at the same time.

His first job was as a baker's assistant at Mrs. London's, one of Saratoga's most famous eateries. He got fired after about six weeks for prepping a batch of roll batter that had too much salt, and for his inability to keep the whites of the eggs from oozing all over the counter when he separated the yolks. He fared no better at Ann's Coffee Park Diner, where he got into a dispute with Ann over the adequacy of the lighting in the kitchen.

While Ben was working, Jerry hung out at the apartment and began looking for a location for the shop. On weekends they would take road trips to try to scour up used restaurant equipment at auctions. In his enthusiasm, Ben would sometimes lose track and bid against himself.

On one of the road trips they came upon a Lightning sailboat in someone's garage, with a For Sale sign on it. It wasn't on their required equipment list and Ben wasn't even close to having his $4,000 grubstake, but at $2,000, complete with trailer, it seemed to him like too good a deal to pass up, especially since they were living on the lake. Neither had sailed before, but that wasn't much of a concern. Whenever they took the boat out, Ben would read the instructions in the owner's manual out loud, and they would toss Chee-tos in the water to measure how fast they were moving.

Jerry and Ben were having a great summer in Saratoga, and their business venture seemed to be progressing, if not rapidly, then at least in an orderly manner. One can only imagine their dismay when another homemade ice cream shop opened up in Saratoga in August. They quickly came to the conclusion that the competition was probably better capitalized than they were, and had to know a little bit more about what it was doing. Discouraged, they began searching for a new location.

This time they settled on Burlington, Vermont, a town that Ben had become familiar with while teaching at Highland. The city proper had a population of 40,000, but more than 100,000 people, approximately 20 percent of the state's entire population, lived within a ten-mile radius of downtown. In addition, there were more than 12,000 students at the University of Vermont and three other smaller colleges. Burlington, only forty miles south of the Canadian border, was by far the coldest college town they had yet to consider, which was why it hadn't been on their original list. But the cold weather probably also accounted for the lack of competition. Vermont was the only state that didn't have a Baskin-Robbins franchise.

In downtown Burlington, two shops sold ice cream. Sewards, a dairy based in Rutland, Vermont, operated a coffee shop/ice cream operation that was connected to the bus station. It was hard to tell where the bus station ended and Sewards began, and Ben and Jerry were sure they could make better ice cream. The other shop was more of a pinball arcade, and it sold a nondescript, commercial line of ice cream. Neither seemed to present the kind of formidable competition that would prevent them from carving out their niche in the market.

They rented a house on West Shore Road in South Hero, a town located on an island in the northern part of Lake Champlain, about thirty minutes from downtown Burlington.

Jerry and Ben were settled in their new home by late September, and they once again started looking for a storefront to rent. At the same time they began to work on the business plan that they'd need to secure a bank loan.

To help them put together their loan proposal, they enlisted the services of Jeff Furman. Jeff was a short, wiry guy who, at thirty-four, already had a considerable amount of gray in his long, thinning hair and his free-flowing beard. He had degrees in law and accounting, but he didn't practice either. Ben had met Jeff by way of Highland, where he had been the bus driver before Ben arrived. Jeff had remained in touch with the school, returning briefly as its administrator. He eventually wound up in Ithaca, New York, working as a consultant to small businesses.

Jeff came up with a copy of a business plan that a pizza parlor in New York had used, and suggested that Jerry and Ben change the word "slices" to "cones," and use it as the model for what they were going to submit.

If they were to have any chance at all of getting the loan, it was clear that the business plan was going to have to be convincing. "We didn't have a whole lot going for us," Jerry admits. "We had no assets or collateral to speak of. We were new to the area. We were young. We weren't married. And we had no business experience."

An initial conversation with Fred Burgess, a local banker, convinced them that in order for their shop to survive the winters in Vermont, they'd need to offer something other than frozen desserts. After going through some cookbooks, they settled on soups and crepes, which they thought would be a natural complement to the ice cream. In the business plan, they pointed out that "almost every nationality has developed its own version of a thin, filled pancake—the Hungarian palascinta, the Mexican enchilada, the Jewish blintz, Italian cannelone, Russian blini, Scandinavian platar, Greek krep, and others." It wasn't clear what this gastro-geography lesson meant in terms of potential food sales in Burlington, Vermont, but Jerry and Ben were obviously well-read on the subject.

Not satisfied with having done exhaustive historical research into the new product line, Ben dragged Jerry and a friend, Lyn Severance, up to Montréal for "Crepes Research Day." Ben was intent on finding out how crepes were made in a French-speaking city, and how big their griddles were. "I remember going into a very fancy crepe restaurant, and right away Ben pulled out his tape measure," says Lyn.

Originally, Ben wanted to call the business "Josephine's Flying Machine," after a song he'd learned as a kid. Jerry wasn't too crazy about the name, and argued that homemade ice cream parlors were traditionally named after the proprietors. "It reinforces the concept," Jerry argued. Whose name to put first was debated back and forth. They settled on Ben & Jerry's because it had a better ring to it. "Things that end in e sound better, which is why people put e's on the end of things that don't end in e," Ben explains logically. "Fran becomes Franny, Fred becomes Freddie. It could have been Jer and Benny's. We didn't consider that at the time, because my mother would never allow me to be called Benny."

The business plan started out by describing the menu and the decor. "Ben & Jerry's is an Ice Cream and Crepe Parlor featuring homemade ice cream, frozen yogurt, sundaes, and fountain drinks, as well as main dish and dessert crepes. . . . Ben & Jerry's will be appealing to people who appreciate high quality, good tasting and nutritious food in a warm, friendly atmosphere."

The plan went on to cite government statistics that predicted an ever-increasing percentage of food dollars being spent away from the home and a national trend toward more specialized eating establishments. "These facts bode good tidings for Ben & Jerry's," they concluded.

The loan proposal included a list of all the items they intended to offer, with the cost of goods sold calculated both in dollars and as a percentage of sales. A one-scoop cone would sell for forty-two cents, two scoops for seventy-one. They actually had no idea how much it was going to cost them to make anything. Having guessed at a reasonable selling price, they worked backwards, applying a targeted cost of goods sold of 40 percent. So it wouldn't look as though they had plugged in the numbers more or less arbitrarily, which is exactly what they'd done, they put some items in at a few points over 40 percent and some a few points under.

In an attempt to make them seem as credible as possible, the backgrounds of the two would-be entrepreneurs were sanitized and expounded upon as needed. ("Mr. Cohen has held various other jobs in the food-service industry. . . .") Their personal financial statements were somewhat less inspiring. Jerry listed assets of $8,000 in cash and a 1970 four-door Volvo worth $1,400. Ben had $4,000 in cash, a '69 semi-camper Ford van, the sailboat, and a quadrophonic stereo. He also listed unemployment insurance payments of ninety-five dollars per week as a source of income.

The $4,000 in cash that Ben listed wasn't actually all his, free and clear. His investment in the sailboat had been too big and too recent a setback to his cash position, and he was forced to turn to his father for half of the money. His father, pleased that his son was getting out of crafts, was happy to make the loan. "He saw this as a transition from my being a hippie to becoming a businessman," Ben recalls.

At the end of the plan were the projections: first-year sales of $90,000, and a pre-tax net profit of $7,746. When the first set of numbers didn't come out right, they changed them. "Who knew how often how many people would come to our store and buy how much ice cream?" Jerry acknowledges. "We probably thought it was a stretch at the time."

When the plan was finished in mid-October, it was typed and stuck into a nice-looking binder. The boys combed their hair, put on coats and ties, and headed back to the Merchants Bank to see Fred Burgess. The plan called for a $20,000 loan, bringing the total investment in the business to $28,000. Fred was impressed by the plan, and by the fact that they had taken a course at Penn State in ice cream making. At the time, he didn't know it was a mail-order thing. Fred thought that young people with ideas, energy, and some intelligence deserved a chance to prove themselves, and he was ready to do the deal if he could get the Small Business Administration to guarantee it. He sent the application to the SBA office, and it came back approved, contingent on only one thing—that they find a "suitable location."

Their first choice was an old drugstore that had a beautiful soda fountain with a marble counter top and a row of upholstered, floor-mounted, chrome-based stools. It had been vacant for years, and the original equipment hadn't been touched. It would have been a great location, but the estate that controlled the building was in probate, and there was no way to rent the space until things were sorted out by the courts.

Their second choice was an abandoned gas station on the corner of St. Paul and College Streets. It was across the street from City Hall park, one block removed from Church Street, the city's retail center. It had been years since it had actually been used as a gas station, and the pumps were long gone. More recently it had been a plant store and a farmers' market.

The only problem with the gas station was that they couldn't get more than a one-year lease, and without a longer term, the SBA wasn't willing to do the deal. Fred informed them of the news, but, as a consolation, offered to loan them $4,000 collateralized by the equipment they were buying.

They were faced with the choice of trying to find another location and salvaging the original loan proposal, or sticking with the gas station and scraping by on less than half the money they figured they needed. By this point they were convinced that the gas station was the perfect location, and they were anxious to get the business up and running. They decided to take the $4,000 from Burgess.

With the loan approved, the two boyhood friends formalized their business relationship. Ben & Jerry's Homemade, Inc., was incorporated and registered with the Vermont Secretary of State on December 17, 1977. Jerry was given the title of president because they had put Ben first when they had named the business.

They were scheduled to start renovating the gas station in February, with the intention of being open for business by May 1978. To kill time between Thanksgiving and Christmas, they opened a little hot-drink stand in the basement of Bennington Potters North, a crafts and housewares store two doors down from the gas station.

To amuse themselves and the customers, they kept a jigsaw puzzle and a couple of games at the stand, such as Shoot the Moon and Labyrinth. If you put five pieces in the puzzle, or were particularly adept at one of the other games, you got a free drink or cookie. Most of the customers wound up paying for about half of what they ate.

The gas station was the embodiment of funk—which, like pornography, is hard to define, but easy to recognize when it's staring you right in the face. It had been built in the 1940s, and the exterior walls were covered by a white baked-enamel aluminum skin that was sectioned off into large, two-foot squares, giving the station an almost igloo-like appearance. The roof was flat, and the right front corner of the building was curved in a wide, sweeping arc that visually softened the impact of the structure as it protruded into the lot.

There was no heat in the building, and a three-to-four-inch layer of ice covered the floor when they took possession in February of 1978. The ceiling in the bays had been insulated with batts of fiberglass and covered with plastic, but never drywalled. The insulation was soaked and the plastic had bagged down with water that had seeped through the roof. Junk was strewn everywhere.

To supplement their limited construction skills, they enlisted the help of Darrell Mullis, a former houseparent at the Highland Community who was now working for a local building contractor. When Ben & Jerry's was incorporated, and they needed to name a third member for their board of directors, Jerry and Ben had chosen Darrell, one of the few people they knew in the Burlington area.

There was no money to pay Darrell, so, in exchange for his services, he became the charter member of the "Ice Cream for Life Club," which guaranteed him an unlimited supply of product for as long as Ben and Jerry managed to stay in business.

They had rented only one of the two service bays and the office area, so they framed up a stud wall to delineate their space. A local farmer, who had sold produce in front of the gas station the previous summer, remained as the building's other tenant.

The bay was renovated into the kitchen and serving area. The front counter was set back enough from the overhead door so that the customers would have room to congregate. Behind the counter were the dip cases, and behind them a stove, the crepe griddle, and two homemade work tables that they had built out of green, rough-cut lumber purchased directly from the mill. "It was the cheapest wood we could get because it hadn't dried out yet," Ben recalls. "We would nail it and it would squirt at us."

Looming large behind the stove was a six-foot-wide, antique oak refrigerator cabinet. Tucked behind it were the sinks. They couldn't afford the standard, stainless-steel three-bay sink that was required by the health department, so they bolted three fiberglass laundry tubs together.

Without the SBA loan, they were forced to eliminate a lot of the equipment that had been on their original list. They never would have made it except for an auction in Gorham, New Hampshire, that almost no one else showed up for, at which they picked up five or six major pieces of equipment. The only new thing in the shop was a chef's knife, a thirty-five-dollar item that they purchased only after comparison-shopping for the better part of an afternoon.

The gas-station office was renovated into the customer seating area. One of the cinder-block walls in the office was covered with boards hung diagonally. It was their "fancy wall," and one of the few things that was strictly for aesthetics.

To help with the plumbing, they had hired Lanny Watts, Burlington's alternative, hippie plumber. Lanny didn't advertise, and wasn't even listed in the Yellow Pages. He got work by word of mouth, and his name had been passed along to Ben and Jerry as someone who could work on a tight budget. Lanny plumbed in all the kitchen equipment and got the toilets working again. Rather than rip a broken urinal off the wall, a job that looked as though it could lead into a bunch of other work, he covered it up with a plywood box.

Lanny was working for his regular hourly rate and charging for materials. At some point on the job, however, he lost track of how much stuff he'd brought onto the job site, and rather than crawl around the gas station measuring copper pipe and counting up the fittings, he asked Jerry if it would be okay to ballpark it. Jerry thought it over, mentioned that they were a little tight on cash, and counter-offered with the same deal they had given Darrell, free ice cream for life. Lanny seemed interested, but wanted to clarify the offer.

"Well, does this cover your franchises?" he asked. By this point, Ben had joined Jerry in the negotiations, and they were clearly amused by Lanny's foresight. Neither Ben nor Jerry had ever entertained the notion that their business might someday grow beyond the four walls of the gas station.

"Sure, Lanny, it includes our franchises," Jerry answered.

"Well, I'm not just talking about your Vermont franchises now, I'm talking about all the franchises, coast to coast," he said, completely serious.

So here were Ben and Jerry, in the midst of the rubble that was being transformed into what they fully expected to be their first and only outlet, trading the promise of free ice cream from a nationwide chain of stores that existed only in their plumber's mind, for a couple of hundred feet of copper pipe.

"Sure, Lanny, coast to coast. No problemo."

They worked incredibly long days on the renovations, starting first thing in the morning, and going long into the night. When they couldn't stand the cold anymore, they took a break at the bus station down the street, where they'd warm up and use the bathrooms. They were trying to conserve all their cash, living on saltine crackers and tins of sardines that they got at Woolworth's, three for a buck.

By the time they got home, they would fall into bed, only to wake up exhausted in a freezing cold house. The house, which was really a summer cottage, wasn't insulated, and the wind would whip up off the lake and blow right through the walls. Eventually they stopped driving home at night and started sleeping in the gas station. Ben slept on top of the chest freezer in the back room; Jerry was out front on a cot that he'd bought at the army-navy store.

When the weather warmed up, and the ice and snow melted, they turned their attention to the roof. It was really in need of being completely redone professionally, but they obviously didn't have the money for that. Instead, Ben patched it with a generous amount of roofing tar and scrap aluminum sheets that he picked up at the *Burlington Free Press* for thirty-five cents each.

At the same time they were renovating the gas station, they were, in Jerry's words, "figuring out how to make ice cream unencumbered by experience." After taking the Penn State correspondence course, they picked up the definitive industry textbook, *Ice Cream*, by Wendell S. Arbuckle. Jerry, relying on his biochemistry background, would read the book with a calculator in hand, trying to work out the formula for their base ingredients, known as the ice cream "mix." Their mix consisted of cream, milk, cane sugar, egg yolks, and a natural stabilizer to help improve the product's texture. In each instance, they chose the highest quality ingredient available to them. "Our original concept for the store was 'Ice Cream for the People,'" Jerry recalls. "We wanted to make the best ice cream available and sell it at a price that everyone could afford."

They had a small electric rock salt and ice freezer, and Jerry was making test batches at home all the time. The freezer was incredibly noisy, and it leaked, so they put it in the bathtub and shut the door. In the winter months they were getting the ice for the freezer right off Lake Champlain, sending their dinner guests out to the shoreline with a hatchet. Most of the ice cream came out fine. The most notable exception was a batch of rum raisin that all but bounced. "It was overstabilized by a factor of ten," Jerry reckons. "Very, very stretchy."

They were getting close to finishing the renovations, and still hadn't found the freezer in which they were going to make the ice cream at the store. They couldn't afford to buy a new one, so they'd been placing classified ads in a bunch of antique magazines and *The New York Times*. With less than a month to go, Mark Mumford, aka Mumpo, a friend from Highland who was living in Boston, spotted an ad in the *Globe* for a secondhand freezer. He called Jerry and Ben and they drove down to Massachusetts and picked it up for around $1,200, less than half the cost of a new one. At the same time they picked up Mumpo, who moved in with the boys at South Hero, and helped with the final month of renovations.

The four-and-a-half-gallon White Mountain rock-salt and ice freezer that they brought back to Vermont in Ben's van was essentially a large-scale, motorized version of the old-fashioned hand-cranked models in use since the nineteenth century. A stainless-steel cylinder would be filled with the mix, and then extracts or fruits would be added, depending on what flavor was being made. The cylinder sat inside a wooden tub that contained ice and salt, which acted as the refrigerant. Inside the cylinder was a blade, called a dasher, that would turn round and round and scrape a fine layer of frozen ice cream off of the inside wall of the barrel as the mix dropped in temperature.

As the dasher turned, air would be incorporated into the mix. The amount of air in ice cream is known as "overrun." A commercial ice cream might have an overrun as high as 100 percent, which means that one gallon of mix gets whipped into two gallons of ice cream. The finished product will be pretty light, because half of it is air. A really good homemade ice cream has an overrun of between 20 and 40 percent, and pint for pint, or gallon for gallon, it weighs quite a bit more than the commercial products because it has a lot less air in it.

It was hard to control how much air got whipped into the ice cream on the rock-salt freezer, but it was largely dependent on how fast the dasher was turning. One of the research projects that Jerry and Ben had done on their road trips was to surreptitiously count the revolutions per minute on the ice cream freezers at other homemade scoop shops. If twenty per minute worked for Steve's in Cambridge, they figured that twenty per minute would work for them. They had a local tool-and-die man build a gear-reduction setup that slowed the machine down to where they wanted it to be.

After thirty minutes or so, the mix in the barrel would be in a semifrozen state, much like soft-serve ice cream. At this point, chunks of cookies or candy could be added in, and once mixed throughout, the ice cream would be poured off into two rectangular, two-and-a-half-gallon coated-cardboard tubs. It was then placed into a hardening freezer that would drop the temperature down from twenty-two degrees above zero Fahrenheit to twenty degrees below.

Ben and Jerry set out to make an ice cream that was rich, creamy, smooth, dense, and chewy. That meant a low overrun and lots of butterfat, well above the 10 percent minimum that by law has to be in a frozen dessert in order to call it ice cream. Their product was also going to be very heavily flavored, largely as a result of Ben's sinus problems. "It tastes great," he'd tell Jerry when asked to evaluate a new test batch, "but I can't tell what flavor it is." Jerry would go back, up the dosage, and usually wind up putting in about one and a half to two times the amount suggested by the manufacturer.

To compensate for Ben's inability to distinguish subtle flavor variations, they decided to put lots of chunks or add-ins in the ice cream. Many of the flavors were developed with the idea of creating texture variations and a "mouth feel" that Ben could respond to.

Making the mix was beyond the scope of their operation, so they started to work with the University of Vermont dairy science department, which did scale-ups of the formulas that Jerry came up with. He would then run test batches on the new freezer, and make adjustments based on the results. Once the formula was finalized, they contracted with a small dairy in Middlebury, Vermont, which agreed to make the mix to their specifications and deliver it to the gas station in a six-gallon "bag in a box."

The impending grand opening of Ben & Jerry's Homemade was announced by way of an ad in the *Burlington Free Press*. Unfortunately, the wrong date was somehow used in the ad, which inadvertently moved the embarkation up a week. As a result, Jerry and Ben pulled in all the friends they could find to help with the nonstop, frenzied effort to get the shop ready to open on time.

One group of friends painted the inside walls and ceiling with an orange color that Ben had picked out. Just as the crew was finishing up, Ben announced that it was the wrong color. Or rather, it was the right color, but the wrong shade.

"It looks like Grossman's," Ben announced. "It's too bright. I wanted more of a burnt orange."

So they painted it again. Jerry didn't realize it at the time, but it was a foreshadowing of things to come. As soon as something was done, Ben needed to change it.

The logo for the business was designed by Liz Gallerani, another former Highland staffer. It featured a player piano with a huge ice cream sundae on top, and a banner through it that read Incredible Ice Cream . . . Amazing Crepes. Liz painted it directly onto the windows, surrounded by a wide black oval with the words "Ben & Jerry's Home-made" appearing in white. Another sign, which read simply "Ice Cream and Crepes," was painted on the bulkhead above the doors.

A party for family and friends was held the night before the grand opening, during which the crew kept working on the renovations. Mumpo and Vinny Vito, who had been living off and on at the house in South Hero, bolted the table bases to the floor. Jerry was making up batches of ice cream. And Ben? Ben was using a circular saw with a masonry blade, cutting through a cinder-block wall, sending a dust storm throughout the store in the process. In a last-minute setback, the health department had insisted that while it was okay to have two single-use rest rooms that weren't designated by sex, at least one of the toilets had to be accessible from the inside. Fortunately, the fixtures didn't have to be moved to accommodate the new egress.

It was little more than a year since they had first conceived their venture together, and once a new, used door was framed into place on the bathroom, they were ready to go.

CHAPTER THREE

What You Are About to See Will Astound and Amaze You

The gas station opened officially on Saturday, May 5, 1978. Nothing clearly distinguished the end of the renovations and the start of the business. People started to wander in to buy ice cream at around ten-thirty in the morning, oblivious to the construction that was still going on around them.

The grand-opening advertisement had promoted a "buy one, get one free" cone offer, and a line formed early and lasted most of the day. Small cones went for fifty-five cents, including tax, up slightly from what had been projected in the business plan.

With the store open, Jerry and Ben were now faced with figuring out how to run it. There was no time to rejoice as the register filled with cash. It was all they could do to keep up with the business. Jerry fell into the role of chief ice cream maker, and Ben made the soups, crepes, and brownies. Everyone worked the counter, including Mumpo and Vinny, who made the transition from banging nails to scooping cones.

Business kept getting better and better, and on or around the ninth day it was so good that they ran out of ice cream, and had to close early. To convey the bad news to their customers, they invented the "International No Ice Cream Cone" sign, a picture of an ice cream cone inside a red circle with a slash drawn through it.

It only took about a half hour to make four and a half gallons of ice cream in the rock-salt freezer, but each batch had to be hardened overnight. One of the casualties on the equipment list when the SBA loan didn't come through had been a freezer specifically designed to harden ice cream to minus twenty degrees. Without it, there were limits on how much ice cream they could produce.

Instead of the hardening freezer, Jerry and Ben were using a used six-hole dip case, which they could get down to minus twenty when it was empty, but which went up above zero as soon as they put about eight tubs of soft, twenty-two-degrees-above-zero ice cream into it. Even after twelve hours overnight in the dip case, the ice cream was sometimes still too soft to serve the next day. Any of the ice creams that had alcohol-based flavorings, like rum raisin, were the last ones to harden. Customers were often encouraged to take those flavors in a dish. Running out of ice cream was a regular occurrence at the store until the cash flow coughed up enough money for a hardener in late June. Other than the chef's knife, it was the first brand-new piece of equipment that they purchased.

Directly in front of the customers as they walked into the serving bay, beneath a sign that proclaimed "Today's Orgasmic Flavors," were the handwritten strips that listed the flavors that were currently available. On any given day as many as twelve might be offered, including basics such as vanilla, chocolate, coffee, and chocolate chip, and more unusual combinations like Mocha Chip, Piña Colada, Burgundy Cherry, Banana Rum, Coconut, or Carob. Some of the flavors were sweetened with honey, such as Honey Almond Mist and Honey Cinnamon. Some were flavored with fresh fruit, like strawberry, banana, and cantaloupe. The key to making a great banana ice cream was to use overripe fruit, which was a plus because they were able to get it dirt cheap.

With the rock-salt freezer, there was really no limit to how many different flavors they could make. When the base mix was almost at temperature, Jerry could toss just about anything he wanted into the cylinder. It wasn't unusual for a customer's homegrown blackberries or rhubarb sauce to wind up in a batch of ice cream. Jerry liked experimenting with ingredients, and to this day maintains that there is no such thing as an unredeemable batch of ice cream. Nevertheless, he managed to come up with a few combinations that didn't send anyone's salivary glands into overdrive. Lemon Peppermint Carob Chip and Honey Apple Raisin Oreo ("The Oreos were a mistake. They were supposed to be walnuts.") were two one-time batches that weren't repeated. The best-seller at first was Oreo Mint, a peppermint-based ice cream with Oreo cookies that they smashed up with a hammer.

One of the most prominent fixtures in the gas station was a player piano that Ben and Jerry had gotten for next to nothing through a classified ad. They had completely overhauled it using a how-to book, at the same time they were renovating the gas station. "Like a lot of things we fixed," Jerry says, "it leaked a little, and it wasn't quite exactly right . . . but it worked."

A couple of weeks after they'd opened, a guy by the name of Don Rose walked into the store, ordered up a fresh squeezed orange juice, and sat down at the piano while he waited for his order. Don worked second shift at the local IBM plant, and occasionally played at local restaurants. He rattled off a blues shuffle, got Ben and Jerry and the scoopers bopping just a bit, got his juice, and left.

About three weeks passed until he came back to the gas station, and he was greeted by an exuberant "Where you been?" from Jerry. Don took that to be an invitation, and he quickly became a fixture at the store. He was well over six feet tall, with broad shoulders and some extra girth—just the kind of guy you'd want banging out tunes while people waited in line for ice cream. Most days he would be at the gas station before it opened at 11:00 A.M., and stay until around 2:30 P.M., when he left for work. On weekends and days off, he'd usually be there all day.

Don's music was a blend of barrelhouse blues that ranged from honky-tonk through ragtime and Delta blues to boogie-woogie, influenced by the likes of Otis Spann and Memphis Slim. Like the piano players at the silent movies, he'd adapt what he was playing to what was up on the "screen." When the line got longer, and the scoopers were hustling, he'd be boogying, and when the customer counts were down, he'd play the blues.

Since they couldn't afford to pay him, Jerry and Ben rewarded Don the only way they could—with free food and ice cream, anytime he wanted. One day, Jerry came around from behind the counter, threw his arm around Don, and officially inducted him into that most exclusive of gastro-fraternal organizations, the Ice Cream for Life Club.

Don joined Darrell Mullis as the club's only members. Lanny Watts, in one of the most shortsighted business transactions any plumber, hippie or otherwise, has ever made, had dropped out of the club about six weeks after the store opened. Lanny liked the ice cream well enough, and he was stopping by the shop once a week for a dinner and dessert crepe, but he ran into some cash-flow problems of his own, and went back to Jerry and Ben and asked them if he could cash out of his deal. He crawled around the gas station and measured off the pipe, and after deducting fifty bucks or so for the food that he'd already eaten, he presented the boys with a bill for about three hundred fifty bucks. It's Lanny's fish story. The one that got away.

Jerry and Ben knew next to nothing about waiting on customers, and standing in line for ice cream at the gas station became the norm. They tried to get their scoopers to strike a balance, being friendly and personable with the customers, but not talking with them so much that it slowed down the line. They also hired waitpersons to serve the customers who sat down at the tables, but only scheduled them to work during the busiest times of the day. It was never really clear when you needed to go up to the counter to get the food yourself, and even when the wait staff was working, the service was inconsistent at best.

Jerry and Ben had decided early on in their business careers that they would only do the jobs they liked to do. Of necessity, firing people was a notable exception. Jerry argued that he was constitutionally unable to fire people, and that Ben's employment history had given him the firsthand experience it took to do the job. They worked out an arrangement between themselves whereby Jerry did the hiring and Ben did the firing.

There were two primary reasons why someone would get axed—overscooping or slow scooping. When they knew that someone had to go, they'd say to each other, out of earshot of the staff, "The monster is hungry, the monster must eat." That was Ben's cue to start practicing his routine, and he would start to emit a low-grade rumble. At one point they talked about getting him a mask to pull over his head.

It wasn't easy for Ben to be a boss. The closest he had come to supervising anyone up to that point in his life had been his dog Malcolm. You only had to ask the chickens at Highland how good a job Ben had done on that one. Ben had spent his entire life questioning authority, and resented being told what to do by others. The thought of now being in the position where he would have to do unto others what others had done unto him was disconcerting.

Ben, who had been on the receiving end more times than he could remember, actually worked out a fairly compassionate speech that he used to soften the blow. Not being great at scooping ice cream, he'd explain, really wasn't something to feel bad about. Most of the scoopers were college kids who were working part-time to earn a little extra cash. Ben assured them that their future careers as lawyers, doctors, or whatever wouldn't be affected by the fact that it took them too long to roll a scoop of ice cream onto a sugar cone.

If firing people was the exception, accounting proved the rule. Neither Jerry nor Ben liked to keep the books, and their recordkeeping was almost nonexistent. Within two months of opening, there was a sign on the front door of the gas station that read "We're closed today so we can figure out if we're making any money." They spent the day with an accountant, who tried to set them up with a system that would keep track of their sales and expenses.

At first Jerry paid the bills, but when they ran into cash-flow problems, Ben took over. Ben stopped paying the bills, and cash flow improved immediately. The deposits were made up by whichever of the two closed up at night. The cash got counted, stuffed into a night bag, and dropped off at the Merchants Bank, where it was opened and deposited into their account the next morning. The bank's count almost never agreed with theirs, and they put candy bars in the bags to compensate the tellers for the extra work involved in reconciling their account.

They averaged about $650 a day in sales during the summer months, but as far as they could tell, they weren't making any money. Their checkbook balance hovered around zero, and unpaid bills continued to accumulate, although they did everything they could think of to conserve cash and cut costs. They were only paying themselves a hundred and fifteen bucks a week by way of their paychecks, and skimming a few bucks more out of the register. Payments to their suppliers had been stretched to the limit, and they always called around to get the best prices, going so far as to order their lemons from one supplier and their bananas from another in order to save a couple of cents per pound. Whenever possible, they made batches of ice cream with samples of ingredients that they got from suppliers by way of the customer-response cards in the dairy food trade magazines. They knew they were losing money by overscooping, but other than watching over the counter and firing the worst offenders, they didn't have a clue about how to deal with the problem.

As the summer ended, the exhilaration of being in business gave way to exhaustion from working endless hours, seven days a week. One night Jerry was so tired when he left the store, that he dropped the night deposit bag into the mailbox on the corner by mistake. Another night, Ben went outside while Jerry did the final mopping, and fell asleep in the gravel parking lot. They were approaching spent cookiedom, and it was only made worse by the fact that they had little to show for their efforts. They also knew that when sales dropped off as winter approached, they'd only have to work harder to keep their heads above water.

Being open for business did lead to one major improvement in their lifestyles: the budgetary restrictions on their diets were lifted, and saltines and sardines gave way to crepes and ice cream sundaes customers left behind. The deal was that whoever found the food would call the other one over. They'd usually meet out back behind the oak refrigerator, where they'd scarf it down out of view of the customers.

Nothing got a bigger response from the human composters than when a half-eaten dinner crepe made its way to the backroom. The crepes, like the ice cream, were delicious. The Coquilles St. Jacques crepe, which had huge sea scallops, mushrooms, and onions in a very airy, slightly sourdough crepe batter, was the best-seller.

Outside of a Mother's Day promotion, which they ran the weekend after their grand opening, they did virtually no advertising through the end of the summer. They were too busy to think about it, and they were selling all the ice cream they could make. On Mother's Day they had given free cones to all moms. Any woman who came in with her kids, pictures of her kids, gray hair, or stretch marks qualified. Visibly pregnant women got two cones.

When summer ended and sales started to taper off, they figured it was time to start promoting the store, and they got in touch with Lyn Severance, who had gone to Montréal with them the day they had researched crepes. An eighth-generation Vermonter, Lyn had grown up in Burlington and studied communication design at the Parsons School of Design in New York. To the horror of her teachers, who thought that she was tossing away a very promising career as a graphic artist, she moved back to Vermont after graduating with honors in 1976. Lyn had been a regular at the hot-drink stand in the basement of Bennington Potters North, which is where she had met Ben and Jerry.

Most of the early promotions were an attempt to increase awareness of the non-ice-cream food items on the menu. While the ice cream had been an instant hit, the crepes never seemed to get off the ground. This was somewhat dispiriting to Ben, who watched with envy as Jerry's ice cream flew out the door, while demand for his crepes flat-lined. No matter how they were advertised, or how many varieties they offered, it seemed that they would sell about twenty crepes a day.

They started to experiment with other food items, from vegetarian sandwiches to lasagna, but none of them proved any more popular than the crepes. The best-selling items on the food menu were the soups, which were served with homemade bread. Broccoli mushroom became the mainstay, probably owing in part to Don Rose's personal addiction.

The graphic image that Lyn created for the business was in many ways born of necessity. Ben asked for something that looked funky and homemade, and put strict limitations on how much money he was willing to pay for design work. To create the image, Lyn put herself into the mindset of a five-year-old in an ice-cream-eating mode, and came up with a naive, childlike, unsophisticated look.

A key to the image was the decision to hand-letter everything. Even the lines around the ads were hand-drawn, with just enough of a wiggle to let you know that it hadn't been drawn with a ruler or laid out with a roll of border tape.

The hand-lettered look not only reinforced the homemade image, but also saved money. At six dollars an hour, it was cheaper to pay Lyn than to have the ads typeset. One of the alphabets she created came to be known as "Ben & Jerry's Chunk." Chunk-style lettering was big, bold, friendly, and very noticeable, and Lyn used it when she redesigned the logo. She kept the oval, because it was a nice shape and it stood out, but tossed out the piano because she didn't think it was representative of what the business was all about. In its place she created the "man making ice cream" drawing that would eventually be used on the pint containers.

At first, both Ben and Jerry would sit in on the meetings with Lyn at which the graphics and ads were discussed. A few months later they sorted out their respective roles, and Lyn started working exclusively with Ben on sales and marketing. Without Jerry's moderating influence, working with Ben was a handful. "He didn't always know what he wanted, but he wanted it really cheap because he had no money, and he wanted it really fast, because he was always doing things at the last minute," Lyn recalls. "And he usually didn't like anything after it was done, convinced that it could have been better if we had changed this or that detail."

Shortly after opening, the boys printed up bumper stickers that said "Lick It," which were left on the counter and given away for free to their customers. The slogan, which also appeared on the backs of the logo T-shirts they sold in the store, was a reference to their products, not to their anatomy, but it nevertheless created a bit of an uproar in the local lesbian community, who had taken to hanging out at the gas station in relatively large numbers.

Commonwoman, an alternative weekly newspaper, cited the bumper stickers as an example of offensive behavior in the local business community. Ben and Jerry responded by placing an ad in the newspaper that read as follows:

> Despite the fact that *Commonwoman* displayed our bumper sticker as an example of sexism in Burlington, and
>
> Despite the fact that *Commonwoman* published an article advocating stealing from businesses, and
>
> Despite the fact that *Commonwoman* disapproves of and threatens not to accept this ad because they fail to see the humor in it,
>
> Ben & Jerry's would like to thank *Commonwoman* for its service to the community and would like to thank its many readers for supporting our store these many months.

Ben thought the slogan too good to drop, but Jerry and Lyn prevailed upon him, and "Vermont's Finest" replaced "Lick It" as the slogan of choice on the bumper stickers and shirts. With the change in slogans, amicable relations with the lesbian community were restored.

Print advertising wound up being a very small part of Ben & Jerry's marketing, mostly because it was too expensive. Instead, they turned to creating events that drew attention to their business, while giving them a chance to celebrate with their customers. The first was an end-of-summer celebration that they put on together with some other like-minded businesses from their part of town.

The celebration, called "Fall Down," was held at or near the intersection of St. Paul and College streets, and spilled out from in front of the gas station into City Hall Park, across the street. It featured a round-the-block stilt-walking contest, an ice-cream-eating contest, and an apple-peeling contest in which the person with the longest unbroken peel won a dinner for two at a local restaurant.

Much more exciting was the Mark Twain Memorial Frog Jumping Contest. Jerry and Elizabeth Skarie, who started living together again just after the gas station opened, had personally caught all the frogs in a swamp down the street from their house that morning. They made a mark on the pavement, and then drew a series of concentric circles around it to measure how far the frogs had jumped. The contestant would pick out his or her frog, place it in the middle, and try to make it jump as far as possible in a single hop.

A local dance company did a specially choreographed performance that featured the dancers in the roles of ice cream, hot fudge, and whipped cream. At the end they wound up falling all over each other, in a giant ice cream sundae. While all of this was going on, Don Rose played the piano and jugglers and unicyclists wandered throughout the crowd.

By far the highlight of the day was the Burlington debut of the dramatic sledgehammer-smashing of a cinder block on the bare stomach of "Habeeni Ben Coheeni, the noted Indian mystic."[1] It was a routine that Jerry had learned in a carnival techniques course he'd taken his senior year at Oberlin. Fall Down marked the second time they had done the act, the first being at a party in Saratoga the previous summer. Jerry had given Ben the option of whether he wanted to be the smasher or the smashee. ("There was no hesitation on my part," said Ben. "I didn't want the responsibility.")

As the crowd gathered in anticipation, the song "Rubberband Man," by the Spinners, was cranked out over the makeshift PA system. Ben (aka Coheeni), draped in a bed sheet and perched on a platform in the lotus position, was carried onto the scene by six bearers, while chanting incoherently, a cross between a hum and a groan.

"Feel the vibrations. The profound mound of round, here before us," Jerry exhorted to the crowd. "His ever-expanding consciousness exceeded only by his ever-expanding width."

After completing his entrance, Habeeni took his place alongside Jerry, who was dressed in safari clothes and a pith helmet. As Habeeni continued to chant, Jerry launched into the story of how His Holiness had come to be before them today.

"Ladies and gentlemen, what you are about to see will astound and amaze you. What we have before us here today is the genuine article, the real thing. Born in India, Habeeni was abandoned as a baby, but rescued and raised by the Indian fakirs, those magical and mystical

1. Habeeni was actually billed on the Fall Down posters in 1978 as Habenni Ben Coheen. In 1979 he appeared as Habenni Ben Coheni, in 1980 as Habenni Abdul Ben Coheni, and in 1981 (after changing publicists one last time), as Habeeni Ben Coheeni, which was, after all, his real name.

people. One day, Habeeni was studying at the temple of Rishakesh, when disaster struck—an earthquake. The building crumbled, rubble and stones tumbling all around. However, Habeeni was able to survive by placing himself in a metabolic trance, which he will simulate here before us today."

While Jerry invited a few kids up to verify that the cinder block and sledgehammer were real, Coheeni went metabolic, falling backwards into the hands of his attendants, who suspended him in a supine position between two chairs. Once settled in place, Jerry looked around for an appropriate opening in the sheet so as to expose only the mystic's belly, on which he placed the cinder block.

"And now I ask for your total silence as I bring the sledgehammer high above my head. No loud noises, no lighting of matches, no flash photography. Keep your eyes on the belly, as this will be over in an instant. Ladies and gentlemen, one time, and one time only. . . ."

Whereupon, Jerry took the sledgehammer and, in one fell swoop, brought it crashing down on the cinder block, smashing it into lots of little pieces that, fortunately for insurance purposes, didn't go hurtling into the crowd, but fell away harmlessly.

"Habeeni Ben Coheeni, ladies and gentlemen, the noted Indian mystic, Habeeni Ben Coheeni," Jerry shouted over and over, as "Rubberband Man" once again cranked out over the speakers.

Habeeni, restored to his platform, left in triumph, carried out by his handlers and tossing flower petals to the pumped-up crowd.

As a warm up for Habeeni, Jerry had done his "Dr. Inferno" fire-eating routine, which he had also learned at Oberlin. His torches were straightened-out metal coat hangers with wads of cotton that had been dipped into 151-proof rum and tied onto the ends with picture-hanging wire. After a brief introduction about fire and its relationship to mankind in the history of civilization, Jerry began with the "flaming single," whereupon he placed a single torch in his mouth, and snuffed it out.

He then moved on to the most dangerous of all fire-eating feats, the flaming tongue transfer. The intent of the trick is to transfer the flame from one torch to another, using his tongue as the intermediary. Unfortunately, Jerry put a little too much rum on the wads ("If you eat fire as often as I do, you sort of forget how much to put on"), and it kind of dribbled out the side of his mouth, which set his chin on fire. This, of course, got a great reaction from the crowd, who had no way of knowing that it wasn't part of the act until a sense of panic came over Jerry, whereupon it was clear to everyone that something was terribly awry. Ever the showman, Jerry extinguished his face and went on with the act, finishing up with the "flaming triple," swallowing three torches at once while bending over backwards as far as he could go.

Fall Down was a great success, and it would be repeated and improved upon in subsequent years.

All too soon after fall came winter, and, as expected, the colder it got, the less and less ice cream they sold. As an incentive to get people into the shop on the really cold days, they ran the POPCDBZWE (pronounced "pop si biz we") promotion, which stood for "Penny Off Per Celsius Degree Below Zero Winter Extravaganza." POPCD-BZWE became one of the most written-about promotions that the company ever did, but converting Fahrenheit to Celsius drove the scoopers nuts, and the incentive of a few cents off wasn't enough to increase traffic all that much.

As an alternative to POPCDBZWE, which focused people on how cold it was, Ben next tried to promote winter ice cream sales by putting forth his First Law of Ice Cream Eating Dynamics, which held that the reason you got cold in the winter was the difference between your internal temperature and the external temperature. If you bought into it, you realized that you could warm up on a really cold day by eating lots of ice cream, thereby lowering your internal temperature a few degrees. Ben professed this theory to all who would listen, but he was preaching to the converted who had already wandered in for a scoop in spite of the cold, and his breakthrough in thermal physics yielded no tangible increase in sales.

Despite the huge drop-off in sales through the winter months, the business survived. The onset of warm weather in the spring of 1979 brought with it a much-needed increase in sales. In an attempt to get ready for their second summer, they converted the second bay of the gas station, which they now rented, into the Mark Mumford Memorial Dining Room, featuring booths for additional seating and shelving for storing ingredients.

At Lyn's urging, the whole shop was repainted in white and bright primary colors, covering up the browns, oranges, and wood tones. The concrete floor in the seating areas, which had originally been painted gray, was covered with black and white tiles arranged in a checkerboard pattern. Outside on the bulkhead, the relatively small "Ice Cream & Crepes" sign, which had been painted with one-foot-high letters, was replaced with "Ben & Jerry's Homemade" in huge, black, three-foot-tall, chunk-style letters.

Ben also put in a few days trying to effect a permanent solution to the latest batch of leaks brought on by the warm weather. As a temporary solution, they had hung a plastic sheet just underneath the ceiling, with a few buckets strategically placed to capture the runoff, so their customers didn't get soaked.

While Ben was up on the roof, he also installed the first pieces of roof art, which were cut out of plywood and painted by Lyn. There were three ice cream cones and a giant, eight-foot-by-eight-foot coffee cup complete with checkered tablecloth. The coffee cup was strategically placed in front of the chimney for the woodstove, which gave the visual impression that there was steam coming off of the cup.

One day in the spring, Jerry and Ben were sitting outside, staring at the side of the three-story building next door, which loomed large over the paved and graveled area in front of the gas station. It occurred to them that they could put the wall to good use by showing outdoor walk-in movies downtown during the summer.

The only apparent obstacle to the idea was presented by a couple of streetlights that illuminated the corner. They approached the electric company about shutting off the lights for a couple of hours, once a week, but were informed it would require a switch that could only be installed with the approval of the city's board of aldermen. So they went before the board and were somewhat surprised that their proposal was greeted with a healthy dose of skepticism. One member of the board had already made up his mind. "There'll be free movies in Burlington over my dead body," he announced.

Ben and Jerry left the meeting somewhat amused and somewhat confused, but still very much determined to show free movies. They circulated a petition among other local businesses, offered to pay the $750 bill for installing the light switch, and personally agreed to provide security during the screening. The aldermen ultimately relented.

The movie festival was announced via a black-and-white poster that featured a huge sling chair and the movie projector, to drive home the point that it was a bring-your-own-chair event. Jerry, who took the commitment of providing security seriously, broke out his pith helmet and walked the grounds with a flashlight during the shows. Ben ran the projector, which was only appropriate since they were using one of his bedsheets as the screen.

In May, on the shop's first anniversary, Ben and Jerry held their first Free Cone Day, scooping ice cream to all comers to celebrate their having survived their first year in business. A quote, attributable to each of the founders, was used on the flyers that announced the event. "If it's not fun, why do it?" was Jerry's. Ben's was "Business has a responsibility to give back to the community from which it draws its support."

The line went out the door all day long, and Don Rose played for over twelve hours straight.

Giving away ice cream came to them naturally, and they did it without a premeditated calculation as to what the payback might be down the road. They truly believed that the joy was in the journey, and were determined to seize upon every opportunity to have fun that came their way.

Ben and Jerry came to describe their business as being "funky," which to them meant honest, no frills, handmade, and homemade. It was on the opposite end of the spectrum from slick, refined, polished, or packaged. It was as much a description of themselves and their emerging business philosophy as it was of the physical surroundings or graphic image.

Sales in their first year were almost double the $90,000 they had projected in their original business plan. Still, they didn't make a penny of profit, nor had they figured out a business strategy that would ensure their ability to survive over the long term. But as Caryl Stewart, who was subletting the gas station to them, recalls, "They had connected with their customers, who felt like they were an integral part of what was happening, not merely a source of revenue to some faceless businessmen. Walking into the gas station was very different from walking into any other retail establishment, getting what you needed, and going. There was a sense from the beginning that this was something special."

CHAPTER FOUR

We're the Guys Who Make It

There were two reasons why Ben and Jerry started wholesaling their ice cream. First, they became resigned to the fact that they were never going to figure out how to control the portions in the scoop shop, and as a result, they would never make any money. More important, Ben had become envious of the salespeople who were coming into the store to try to sell them supplies and ingredients. These guys, Ben thought, had a great job, driving around the state, listening to their tape decks, and stopping off every now and then to try to sell some stuff. Ben figured it was the kind of work he'd like to do. After six months or so of trying to peddle his cooking to an unreceptive audience, he was more than ready to give up the crepe griddle and hit the open road, and in January of 1979, he did.

They had actually started selling ice cream to restaurants during their first summer, responding to a few unsolicited requests. Expanding beyond those few accounts wasn't easy. The few high-quality establishments that were willing to pay the premium price they were charging were spread out all over the state. Many of these restaurants were at the ski areas that were being affected adversely by a decided lack of snow that winter, which made them all the more reluctant to trade the low-cost brand of ice cream they were currently serving for a higher-priced alternative.

In all, Ben lined up about thirty accounts, including some across the lake in upstate New York. He drove a different route each day of the week, and Jerry would call the accounts a couple of days in advance to get their order. "I'd try to speak with the chef or the owner, and ask if they wanted any ice cream that week. Half the time they wouldn't be there, half the time they didn't know, and half the time they said they'd call me back. Every once in a while somebody would order one or two tubs."

Ben had traded in his camper van for an orange Volkswagen squareback, which was pressed into service as the company's delivery vehicle. They made a cooler for the back out of a high-efficiency insulated material that kept the ice cream cold without the benefit of refrigeration or dry ice. As long as Ben drove fast, a natural tendency, he made it to the accounts before the ice cream melted.

Ben drove the routes every day, regardless of how much had been ordered. It wasn't unusual for him to drive a seventy-mile round trip, just to deliver two or three tubs.

Most of the restaurant accounts had been added during the winter, when the volume at the scoop shop had dropped precipitously. With sales picking back up at the gas station as the weather once again got warmer, they realized that the rock-salt-and-ice freezer wasn't going to be able to keep up with demand. They went back to Fred Burgess at the Merchants Bank and, in May of 1979, received a $30,800 SBA-guaranteed loan with which they could equip a separate manufacturing facility. Their lease at the gas station, which they'd just renewed, was still only for one year, but apparently, since they were an ongoing business, the SBA no longer viewed that as a problem.

The space they rented for their new venture was in an old spool and bobbin mill, about five blocks from the gas station. It was a huge brick building, typical of the textile mills that had once thrived throughout New England. The building was slated to be converted into apartments, and it had a bombed-out look. Most of the windows had been broken, and there was glass and garbage all over the place. Despite outward appearances, Jerry and Ben believed they could create a sanitary dairy manufacturing plant out of the rubble. Besides, the price was right, and utilities were included. "They only had one meter for the building," Ben recalls. "We tried to tell them we were heavy users."

To enclose their 750 square feet, Ben and Jerry framed up some stud walls that they then drywalled and painted white. Overhead, they hung a dropped ceiling with recessed fluorescent lights. There was no floor drain, but with Ben's expertise in mopping, they figured they could do without one.

To make the ice cream, they picked up a used ten-gallon batch freezer made by Emery Thompson, which was affectionately called

Emery. It worked on the same basic principles as the White Mountain freezer at the gas station, only it used freon as the refrigerant instead of rock salt and ice. A variable-speed motor was installed to slow Emery down and limit the amount of air that got pumped into the ice cream.

To most consumers, there was no perceptible difference in the quality of the ice cream that was produced on the two freezers, although in theory, Emery, which froze the mix faster, produced a slightly smoother and creamier product. The texture of the ice cream at the new plant was also enhanced by a brand-new, eight-by-ten-foot walk-in freezer, in which they hardened and stored the ice cream.

With the new manufacturing capacity up and running, the box in Ben's squareback was no longer big enough for all the ice cream they were going to sell. From an ice cream distributor in Massachusetts they purchased a 1969 International truck with 240,000 miles on the odometer. They paid $3,500 for it, and although the truck was sold "as is," Ben was assured that the refrigeration system was in good working order. Compared to the box in the squareback, it probably was.

The truck was a six-door "reach-in," which meant that all the ice cream had to be loaded and unloaded by hand into one of the three doors on either side. It looked like the quintessential ice cream truck, which is just what Ben had in mind. Just so there'd be no mistaking what product he was trucking around the state, Lyn came up with a paint scheme that featured two giant hands that wrapped completely around the body, each holding a huge ice cream cone.

When summer came, Jerry worked in the plant all day, making batch after batch of ice cream, while Ben was out on the road delivering product and trying to sell new accounts. Concerned that sales to restaurants might not be enough to offset the increased overhead of the new plant and truck, they also set up four seasonal scoop stands around Burlington. Since the stands had been Ben's idea, he was also responsible for running them. Unfortunately, the stands turned out to be a lot more work and a lot less successful than they'd anticipated. "The seasonal stands are what put Ben into therapy," Jerry concedes, which isn't to say that he wouldn't have wound up there anyway. "Three out of the four locations were somewhat questionable, and the people running them were more than somewhat questionable. One scooper just disappeared one day, never to be heard from again, taking the day's receipts with him." There were also a few problems that were beyond Ben's control. In the summer of 1979 there was a nationwide gas shortage that kept the tourists out of state and cut down on trips by the locals to the shopping centers.

Some might have taken the summer without gas, coming on the heels of the winter without snow, as an omen to head back to the gas station. Things there, actually, had taken a decidedly upward swing. In order to devote their time to the wholesale business, Ben and Jerry had hired a manager to run the scoop shop for them, and as a result of increased sales and more effective control of the costs, they started to make some money. Of course, they were now losing whatever they made at the gas station on the wholesale operation, and they repeatedly kicked themselves for diversifying.

By the end of the summer of '79, it was pretty clear that a wholesale business selling two-and-half-gallon tubs to restaurants wasn't going anywhere. The scoop stands, which were a key part of their strategy to increase their volume, had been a bust, and they were heading into another winter when the sales at the gas station would once again plummet. Then one day, Ben seized upon the idea that would transform the business. In order to make the truck routes he was driving viable, they would package the ice cream in pint containers and sell it to the mom-and-pop grocery stores and supermarkets that he was passing along the way.

Jerry's initial reaction to Ben's brainstorm was muted by his knowledge that it would wind up being more work for him. "I really don't think I embraced too many new ideas from Ben with open arms," he admits. But he eventually relented, and they went to Lyn to get her to design the package.

Lyn did a bunch of thumbnail sketches, at first suggesting a pastoral scene of green fields, blue sky, and black-and-white cows. The cost of printing a pint container with that many colors was prohibitive, and they finally decided to use the oval logo featuring the man making ice cream. Underneath the logo they added the words "Vermont's Finest All Natural Ice Cream," a slogan that Ben had used in the advertisement for the grand opening of the gas station. "I knew we could make the claim," Ben says, "because we were Vermont's *only* all-natural ice cream." Lyn argued for a pink container. Ben wanted something that was stronger and bolder, and they settled on claret, a deep shade of red.

On the lid, Lyn proposed that they put a picture of the two entrepreneurs. With the start of the wholesale business, neither Ben nor Jerry was spending any significant time at the gas station. The picture was Lyn's way of reconnecting them to their product. At first, Ben didn't like the idea of having his face so prominently displayed, but Lyn argued forcefully, and she finally prevailed.

In November, Jim O'Donnell, the sales rep from Sweetheart Paper, showed up at the gas station after getting a message that there were a couple of guys in Burlington who wanted to get their picture on the lid of a pint cup. The only way to do it, O'Donnell explained, was to use process printing, and the plates alone would cost between six and ten thousand dollars. There was no way Ben and Jerry could afford that, and they kept insisting that there had to be another way to do it. Having shed his initial skepticism about the idea, Ben was now dead set on it, and he wasn't willing to accept that it couldn't be done for less money. After phoning the art department at Sweetheart's Maryland headquarters, O'Donnell came back to the table with word that if they supplied a black-and-white negative with a sixty-five-line screen, he could get them a reasonably good three-dimensional picture on the lid.

Ben showed up for the photo shoot with a yellow porkpie hat that he wore on occasion. The photographer, Marion Ettlinger, had them sit on straight-backed chairs in front of a small folding card table. Ben held a cone, Jerry a dish and a spoon. The photo they picked captured the two entrepreneurs perfectly, but if you looked closely, you could see the ice cream melting down the side of the cone in Ben's hand, a flaw that is still visible on the pints today.

For the back of the containers, Ben and Jerry wrote out a sales pitch to try to persuade the consumer to give their ice cream a try. Lyn edited it down, fitting in as much of their original copy as she could, and added a few small illustrations to make it work graphically.

> This carton contains some of the finest ice cream available anywhere. We know because we're the guys who make it. We start with lots of fresh Vermont cream and the finest flavorings available. We never use any fillers or artificial ingredients of any kind. With our specially modified equipment, we stir less air into the ice cream creating a denser, richer, creamier product of uncompromisingly high quality. It costs more and it's worth it.

They signed their names, and offered to refund the purchase price to any unsatisfied customer. The idea behind the money-back guarantee was twofold. At $1.69 to $1.79 per pint, the ice cream was expensive compared with the other packaged products in the market-place. The guarantee was intended to give consumers the confidence that if they did fork out the money, at least they'd be happy with the purchase. Ben also viewed the guarantee as a way to keep an eye on quality, figuring that if for some reason Jerry started slipping, they'd find out about it before it was too late.

The pints were launched in February 1980, less than five months after Ben had first proposed the idea. Considering the lead time for getting the artwork produced and the printing plates made, it was an incredibly fast turnaround. There was one generic container, and a different-colored lid for each of the eight flavors—Oreo Mint, French Vanilla, Chocolate Fudge, Wild Blueberry, Mocha Walnut, Maple Walnut, Honey Coffee, and Honey Orange.

In all, they had over $10,000 tied up in packaging for the new product line, which was a staggering amount of money at that time. Fortunately, selling the pints turned out to be a cinch, and it didn't take long to realize they'd made a good investment. It wasn't a big deal for a small grocery store to put a new product into its freezer, especially when Ben offered to refund the store's money if it didn't sell through. Within a few months, they had gone from thirty-five accounts to more than two hundred. Ben kept waiting for the bottom to fall out, not yet convinced that it wasn't just a fad, but week after week, the stores kept selling more and more of the stuff.

They then approached a couple of the local supermarket chains. Although they were a tougher nut to crack, Ben & Jerry's eventually got authorized by Grand Union for a nine-store test, and the other area supermarkets soon followed. To promote the product, Jerry and Ben did demos, setting up a dip case and scooping free samples for the shoppers.

While Jerry had been able to manufacture the bulk tubs by himself, packing pints was a two-person job, and he was now working with a full-time assistant, Cia Rochford. Unlike the two-and-a-half-gallon containers, which were filled by hand, the pints were filled automatically—or at least semiautomatically.

The filler they were using was circa World War II, and was a Rube Goldberg–style piece of equipment. It was roughly configured like a person standing upright with his arms extended out on either side, parallel to the ground. The "torso" was the base of the machine, which was massive enough that the whole thing didn't tip over. The "head" was a triangular stainless-steel hopper, which was where they dumped the ice cream. The "arms" were a set of steel springs and pulley wheels that moved the containers, automatically stopping each one directly underneath the hopper.

There were two holes at the bottom of the hopper, both of which fed into a cylinder that had a plunger inside. When the plungers moved up, they sucked the ice cream through the hole and into the cylinder. When the plungers moved down, they pushed the ice cream out into the pint container waiting below.

Their machine was missing the vertical stations that automatically dropped the empty cups onto a conveyer at one end and put the lids on the filled pints at the other. Instead, both of those jobs were done by hand. Eight pints, a gallon of ice cream, went into a square corrugated cardboard box, which got placed in the storage freezer where the ice cream hardened overnight.

Getting the right amount of ice cream into each container was their largest problem. The plungers were adjustable by volume, but there were always incomplete fills. They kept a large spoon nearby, and when a half-filled pint came down the line, they'd fill it up the rest of the way by hand.

The flavor that had the most incomplete fills was Oreo Mint. The Oreos would get stuck in the holes, which would prevent the ice cream from getting through. When it clogged completely, they had no choice but to stick their hands into the hopper, reaching down through the ice cream to get to the offending cookies. This exacerbated the ongoing debate between the partners about what was the appropriate-sized chunk for their ice cream. Ben always argued for larger chunks. Jerry, whose forearms were suffering the consequences of the clogs, preferred smaller ones.

Jerry and Ben had philosophical discussions about chunks going back to the early days at the gas station. At the time, they debated whether their customers would prefer fewer but larger-sized chunks, or a larger number of smaller-sized pieces. "I argued that if the chunks were too large, you might not get a chunk in every bite," says Jerry. "Ben was willing to take that risk, convinced that it would be more than offset by the euphoria of finding a really huge chunk in the next spoonful."

What started out as an academic discussion was now a matter of much greater consequence. One day, Ben was helping Jerry package some Oreo Mint, and every single pint was filling up halfway, which was driving Jerry crazy. They were making batch after batch, and essentially filling every pint by hand with the spoon.

Finally, Jerry burst out, "There's no way I'm gonna keep doing this, Ben, I've had it."

"Hey, I'm out there on the truck every day, breaking down all over the place. I don't have it so easy either, you know," Ben shot back.

It was rare for the two lifelong friends to be at odds over anything to the point where either of them raised his voice. Jerry backed down immediately, acknowledging that Ben was putting up with just as much crap in doing his job as Jerry was in doing his. In the two years since they'd opened the gas station, it was their most vocal disagreement. "It'll be a big scene in the movie," Jerry predicts.

Ben was unwilling to give up on the large chunks, so they took the plungers to a machine shop and asked them to make the holes larger. While things improved somewhat, underfills were a fact of life that Jerry learned to deal with.

Sales of approximately 80,000 pints in 1980 increased the wholesale business more than 300 percent over the previous year, to $135,000, on top of the $238,000 in sales at the gas station. Disregarding the fact that they were paying themselves only about $8,000 a year each, the business actually showed a profit of $33,000, split roughly down the middle between wholesale and retail.

To help keep track of all the bills and invoices for the growing business, Ben and Jerry hired a bookkeeper, Diane Cadieux. When he was out delivering ice cream, Ben would put the money or check he collected together with the invoice, crumple them up together into a ball, and then shove the wad into his pocket. When he got back to the plant, he'd take all the wads of paper and put them in a bag that Jerry would drop off at Diane's house the next day. None of the invoices were priced out, and it was Diane's job to try to make sense of it all and make up the deposits for the bank.

By the end of 1980, Ben began to devote full time to sales, and they hired a driver to take over the routes. Whereas Ben had no choice but to put up with the idiosyncrasies of the International, the hired help was less patient. The truck broke down so often that the drivers would often quit in frustration. One guy just stopped showing up for work. When they called to ask where he was, his wife told them that "he was awful mad at that truck."

All of which made them ripe for an offer that came their way in early 1981. Real Ice Cream, a distributor based in Lebanon, New Hampshire, proposed taking over distribution of their product. On its face, the idea made sense. Rather than try to keep their one truck on the road and sell a single product to a couple of hundred small accounts, they could concentrate on manufacturing, and sell their product in quantity to Real, who would resell it to grocery stores along with all the other ice cream products they carried.

The only thing Real did was distribute ice cream. At many mom-and-pop grocery stores, Real owned the freezer, supplying it to the retailer in exchange for having some control, within reason, over what frozen dessert products were sold at the store.

They began to negotiate a contract with Real. The owner, Frank McIntosh, quickly insisted that he get exclusive rights on the product for the market area in which he distributed. A distributor was at an advantage if he carried a product that his competition couldn't get. For one thing, it allowed him access to accounts that other distributors were servicing. More important, it ensured that he could sell the product at a decent markup, without worrying about somebody else undercutting his price. Once a product was in the hands of lots of distributors, it was likely to be "footballed," which meant that the wholesale price would get knocked down, as everyone tried to get into his competitor's accounts.

From the manufacturer's perspective, the exclusive arrangement had drawbacks, especially if there were no requirements in terms of sales volume that guaranteed the distributor's performance. In the most extreme situation, a distributor could "bury" the product in favor of other brands on which they were making a higher markup, by not aggressively pushing it to their accounts, or by limiting the shelf space they gave the product in the freezer.

Ben and Jerry knew enough to know they'd be better off not giving exclusive rights, but they were so anxious to get out of distribution that it wasn't a deal-breaker. Real got exclusive distribution rights for Maine, New Hampshire, and Vermont, along with a right of first refusal for Massachusetts. All the existing Ben & Jerry's accounts were notified, and as of February 11, 1981, if they wanted to buy a pint or tub of Ben & Jerry's ice cream, they had to buy it from Real.

It didn't take long for the deal to unravel. Ben & Jerry's was only a small part of Real's total business, and the distributor didn't give it the same attention the boys had given it. Stores weren't serviced as frequently as they needed to be, which created a lot of out-of-stocks.

That meant the consumer would find either a limited flavor selection or no Ben & Jerry's ice cream at all. Most consumers faced with that predicament surveyed the freezer and picked out another brand, which resulted in lost sales for Ben & Jerry's.

Attempts to resolve their problems with Frank proved fruitless, and in July of 1981, less than five months after they had signed the contract, they decided to terminate the agreement. Jerry and Ben drove to New Hampshire together, convinced that Frank wouldn't take too kindly to the news. Expecting a big blowup, Frank surprised them, showing a philosophical side that they hadn't seen in him before. "A hundred years from now," he told them, "no one is even going to remember Real Ice Cream or Ben & Jerry's." When he left the meeting, Frank got back into character, called his lawyer, and sued.

Frank's lawyer filed immediately for a preliminary injunction that would force Ben & Jerry's to continue to use Real as a distributor until the lawsuit had run its course. The judge denied the motion, and a year later the parties settled out of court, with Real accepting the dissolution of the relationship.

The experience with Real taught Ben & Jerry that no one else was going to make the same commitment to their product that they did. For them, Ben & Jerry's was their life. For Frank, it was just one more product line he was marking up 25 percent. It was also clear to them that business relationships were strongly influenced by how much leverage one participant had over the other, and that a written contract, no matter how well drafted, wasn't enough to level out the playing field. They were good lessons to have learned, which is not to say they weren't forgotten later.

In April of 1981, Ben and Jerry moved out of the spool-and-bobbin mill, and into a flat-roofed, metal-walled, structural-steel building on Green Mountain Drive in South Burlington. Most of the building was occupied by a truck-repair shop. That wasn't why they chose the space, but since they were back to delivering their product in their own truck, it certainly would come in handy. The three thousand square feet they'd rented was roughly four times larger than their previous location. It gave them room to expand production to meet the increasing demand for their pints. Still, Jerry confidently predicted, "We'll never fill this space up," when they walked in the door.

It was raw, unimproved space when they signed the lease. After pouring a concrete floor, they sectioned it off into different functional areas. In the production room they hung a dropped ceiling and put white hard-plastic panels on the walls. It was the same material dairy farmers used in the milk rooms of their barns to create a sanitary space away from the hay and manure, and it made it possible to hose down the entire space at the end of the day.

Adjacent to production was the warehouse, which doubled as the receiving bay. There was no on-grade loading dock, and all of the trucks had to be unloaded and loaded without the benefit of a forklift.

At the rear of the warehouse was the storage freezer, which they had purchased used from a regional dairy in New Hampshire that had gone out of business. The freezer consisted of modular panels that interlocked together, and Ben and Jerry spent two days disassembling it ("the heaviest, hardest, dirtiest work that either one of us had ever done, before or since"), and at least as long putting it back together. Assisting with the reconstruction was Dick Soule, the refrigeration man they had used since the early days at the gas station. The "Soul Man" was a huge guy who, like Ben, was prone to show a little crack when he bent over. "He had an amazing capacity for work," Jerry recalls. "He lifted and moved things that I never would have guessed in my wildest dreams could be lifted or moved."

At the front of the building was a small office that also served as the employee lounge. Ben worked at a huge, antique draftsman's table that took up about one-fourth of the space. His desk was perpetually covered with a layer of papers, sometimes two or three inches deep, and the spiral notebooks in which he liked to write notes to himself and others. Jerry, who was usually working in production, had a desk but no chair. More often than not, if Jerry was in the office, he was in a recumbent position on a very worn red vinyl couch that rounded out the decor. In between the two was Diane, who did all of the bookkeeping and secretarial work.

With their increased volume, Ben and Jerry needed to find a new source of mix. They had outgrown the capacities of the University of Vermont dairy, which had picked up the account when their original supplier decided that producing a custom-formulated mix for the boys wasn't worth the hassle it entailed. The only supplier who could meet their needs was Weeks, a regional dairy in Concord, New Hampshire. Although Weeks received a significant portion of their milk from farms in Vermont, the majority of it came from New Hampshire. Reluctantly, the raw dairy ingredients in Vermont's Finest All Natural Ice Cream were at least temporarily coming from out of state.

Weeks made mix deliveries to the plant every three or four days. Their tanker truck would back up to the front door, and a two-and-a-half-inch plastic hose would get pulled through the office and connected to the bulk tank, located just inside the production room, about ten feet away. It took about forty-five minutes for the truck to pump off the mix, and in the winter, with the front door open, the temperature in the office would quickly plunge.

The biggest change at Green Mountain Drive was the new production freezer. Emery and the rock-salt-and-ice freezer at the store made one batch at a time. The new freezer put out a continuous stream of ice cream at what was then a mind-numbing rate of one hundred gallons per hour. Overnight, the manufacturing capacity had increased fivefold.

The freezer was a Cherry-Burrell V1D, known in the industry as "The Old Commander." Ben and Jerry found it in the hallway at a dairy auction. It was considered such a dinosaur that it wasn't even listed on the sales sheet. For six hundred bucks, it was theirs.

From the production freezer, the ice cream passed through the fruit feeder, the machine that injected the nuts, cookies, and candies into the product. Originally these machines were used almost exclusively for fruit, which is how they came by their name. Ben and Jerry had modified their fruit feeder in order to get the large chunks that were becoming the trademark of the company into the ice cream. The Oreos, however, were still a problem. The creamy filling was just too gooey, and it gummed up the hole at the bottom of the hopper. To compensate, whenever they ran that flavor, someone was glued to the machine, jamming the Oreos down into the hole with a rubber spatula.

It took three production workers standing around a large stainless-steel table to package the ice cream. The pipe that came off the fruit feeder dead-ended in a vertical position, facing down, about a foot off the top of the table. As the ice cream gushed out, the "filler" would hold a pint under the pipe until it was full, then deftly pull it away, moving another empty container underneath the pipe with his or her other hand. At the same time, the filler would imprint a production code on the bottom of the filled pint and then slide it along the table to the next station. The ice cream never stopped coming until the end of the run, and the filler would keep repeating the above procedure over and over, for hours at a time.

The "capper," standing directly to the right of the filler, put the lid on the pints, and packed them in the corrugated boxes. It was also the capper's job to make sure that any inadvertent drips on the outside of a container were wiped clean. At the spool-and-bobbin mill, most of the pints were underfilled, but occasionally too much ice cream got into the containers, and when the lid went on, it squished onto the outside of the pint. If the mess was minor, a quick flick of the tongue became the wiping method of choice, unless it was a flavor the capper didn't like. Then they used a rag.

The third member of the production crew was the "runner," who would put the boxes of pints in the freezer. To maximize the airflow and reduce the time it took to harden the ice cream, the boxes were spread out all over the floor in the middle of the freezer. By the end of the production day, you couldn't walk into the freezer without squishing pints wherever you stepped. Early the next morning, the hardened ice cream would be stacked along the outside walls, to make room for that day's production.

Hand-filling pints was unique in the ice cream industry. Just about every manufacturer filled its bulk tubs by hand, and many also filled half-gallons manually. There might even have been a few doing quarts, but no one else was doing pints. You simply had to move too quickly, because the containers were so small. Modern automatic fillers were designed for newer production freezers that cranked out ice cream at over a thousand gallons per hour. They could be adjusted, but even at their lowest settings, they didn't run slowly enough to work with the one-hundred-gallon-per-hour flow of the V1D. There was also some question about whether or not the large chunks of cookies and candy would fit through the nozzles on the automatic fillers.

When Ben and Jerry first started manufacturing at Green Mountain Drive, they did two runs a day, one in the morning and one in the afternoon. At some point the crew approached Jerry and asked if they could run straight through lunch, and end the day an hour early. That had the added benefit of eliminating one of the two daily cleanups, during which they flushed out the freezer and broke down, washed, and resanitized all the pipes.

The down side of running nonstop for seven or eight hours was that the staff had given up the only real break they had during the day. The plant was staffed with only one person for each position, and only the runner could even think of walking away for a minute or two. If the runner did get sufficiently ahead, he or she might disappear into the warehouse and fire up a Marlboro, then run back in, shouting, "Garage hits!" Whereupon the other two would take quick breaks in succession, so that everyone got to smoke about an inch.

Giving up lunch didn't, however, mean they had given up food. Every morning at around ten-thirty, a coffee truck would pull up out front and honk its horn, which would prompt Diane to get up from her desk, open up the door to production, and shout out, "Coffee Truck!" at the top of her lungs so she could be heard over the equipment. Whoever was running at the time would take orders and head out to the truck, returning to production with an overflowing cardboard box of sustenance for the crew.

The only alternative to truck food was soft pints of ice cream, eaten right off the line. The ice cream was really flavorful when it was soft, and it went down easily. It wasn't unusual for someone to suck down a whole pint in a single sitting. "Everyone in production had a really thick neck, and was somewhat pudgy," recalls Lanny Watts, who did some of the plumbing at the plant. "Anyone who was new would be getting pudgy real soon."

CHAPTER FIVE

Ward, I'm Worried About the Burger

Taking back the distribution from Real worked out reasonably well, but Jerry and Ben still had to increase sales in order to make the wholesale operation profitable. The only logical way to do that was to add distributors in areas they couldn't service with their own truck. They figured that as long as they delivered to the existing accounts themselves, anything the distributor sold would represent incremental volume. Even if the distributor did a lousy job, they'd still wind up ahead.

In the spring of 1981, Ben was on his way to go tubing down the Saco River with his girlfriend when he drove past an ice cream distributor in Conway, New Hampshire. He was dressed in cut-off jeans, sandals, and a T-shirt, but he decided to stop. Once inside, he asked if he could see the owner.

"Hi, I'm Ben from Ben & Jerry's. Have you ever heard of our ice cream?"

"No," Sut Marshall responded. "Have you ever heard of Abbott's Ice Cream?"

"No," Ben admitted.

"Well, I guess that makes us even," Sut observed.

While Sut listened patiently, Ben launched into his sales pitch, telling him how he and Jerry had started out in the gas station and were now selling pints to grocery stores.

"It sells really well in Vermont," Ben said, adding that a recent article in *Vermont Life* had just hailed the product as the best ice cream in the state.

"This isn't Vermont," Sut dryly observed. "You're a long way from home."

Sut, who, at thirty-nine years old, was about ten years Ben's senior, had been born and raised in New Hampshire. He was a classic New Englander who spoke softly and made his points directly, with as few words as possible.

After a half hour or so, Ben had already done his routine more than once. He was ready to get on with his tubing, and Sut was ready to go back to work.

"Why don't you give it a try?" Ben said, trying to close the deal.

"Okay, you convinced me," Sut said. "Why don't we give it a whirl? I'll take fifty gallons."

The first store Sut sold it to was the Colony IGA, a family-owned supermarket within spitting distance of his loading dock.

"You can put it in as long as you take it out if it doesn't sell," the owner told him.

"Don't worry, it'll sell," Sut assured him. "Ben said so."

It did. Sut was also able to put the product into most of the small mom-and-pops that he serviced, many of which left it up to his drivers to fill the freezer with whatever they needed. He also added sub-distributors in Maine, who had similar success in their accounts.

Ben found three or four other small distributors in the border states around Vermont, and at the same time expanded the company truck routes into Albany, New York. Not sure how well the pints would sell out of state, and concerned about covering the overhead expenses of the new plant, they also decided to start opening franchised scoop shops. Each franchise would be a guaranteed outlet for their ice cream, and since it would be owned and operated by someone else, they wouldn't have to worry about portion or cash control.

Lots of people, including anyone who had firsthand experience with franchising, warned them against it, pointing out that it was more complicated than it seemed. Typically, Ben refused to believe this. A classified ad was placed under "Business Opportunities" in the *Free Press*, and Ben and Jerry started to interview prospective franchisees.

The first store was sold in June to Peter and Mary Ann Palumbo. For a $10,000 franchise fee, in addition to the cost of equipment and leasehold improvements to their storefront, they got the exclusive rights for ten years to scoop Ben & Jerry's ice cream within a defined territory in and around Shelburne, Vermont.

It would have been impossible to duplicate the ambiance of the gas station at the new location. Ben decided that instead the store would have its own personality, which it did. For openers, it was clean. The store was opened on July 31, 1981. Lanny Watts must have been kicking himself.

Ten days after the first franchise opened, *Time* magazine ran a cover story on ice cream that began, "What you must understand at the outset is that Ben & Jerry's in Burlington, Vt., makes the best ice cream in the world." The first paragraph continued with the somewhat conflicting opinion that Mayfield's, in Athens, Tennessee, was the world's best ice cream, and that the best ice cream in the universe was found at either Lickety Split in Denver, Bob's Famous in Washington, D.C., or Gelato in San Francisco.

The point of the article was to highlight the nation's growing infatuation with high-butterfat, superpremium ice creams, not to crown one of the many homemade ice cream scoop shops or nationally packaged brands as the best. Taken out of context, however, the quote was as effective as it was misleading, and Ben played it for all it was worth.

The impact of the *Time* article was huge and immediate. Already popular with the locals, the article made the gas station an attraction for out-of-towners. On weekends, a line would form before the store even opened, and there would be a nonstop stream of customers stretching out the front door until eleven o'clock at night.

In an effort to accommodate the increase in business, Don Miller, the store manager, converted part of the Mark Mumford Memorial Dining Room into Cone Express, the equivalent of the eight-item-or-less checkout line at the supermarket. If you just wanted a cone, and were willing to choose from a limited flavor selection, you could get in and get out a whole lot quicker.

With more customers than ever coming through the gas station, Ben was always harping to Don about the need to control overscooping. It hadn't been until about a year after they opened, when they were sitting in City Hall Park with a pocket calculator, that they realized just how much money they were losing if they were overscooping each cone by half an ounce. Ben went so far as to put small scales on the counter and instructed the scoopers to weigh every cone. Though effective at keeping costs in line, the scales slowed down the lines and alienated the customers, who thought they were getting stiffed. Eventually the scales were eighty-sixed.

Although the notoriety from being featured in *Time* magazine had a galvanizing effect on the business, Jerry and Ben began to have serious doubts about the future shortly after the article appeared. Both were burned out from three years of working sixteen-hour days, seven days a week. They had been struggling constantly to keep their heads above water, and physically the work had taken its toll, especially on Jerry, who was now sixty pounds overweight.

Ben and Jerry were also turned off by the realization that they were becoming businessmen, a vocation toward which they had developed a healthy skepticism while growing up in the sixties. What contribution were they making to the world by taking in money with one hand and paying it out with the other? They had become a cog in an economic machine whose values they had questioned all their lives. The business had grown well beyond the small, community-oriented ice cream shop they had set out to open. They were now running a company whose pints were available in four states and that was selling franchises to other would-be entrepreneurs hoping to duplicate their success.

At the end of the year, Jerry forced the issue when he announced his intention to follow his girlfriend Elizabeth to Arizona. She had been accepted to graduate school and was going to pursue a Ph.D. in psychology. Ben briefly considered keeping the business himself, or bringing in another friend to take Jerry's place, but after reviewing all their options through the winter, they decided to sell the company.

On the first day of spring, 1982, they signed a listing agreement with Country Business Service (CBS), a group of brokers in Vermont that specialized in selling rural businesses. The asking price was $510,000 plus a 3-percent royalty on sales over half a million dollars. The buyer would get all of the company's assets and the rights to continue to operate the business under the trade name, Ben & Jerry's.

Ed Kiniry, the president of CBS, drew up a seven-page summary of the business that briefly described the company's history and success to date. More than one hundred copies of the offering were distributed to potential buyers. Within a month they received a letter of intent from a former executive with M&M Mars.

Thomas P. Hawe was a straitlaced forty-one-year-old who had been a treasurer at Norton Simon prior to joining M&M Mars, where he had responsibility for coordinating the financial audit at the privately held, multibillion-dollar candy company.

Hawe enclosed a $5,000 down payment that went into the CBS

escrow account, and proposed that a purchase and sales agreement be drafted by July 10, and that the deal be closed five days later.

There were still several issues that had to be negotiated, the biggest of which was the security that Hawe was willing to pledge as a guarantee for the note that Ben and Jerry were taking back as part of the deal.

Other than asking for his statement of net worth, Jerry and Ben didn't respond immediately to Hawe's letter of intent. Meanwhile, Hawe and his attorney were working on the assumption that the deal was going ahead as planned. They met with Ed Kiniry on June 28, and the next day Ed wrote a letter to Ben and Jerry outlining the documentation that was needed prior to the closing to ensure a smooth transition.

A week later, Ed met with Jerry in the parking lot outside the plant and pressed him for an answer.

"What can I do to get you to act on the offer?" Ed asked.

"There's nothing you can do. Ben's out on the road, and we haven't had time to hash things out," Jerry responded. "Ben has concerns about certain terms of the offer, and we feel like we need to consult with someone about it."

Ed's recollection of the conversation was slightly different. "The problem isn't with the offer," Ed remembers Jerry saying, "the problem is with Ben."

Aside from the matter of the security, there was no doubt that Ben was seriously ambivalent about the decision to sell the company. Here was someone who was prone to second thoughts about almost every decision he made, even those of little or no consequence. This was the decision of a lifetime. Was he really ready to abandon the business that he and Jerry had given life to, nurtured, and worked their hearts out to keep alive? Their involvement in the business was so personal that it was impossible to delineate where Ben and Jerry ended and where Ben & Jerry's began. Selling the business was like severing a limb. A part of them would be lost forever.

All the parties met in Hawe's lawyer's office on July 28 to try to finalize the deal. At first the discussion centered around the idea that Ben would retain a minority interest and stay on as an employee. Under the deal, Ben would work on the company's marketing and make public appearances, acting as a bushy-bearded Colonel Sanders, sans the white suit. It became apparent, however, that Ben and Hawe wouldn't be able to forge a compatible partnership, and the conversation came back to the security that was being offered to guarantee the note.

Hawe thought his overall net worth, which was just under a million dollars, and personal guarantee were sufficient to appease their concerns. Ben, Jerry, and Sam Bloomberg, their lawyer, wanted the loan secured by specific liquid assets that could easily be converted into cash, in their minds the same type of security that a bank would ask for under similar circumstances. As an alternative, they proposed that Hawe provide them with a letter of credit from a bank, which would guarantee their payments.

Kiniry and Hawe were convinced that the questions being raised about the adequacy of the security were a smokescreen for the real problem, which was Ben's unwillingness to follow through on the decision to sell.

By mid-August it was clear that there wasn't going to be an agreement based on Hawe's original offer. In one last attempt to get beyond the issue of security on the note, Hawe came back with a 100-percent-cash offer on September 1. That offer had been reduced by $75,000 because the profits of the business had been less than anticipated during the summer months, and by another $25,000 to reflect the current value of a lump-sum cash payment at the closing, instead of a ten-year note.

By the time the cash offer from Hawe was received, the listing agreement had expired. More important, Ben had made a firm decision not to sell the business.

The man who ultimately persuaded Ben not to sell was an eclectic restaurateur by the name of Maurice Purpora. Maurice was trying to establish a center for the arts in an old carriage house in Brattleboro, Vermont. The project was called the Royal Yard, and was named for an old diner that he had moved onto the property. Maurice had inquired whether or not Ben & Jerry's would be interested in setting up a scoop shop in the diner.

A month or so later, Ben was in Brattleboro trying to sell new accounts, and stopped in to see him. While he made Ben lunch, Maurice talked about his life, which had included traveling the world while working as a chef for steamship companies, and operating restaurants in both Europe and the United States.

Maurice had a Don Quixote look about him—he was in his late

fifties, very dignified, and had long, gray, wispy hair and a big, waxed handlebar mustache. When he talked, he had a twinkle in his eye that conveyed a love of life, and he told tales that showed his willingness to do all sorts of outlandish and hopelessly romantic things. "I'd like to be like this guy when I get to be his age," Ben thought.

When Ben told him that the business was for sale, Maurice stated flatly that he couldn't possibly sell it.

"If it's so valuable to the guys who are considering buying it," he said, "then it's that much more valuable to you. After all, it's your baby."

"It's just a business that, like all others, exploits its workers and the community," Ben argued back.

"You don't have to run your business that way," Maurice responded. "If there's something you don't like about the business, change it."

Maurice argued forcefully that there was nothing to keep Ben from redefining the business so that it was consistent with his personal values, even if they didn't conform with traditional notions of how a business should be run.

Maurice's enlightened approach to capitalism resolved any lingering doubts Ben had about whether he wanted to pass off his progeny to Hawe, whom the boys had come to refer to as "the man from Mars." After Hawe's cash offer was rejected, Ed Kiniry was informed that they weren't interested in extending the listing agreement, and that the business was no longer for sale.

The decision not to sell didn't change Jerry's plans to go to Arizona, which raised the question of how Ben or the company was going to buy out Jerry's share of the business. To help figure something out, they turned again to Jeff Furman, who said he would try to come up with an arrangement that would get Jerry the equivalent of what he would have gotten had the deal with Hawe gone through.

Jeff's plan was to sell some of Jerry's stock to friends and relations, and he wrote out a simple, three-page outline of the private placement. It briefly recapped the company's history and told of Jerry's plans to head west. An income statement for 1981, which showed a profit of $29,000 on sales of $615,000, was attached.

There were a total of 2,800 shares in the company currently outstanding, with Ben and Jerry each owning half. They priced the shares at $250, which put the total value of the business at $700,000.

On the last page of the offering circular, there was a single multiple-choice question by which the recipient could indicate his or her intentions:

____ Yes, Ben, I don't have anything better to do with my money. I think I'd like to buy _____ shares.

____ Sorry, Ben, if I had it I'd do it, but I don't so I won't.

____ You've got to be kidding.

____ Other _____

____ I've got some questions and/or I need more information. Please contact me at _____.

By law, the private-placement offering was limited to no more than thirty-five investors. There was little chance that many of their friends would be interested, so they sent a copy to everyone they knew.

At the same time that Ben and Jerry were consumed with the start-up of their first business, I was equally engaged in mine, a nightclub called Hunt's. The club was one block away and one block toward the lake from the gas station. I had bought the nightclub with two partners in February of 1978, two months before Ben and Jerry opened their doors. It was one of the few nightspots in town that hadn't put up a mirrored ball and switched over to disco. On weekends it featured local R&B, rock, and jazz bands. Six or seven times a month, a national touring act, like Pat Metheny, Asleep at the Wheel, or Junior Walker and the All Stars would be booked.

Ben, Jerry, and I got to know each other through our businesses. I'd go to their place for cones, they'd come to my place for beer. It was at Hunt's where Fall Down had been christened when Jerry Glowka, the owner of Crispin Leather, tumbled out of his chair while the event was being planned. When Henny Youngman came to Hunt's, Ben, Jerry, and Lyn Severance cooked potato latkes for everybody in the house, including Henny.

Like Ben and Jerry, I had grown up on Long Island, but in Queens, which was part of New York City proper. After graduating from high school, I was intent on finding a more rural location to continue my education, a decision largely influenced by a road trip I took with my parents to deliver my older sister, Anita, to the freshman dorm at

Drexel University in downtown Philadelphia. A decaying urban center was not where I wanted to spend four of my formative years, which is how I came to choose Burlington and the University of Vermont.

I started at UVM in the fall of 1970 as a math major, but switched over to the business school after getting a D minus in calculus in my second semester. The grade was an accurate indication of my academic limitations, but equally a reflection of my inability to get out of bed for an eight-o'clock class, five days a week.

Business, unlike differential equations, came to me naturally. When I was three, I had taken the tin container filled with extra buttons from my mother's sewing kit, and walked around the neighborhood, selling them door to door. I sold petunias and tomatoes out of my garden, polished doorknobs, held carnivals in my backyard, did magic shows, washed and waxed cars, mowed lawns, shoveled snow, and delivered papers.

I took a year off after college, and then entered the graduate business program at the University of Southern California. At the time, the school had an MBA program that gave graduate-school credit for undergraduate business courses taken elsewhere. One year later I had my degree.

When I arrived in California, all of the MBA students were singlemindedly focused on getting a job once they graduated. I was too enthralled with being back in school to give much thought to securing gainful employment. Out of the five or six companies I talked with, only one, Union Bank, offered a second interview, which was only a short-term stay of execution.

The interviews notwithstanding, I was having a great time at school. I spent most of my time between classes in the basement of the law school, which was filled with pinball and foosball machines. I also wrote a sports column for the MBA newsletter, reporting on the exploits of the school's intramural basketball team, Gary Gilmore and the Firing Squad. Come spring, I played centerfield and told tales of our softball team, Roman Polanski, and the Baby Sitters.

Sometime during my second semester at USC, right around the time that I was dusted off by Union Bank, I decided that corporate life in L.A. wasn't for me. What I really wanted to do was go back to Vermont and open up a small business. Totally unaware of Ben and Jerry or their plans, I thought that a homemade ice cream shop might work in Burlington, and after some field research, I wrote out a rough business plan and sent it to some friends from college. Two of them bit, and we were looking for a location in January of 1978 when we came across Hunt's, which had been open for less than a year. My partners and I liked beer at least as much as we liked ice cream, and we were really anxious to stop planning and start doing, so we decided to buy the bar and forgo our scooping careers. Which was a good thing, because three months later, Ben & Jerry's opened around the corner in the gas station.

I hadn't been aware that Ben & Jerry's had been for sale, until after it no longer was. On a Saturday night late in the summer of 1982, Ben came into Hunt's and worked his way through the crowd to the far end, where I was tending bar.

"Well, Chico," he said, "I decided not to sell my business today."

"I didn't know that you were thinking of selling it," I replied, somewhat surprised.

It was busy and we only talked briefly. I bought Ben a gin and tonic, and went back to fixing drinks.

A few weeks later I got a note in the mail that Ben had written on a piece of paper ripped out of a spiral notebook, along with a copy of the private-placement offering.

Dear Chico,

What happens to old bar owners? They become Ben & Jerry's stockholders. Why not? The annual meetings should be lots of fun in themselves, and if you come to the next 30 that's only $100 each. You can buy less shares as part of a group but we have to sell a minimum of $3,000 to one entity.

Ben

Ben followed up on the note with a phone call, inviting me to an informational meeting in a conference room at a local motel. To date, the response to the offering hadn't been overwhelming, but a few of Ben's longtime friends had signed up for the minimum amount. At the meeting, about twenty friends and business associates listened as Jeff Furman took them through the proposal, highlighting both the risks and the potential rewards.

After the meeting, I was walking down the hallway toward the door with Danny Cox, the general manager for Green Mountain Coffee Roasters. Ben came up from behind, wedged his body in between us, and threw an arm around each of us. "Why don't you guys come to work for Ben & Jerry's?" he said, somewhat jokingly. We laughed, spoke a little longer about the offering, and then left.

Ben didn't know it, but I was actively trying to sell Hunt's at the time. I had owned the business for about four and a half years, and had built it into what was widely considered the preeminent nightclub in the state. Both of my original partners were no longer active in the business. One had been bought out within the first year of operation; the second still had an ownership interest, but no longer worked there on a regular basis. Although my workload had lightened substantially as the business became more successful, I was still working until four in the morning, three to five nights a week.

I wasn't sure what I was going to do once the business was sold, but I was looking forward to some time off before getting into something new. Ben's offhand comment pricked my interest, though, and I gave him a call and asked him to come down and talk. As Ben and I sat alone at the bar one afternoon before we opened, he told me how he was going to run the business without Jerry. His intent was to hire a general manager who could oversee all phases of the day-to-day operation. That would leave him free to concentrate on sales and marketing. Even if Jerry stayed, neither of them had the managerial or financial skills needed to run a business that was becoming increasingly complex. Recently a classified ad for the position had run locally and in the *Boston Globe*. Jeff Furman had been helping them sort through the résumés and doing some of the initial interviews.

Most of the applicants were "suits," and Ben had his doubts about working with any of them. Jerry, who was anxious to split, said yes to just about everyone. When Ben casually proposed the idea of my working with him, it had a why-don't-we-go-out-and-play tone to it. Jerry, his closest friend and kindred soul, was leaving him behind. Ben needed to fill that void with someone who could do more than just competently manage the business.

Although there was no firm commitment either way at the end of the meeting, both of us knew that I was going to wind up taking the job. "I got the guy," Ben told Jeff over the phone that night.

Ben and I talked a few more times, reassuring ourselves that we could work well together. I went out to breakfast with Jerry and asked him what it was like to work with Ben. (I don't remember what he said, but in retrospect I'm sure he must have left some stuff out.)

We agreed that I'd work part-time until I sold Hunt's. My salary was set at $20,000 a year, the same as Ben's, and on the assumption that I'd put in two days a week at first, I'd get paid 40 percent of that.

I was interested not only in working for the company, but also in investing in it. Until Hunt's was sold, however, I had no cash. Jerry agreed to take a promissory note for $30,000 in exchange for 120 shares of his stock. I talked my parents and sister into investing another $23,000.

Jeff talked Jerry into retaining 10 percent of the company as an investment. His remaining shares were purchased back by the business and put into treasury. The company didn't have the cash to pay Jerry outright for the stock, so instead he received a consulting agreement that paid him roughly $16,000 annually, for ten years. Under the terms of the agreement, Jerry would return to Burlington four times a year to participate in promotions, help create advertisements, and consult as needed.

The employees had never been told officially that the business had been for sale, but most had surmised that something was in works. One night in September, the staff met at Ben's apartment and the activities of the past six months were revealed. Ben also talked openly for the first time about his intention to create a business that gave something back to the community.

The news of Jerry's imminent departure was greeted by a mixture of sadness and fear. Ben spent a great deal of his time out of the office, and of the two, it was Jerry who had the closer relationship with the employees. Jerry was their first line of defense against all of Ben's crazy ideas. Some worried about the loss of balance with the more accessible and approachable partner no longer involved.

Jerry's last day at work was in early November. Cia Rochford, who had worked alongside of him since the days at the spool-and-bobbin mill, took over production. "I taught Cia everything I knew about managing people, planning, and resisting change," Jerry says proudly.

There was one other lasting casualty of the abortive attempt to sell the company. To make the business more salable, they had moved out of the gas station, for which they never had more than a one-year lease, to another location in downtown Burlington. Other than the founders themselves, nothing personified the business more than their original store. Without it and Jerry, Ben was now running a much different business from the one the two friends had started four and a half years earlier.

CHAPTER SIX

Can You Take It in Twenties?

y first day at Ben & Jerry's was the Monday after the Thanksgiving weekend in 1982. One week later, Country Business Services filed suit against Ben, Jerry, and the company, alleging that CBS had procured a purchaser for the business at the price and terms in the listing agreement, and were therefore entitled to their commission of $50,000. They also sought punitive damages of $100,000, and reimbursement of all their legal expenses.

We countersued, claiming they were using the legal process to harass us without merit, and the lawyers for CBS filed motions seeking a writ of attachment on our bank accounts, arguing before the court that they were likely to win the lawsuit and that we were unlikely to pay. As a precaution, our attorney, Sam Bloomberg, advised us to take most of our money out of the Merchants Bank, and deposit it out of state.

I informed Merchants what we were up to, and picked up a check made out to Ben in the amount of $53,815.77. In reality, we had nowhere near that amount of cash. Outstanding checks that hadn't cleared the account yet typically totaled more than twice our balance. It had taken me only a couple of weeks on the job, managing the company's finances, to realize that playing the float was the key to the company's cash flow.

With the check in hand, Ben and I took the ferry across Lake Champlain to Plattsburgh, New York, and pulled into the first bank we came upon.

"We'd like to open a checking account," Ben announced, once we were seated.

"Will this be a business or personal checking account?" the banker inquired.

"Business," Ben stated.

"Corporation, partnership, or proprietorship?"

"Corporation," Ben replied.

"I'll need to see a copy of the resolution from your board of directors in order to open the account," the banker asserted in a flat, unemotional tone.

Thinking quickly, Ben informed the banker that we had inadvertently left the resolution at home. "There must be a way to get around that requirement," Ben said, more as a statement of fact than a question.

But there was no getting around it. We were told to come back with the resolution, whereupon the banker would be happy to take our fifty-three grand. We decided instead to try another bank.

"We'd like to open a checking account," Ben announced when we were seated at the bank just down the road.

"Personal or business?" the banker inquired.

"Personal," Ben stated. "Just a personal account." I nodded approvingly.

We put both of our names on the account, and gave Ben's apartment as the address. Within ten minutes the money was in the bank, and we had a starter book of eighteen checks.

With our money in the Plattsburgh bank, our daily banking routine became a little more complex. We continued to pay all our bills with checks drawn on our account at the Merchants Bank. Every morning I'd call Merchants to find out how big an overdraft had been created in our checking account the day before. I'd then cover the overdraft at Merchants with a check from the Plattsburgh account, which is where we were making all of our deposits, by mail. Merchants had agreed to cover all the checks that were presented on our account, as long as the overdraft was covered by noon each day.

It seemed as if things were under control, but it didn't take long for our interstate banking scheme to unravel. A week or so after opening the accounts, I called the Plattsburgh bank to check on our balance, and the call was quickly transferred from bookkeeping to a Mr. Conners, one of the branch managers.

"It appears that you're using a personal account for business purposes," he informed me. "Haven't you received the letter I've written you regarding this?"

Anything the bank had sent to us was accumulating in Ben's mailbox. He had left town for ten days, right after we had set up the account. I told Mr. Conners that we had yet to receive his letter.

"Well, have you received the deposits that we've returned to you? We haven't accepted any of the deposits you've sent to us since January tenth."

This was a problem. If the deposits hadn't been credited to our Plattsburgh account, then the checks we'd written to cover our overdrafts at the Merchants Bank would start bouncing. And if those checks bounced, every check we had written on the Merchants account would start bouncing too.

I hung up the phone, grabbed my coat, and drove over to Ben's apartment as fast as I could. If Ben's mailbox was locked, we were screwed. Short of bribing the postman, a week's worth of deposits would be out of reach until Ben came back. In the meantime, both the Plattsburgh and Merchants accounts would become hopelessly overdrawn.

I pulled into the driveway, ran up to the boxes, and breathed an audible sigh of relief. Stuffed into Ben's cubbyhole mailbox, in among the bills and the junk mail, and fully accessible to whoever was passing by on the street, were the deposits that Mr. Conners had sent back.

As it turned out, the entire Plattsburgh banking fiasco was an unnecessary exercise. On January 31, the judge denied CBS's motion, noting that there wasn't a reasonable likelihood that they were going to win the suit.

Most of my time during the first six months was spent trying to get a handle on the company's books. For the previous two years, Ben & Jerry's had used a mail-order bookkeeping service in Randolph, Vermont, to compile their financial statements. At the end of each month, some spread sheets were totaled and two weeks later a P&L and a balance sheet arrived back in the mail. The statements were computer-generated, with all the numbers neatly arranged in their respective columns. They were everything one could want in a P&L, except that they were completely inaccurate. This, of course, was no surprise, given the information on which they were based.

The bookkeeping service just crunched the numbers; they never reviewed the results to see if they made any sense. One month the cost of goods sold would be 85 percent, the next month it would be down to 30 percent. Ben and Jerry knew the statements weren't accurate, but they didn't know what to do about it, and they figured that it would all wash out by the end of the year.

The accuracy of the financial statements became an issue when Jeff Furman was putting together the deal to sell Jerry's stock. Relying on misinformation for internal decision-making was one thing; it was another to make representations to outside investors based on statements that everyone agreed were inaccurate. Jeff told Ben to fire the bookkeeping service, and ship everything to him in Ithaca. When the box arrived, he spread everything out on his kitchen table, and, calculator in hand, tried to sort through it. As one might have expected, it made no more sense to Jeff than it had to the folks in Randolph.

Jeff did manage to generate a handwritten P&L for August, before passing the books off to an accounting firm in Ithaca, which put together a statement for September. When I showed up for work at the end of November, I became the fourth person in four months to tackle the company's books.

I knew there was no hope of arriving at an accurate income statement for 1982. My initial goal was to wind up the year with a reasonably factual balance sheet, and put into place procedures and systems that would allow us to generate accurate monthly P&Ls.

I started with the payables, the money that we owed our suppliers. In addition to a file for each vendor, most of which were stuffed with invoices that dated back to the start of the business four years ago, there were huge, bulging folders marked "To Be Filed." As I sifted through the papers, I came across invoice after invoice that hadn't been recorded on our books, some in envelopes that had never been opened. On the plus side, I also found two hundred dollars in cash and Ben's 1981 refund check from the IRS, for which he was extremely grateful. By the time we reconciled the balances on our books with the statements that our suppliers were sending us, we had added over $25,000 in additional debt to the balance sheet, and wiped out all of the "profit" that had been recorded through the first eleven months of the year.

We were still three years away from buying our first computer, and it would take about ten hours to post the month-end numbers to a two-inch-thick manual general ledger, total each account, and run a trial balance on a calculator. A posting or addition error could take another ten hours to find, depending on how big it was (the small ones took longer to unearth than the big ones). Once the accounts were balanced, a P&L statement for the month and year to date could be drawn up.

Whenever I found a discrepancy between the books and the way things actually were, I'd make entries that I labeled as "adjustments to reality." When all was said and done, we ended 1982 showing a loss of about $4,000 on sales of just under a million. More important, the ghosts of accounting practices past were exorcised in the process, and we started 1983 with a relatively reliable accounting system in place.

I also created systems that began to track our manufacturing costs. We developed standards for each flavor, and started to compare the quantity of ingredients that were used each day with the amount of ice cream that was actually produced. We could then compare our efficiency from one day to the next, and make sure that our product matched our specs.

At the same time I started working for the company, Jeff Furman was added to our board of directors, and began to devote about 25 percent of his time to Ben & Jerry's. Though still living in Ithaca, he consulted on legal and management issues, and came to Burlington at least once a month for a two-day board meeting with Ben and me.

In addition to dealing with the registration laws in the states we were starting to sell franchises in, Jeff was also engaged in a letter-writing contest with the Maine attorney general's office. According to the statutes in Maine, you could only use the word "homemade" in conjunction with dairy products that were "manufactured and frozen under conditions normally found in the home." Despite the fact that our corporate name was Ben & Jerry's Homemade, Inc., the Maine AG's office wanted us to remove the word "homemade" from the logo on the side wall of the pint container.

In an effort to placate the AG's office, Jeff proposed that Ben & Jerry's would undertake a promotional campaign to educate the people of Maine on where and how the ice cream was made. When that option was rejected, Ben told Jeff to suggest that we'd add an asterisk to the word "homemade," and place the following copy to the left of the logo:

> * This ice cream is a recreation of the same homemade style ice cream which Ben and Jerry made famous in their original ice cream parlor. Ben and Jerry, however, did not make this particular pint of ice cream in their homes. They made it in their plant. Enjoy.

67

The Maine AG agreed to that change, but only if the copy was set in a typeface that was as large and prominent on the container as the word "homemade." Had we been packing half-gallons, that might have been a possibility, but there was no way to fit it onto the pint.

Jeff had outlasted one assistant attorney general and was just warming up her replacement, but he finally agreed to replace "Ben & Jerry's Homemade" with "Ben & Jerry's Ice Cream." We didn't want to admit it, but identifying what was in the container wasn't such a bad idea.

The plant at Green Mountain Drive, which Ben and Jerry had worried about being too large when they arrived in 1981, was already too small by 1983. We briefly considered moving to a new location, but decided instead to erect a new freezer behind the plant. The Merchants Bank, impressed with the growth of the business and some-what reassured by the arrival of someone who could balance a check-book, agreed to lend us $100,000 for the project.

Shortly after setting the construction project in motion, Ben took a call from John Gaydos of the Heath Candy Company. Heath had apparently shipped three hundred eighteen-pound cases of factory-second Heath Bars to a warehouse in Boston, and wanted to move them quickly. At the time, Heath Bar Crunch was our best-selling flavor, and we were using about twenty cases of Heath Bars a week. John offered the three hundred cases, some or all, at ninety-nine cents a pound, thirty cents less than our regular price.

Ben knew it was a good deal, but he wasn't sure how many cases to order. I was out of the office when the call came in, so he split the difference, and ordered 150 cases.

When I got back, Ben told me about the phone call. I didn't need a calculator to see that Ben had been too conservative. On the three hundred cases, the discount added up to a savings of over $1,600 that could be realized in less than fifteen weeks.

"Ben, you should have taken them all," I said.

"Well, call him back, and up the order," Ben responded.

I did just that, but when I told John that I'd take all he had, he asked me how many I wanted.

"I thought there were three hundred that were shipped into Bos-ton that you were looking to move," I said.

"There are, but I can give you that price on as many cases as you want," John replied.

This set me back in my seat. An unlimited supply of Heath Bars at ninety-nine cents a pound was almost too good to be true. My enthusiasm was only slightly tempered by the fact that we had no place to store that many Heath Bars, and we didn't have the cash to tie up in excess inventory. Thinking I'd figure out a way to deal with the consequences later, I ordered five hundred cases.

Ben, upon hearing the news, was really enthusiastic about the purchase, not so much because of the savings, but because it was the kind of bold, "what-the-hell" type of move that he loved to make. Since the new freezer wasn't scheduled to be up and running until the end of February, I talked John into holding the bars in Boston until the middle of March. Unfortunately, when the ship date rolled around, the new box was just a concrete foundation and a pile of insulated panels in a snow bank. I returned to the plant one day after lunch to find five hundred cases of Heath Bars stacked up directly behind my desk, floor to ceiling, two rows deep. They covered the entire back wall of the office, and my chair was wedged in place behind my desk. The only way to sit down was to step over the arms and slide in.

Finally the new freezer was completed. It was over ten times the size of our old box, and had racks on which the ice cream was stacked three levels high to take full advantage of the twenty-two-foot-high ceiling. That meant we also had to buy the company's first forklift to move ice cream up, down, and around. It was actually a walk-behind straddle stacker, the most basic and cheapest hydraulic lift available. The brand name was Big Joe, but it went into a hibernative state so often that we nicknamed it "Big Joke." It was warrantied to work in a minus-twenty freezer, but apparently Joe had never read the warranty. When Joe wasn't up to pulling down a pallet of ice cream off the upper racks, we had no choice but to do it by hand. One brave soul would climb the racks and toss down the pints to someone waiting below, who would restack them on another pallet.

Sometime in the spring, Ben received a call from a woman who was organizing an ice cream festival in July at the Hyatt Regency O'Hare in Chicago. Apparently she had heard about our ice cream by way of the article in *Time*, and thought it would be a great coup to have us there. The fact that at the time our ice cream wasn't sold in the Chicago area, let alone anywhere west of Albany, New York, didn't faze her in the least.

Nor did it faze Ben. "A great way to kill a weekend," he reasoned.

"We're gonna be out there eventually, we might as well start building the market." Jerry, who would be back for the summer, agreed to come along.

We left Burlington late Thursday afternoon, intent on pretty much driving straight through to Chicago. Along the way, Jerry and Ben reviewed transcripts of their depositions for the trial with Country Business Services, which was scheduled to begin on September 12. It was important that they not contradict in court what they had testified to during the discovery process earlier in the year. Ben entertained us by reading his deposition aloud, almost like an actor trying to learn his lines.

LAWYER: Were you having any feeling of ambivalence or equivocation at all as to whether or not you really wanted to sell the business?

BEN: I had doubts at some times, that's about it.

LAWYER: Throughout the entire period?

BEN: No.

LAWYER: When did you have these doubts?

BEN: I don't recall the dates of my doubts.

LAWYER: I'm not asking you for the dates of your doubts. I'm asking you rather to express whether you had these doubts continuously up to and including the time when you saw Mr. Kiniry's letter or whether they were doubts that had been resolved earlier, or what.

BEN: I did not have the doubts continuously. The doubts did get resolved, I'm not sure of the dates.

The trial, it seemed, was going to come down to "What did Ben doubt, and when did he doubt it?"

The Hyatt Regency O'Hare was a twelve-story luxury hotel that featured an atrium lobby that was the signature design element of the chain. Ben hadn't had a chance to pack, so he had taken all of his clean laundry, which, conveniently enough, was still in a plastic basket, albeit with a broken handle. Looking (and smelling) more than a little ripe from our sixteen-hour trip, the three of us wandered through the lobby toward the front desk, Ben leading the way in full embrace of his laundry basket.

Ben was scheduled to participate in a panel discussion opening the festival, and he started to work on his presentation over breakfast on Saturday morning. As was his standard practice, Ben never started thinking too seriously about a speech until about an hour beforehand. He scratched out some notes on a napkin, and took his place on the dais along with three other industry notables, Harry Bresler of Bresler's 33 Flavors, Vic DeGuilio of Dean Foods, and Ann Bassett, of Bassetts Ice Cream.

All four participants had been given the same assignment—to try to capture in about ten minutes why America was so fascinated with ice cream.

Ann Bassett went first, and took a historical approach, noting that the first ice cream evolved from chilled wines and other iced beverages, that Marco Polo had learned about ice cream from the Chinese in the thirteenth century, and that the first ice cream cone was made at the St. Louis World's Fair in 1904. It was all basic stuff, taken right out of the introduction to any standard ice cream book. Harry Bresler, looking somewhat disheartened, confessed that most of what he had to say had been covered by Ms. Bassett. It reminded me of elementary school, where you always wanted to be the first to read your report because half the class had copied it word for word right of out of the *World Book Encyclopedia.*

Vic DeGuilio had also taken a historical approach to the assignment, and sat down rather quickly after adding one or two facts that the earlier speakers had overlooked.

And then it was Ben's turn. By this time, most people in the crowd were resigned to hearing about Marco Polo one more time. Ben began by noting that the ink on his napkin was still wet, which accounted for why he was the last one to speak. He then proceeded to compare the oral sensations experienced by a newborn infant sucking on his or her mother's breast with those of an adult licking an ice cream cone. This, he concluded, and not Marco Polo, was the essence of ice cream and America's love affair with the dessert.

On the way back to Vermont, we wrote a letter to the president of Hyatt, giving him some feedback on the weekend and suggesting he throw in the Sunday brunch for free next year "for those exhibitors driving over one thousand miles round trip in a trucklike van or a vanlike truck, and endangering their entire corporate structure by placing all their executives and entire board of directors in one vehicle."

To demonstrate our sincerity, we enclosed a copy of an ad we had run once in a local weekly. Under the photo from the pint container, the headline read, "When in Chicago, Ben & Jerry Always Stay at the Fabulous Hyatt Regency O'Hare. For reservations, call 800-228-9000." It was the last and only time that Ben and Jerry offered their personal endorsements for fifteen dollars' worth of food.

The trial for the Country Business Services lawsuit began in September. In the nine months since the suit had been filed, there had been no substantial effort to settle the case out of court. Sam Bloomberg, the attorney who had successfully rebutted the pretrial motion for a writ of attachment on our bank accounts, was confident he would prevail at trial.

That Ben and Jerry had changed their minds and decided not to sell the business was obviously not subject to dispute. At issue was whether Tom Hawe's offer conformed with the terms set out in the listing agreement that Ben and Jerry had signed, and whether the collateral he had offered to secure the note was reasonable.

CBS had retained Robert Hemley, a young, aggressive litigator from a respected local firm, to represent them. In his opening argument, Hemley laid out his case to the jury. He told them that Ben had had second thoughts about selling the company that were never fully resolved, even after the listing agreement had been signed. "My client, Ed Kiniry, has no quarrel with Ben's right to change his mind," Hemley said, "but he's entitled to his commission because he held up his end of the contract by bringing forward a buyer who made an offer consistent with the terms of the agreement." The issue of collateral, Hemley told the jury, was a smoke screen that Ben had raised only because he wanted to get out of the contract without having to pay Kiniry his commission. Hemley's arguments were reasoned, well constructed, and even sounded convincing to Ben. "I thought his opening argument made perfect sense," Ben recalls. "I was ready to convict."

Sam's defense was based on the inadequacy of the collateral that Hawe was offering for the note to Ben and Jerry, and the fact that Kiniry had told them they had the right to reject the security. Hawe's limited real-estate partnerships were inadequate, Sam argued, because they weren't liquid and couldn't be transferred. Furthermore, Hawe's offer required Ben and Jerry to subordinate the note they were taking back to whatever future bank debt the business incurred, meaning that over time, they would be pushed farther and farther down the financial food chain.

Unfortunately, rather than trying to craft an argument that would allow the jury to see the case from Ben and Jerry's perspective, Sam tried to refute Hawe's and Kiniry's accusations one by one, which turned out to be extremely ineffective. Sam had done skillful work in the pretrial motions, but in court he was overwhelmed by Hemley, who was a superior litigator.

When the closing arguments were completed on the morning of the fifth day of the trial, the judge gave the jury its instructions, and sent it off to deliberate. Jeff had flown in for the last day of the trial to testify, and he and Ben, Jerry, and Sam sat together in a room just outside the courtroom and contemplated their fate. At one point, finding himself in the men's room pissing next to Ed Kiniry, Jeff wanted to try to settle the case. "I thought to myself," Jeff recalls, " 'This is where it's supposed to happen, in the men's room, ten minutes before the jury comes out,' but Sam decided not to make an offer."

In less than two hours, both parties were notified that the jury had reached a decision, and everyone filed back in. Ben, Jerry, and Sam stood nervously behind their table, looking up to the jury along the right wall of the courtroom.

The judge asked the foreman if the jury had reached a decision.

"Yes, we have, your honor."

"Do you find that there was a valid brokerage contract between the plaintiff and the defendant?" the judge asked.

"Yes, we do, your honor."

"Do you find that the plaintiff produced a financially ready, willing, and able buyer for the defendants' business according to the agreed terms of sale before the contract expired?"

"Yes, we do."

"Accordingly, you must enter a verdict for the plaintiff and award the plaintiff the commission."

That was a quick $50,000, but the jury was just warming up.

"Do you find that under the contract, the defendants acted in a way that entitles plaintiff to punitive damages?"

"Yes, we do, your honor."

"What amount of punitive damages do you find the defendants under consideration should pay?"

"Twelve thousand dollars apiece for Mr. Cohen and Mr. Greenfield, and $6,000 for Ben & Jerry's Homemade, Inc.," the foreman responded.

Another $30,000. After the jury tacked on Hemley's legal bill of $14,000 and $6,000 for interest, our balance sheet was a nice, round hundred thousand dollars lighter.

Immediately after the verdict, Hemley jumped up and moved to attach the assets of the business. Sam objected, but Hemley had drawn up the papers in advance and already had them in the judge's hands. The motion was granted less than sixty seconds after the verdict was announced.

Ben, Jerry, and Sam stood there stunned. "Quick, go run to the bank and take out all your money," Sam told them before they could sit down. "In cash!" It was the best piece of advice he'd given on the case. Unfortunately, his timing was a little off, and Ben and Jerry now found themselves in a foot race with the sheriff up Church Street to the Merchants Bank.

The bank was only a block from the courthouse, and Jeff had gone ahead to try to start the transaction for them. Ben and Jerry got to the bank just as Jeff got to the front of the line. All three, agitated and out of breath, stood before the teller.

"We want to take out all the money in all of our accounts," Ben told her. "In cash!"

The teller looked at them, somewhat taken aback. "I've got to talk to my supervisor," she said, and she methodically closed and locked her cash drawer and disappeared into the back room. A few minutes later she returned with her boss.

"What's going on?" the supervisor inquired.

"We just lost this court case, and our lawyer told us to get all our money in cash," Ben blurted out, hoping that the sense of panic in his voice might light a fire under someone.

It did. The supervisor, somewhat concerned about the increasing commotion at the teller window, called Dudley Davis, the president of the bank, who ushered the three of them upstairs into his office.

"Now, boys, what seems to be the problem here?" Dudley asked.

"We need our money, we want it all. In cash," Ben repeated.

Jeff briefly explained what had happened in the courtroom.

"Okay," Dudley replied, "I'll help you out. Wait here." Whereupon he left the room.

"Can you take it in twenties?" he asked when he came back in.

"Sure, twenties, whatever, as long as it's in cash," Ben said, beginning to calm down a little.

Dudley left the room again. "The sheriff is here, he's trying to get your money," Dudley told them when he returned a few minutes later. Whatever you do, don't go downstairs."

A short time later, the money arrived in Dudley's office, and they began to count it. There was just under $90,000 dollars.

When things settled down, Ben called me at the plant. I'd been tending to the business throughout the trial, and had only sat in on the closing arguments. It had been enough to convince me that Ben's nightly predictions of impending disaster were probably accurate, so the news didn't take me completely by surprise.

"Chico, are you sitting down?" Ben asked in a very flat voice.

"Yeah, what's up?"

"We just dropped a hundred big ones."

"No," I said.

"Yeah," Ben replied.

"No," I said again.

"I'm afraid so, Chico, we're at the bank, and we're taking out all our money."

"Noooo," I said, this time kind of laughing.

"Yeahhh," Ben repeated, kind of laughing too. We were already beginning to see the humor in it.

Early that evening, Jeff caught a flight back to Ithaca, taking all the money with him in a shopping bag. When he walked into his house that night, he dumped the money on his bed in front of his girlfriend. "Look what I've brought back from Vermont," he announced.

The next day, Jeff put the cash in a safe deposit box at a local bank, and we once again embarked on a series of convoluted out-of-state banking transactions, which, though legal, were worthy of any money launderer.

Sam, who had been taken aback by the verdict, was confident he could win on appeal, and he filed a twelve-page brief supporting motions for a new trial. Jeff was convinced an appeal would be a continued financial and emotional drain on the business, and that we had to get the case behind us. He told Sam he was going to try to settle with Hemley.

Having lost the trial, we had very little leverage in the negotiations. All we could hold over their heads was Sam's threat to appeal the case, which would tie them up in additional litigation and put their judgment at risk. It also didn't hurt that we had gotten our money out of state, where they couldn't get their hands on it.

A couple of weeks after the verdict, Jeff talked by phone with Stewart McConaughy, a lawyer who had assisted Hemley during the trial. McConaughy followed up the conversation with a letter offering to settle the case for $80,000, provided the deal was done within two weeks. McConaughy also made it clear that the offer wasn't his opening gambit in a protracted back-and-forth negotiation. "This offer is a one-time-only, take-it-or-leave-it proposition," the letter stated. "The mere mention of a smaller figure or a later date will cause its automatic revocation."

Somehow, Jeff did mention a lower figure, and within a week both sides agreed to $75,000. That was a huge amount of money relative to our sales, earnings, and, most important, our cash flow. Fortunately, we'd just raised some cash by selling to friends and employees some of the stock the company had taken back from Jerry. The money had originally been earmarked to pay for an expansion of the plant, but in mid-October it was paid to Kiniry, which finally put the matter to rest.

In retrospect, we could have settled the case out of court for less than we wound up paying Sam in legal fees. Given that it was a no-up-side lawsuit, that's what we should have done. Going to trial, the best we could have hoped for was to pay our lawyer a lot of money and be found innocent. Why not pay the plaintiffs some money and be done with it? That approach would have eliminated a major distraction for our senior management, as well as the risk of getting creamed in court, which is what happened.

"They could have found us innocent, guilty, really guilty, or really, really guilty," Ben tells people when he speaks of the trial. "They found us really, really guilty."

CHAPTER SEVEN

Send in the Clones

With the lawsuit behind us, we were once again able to focus all of our attention on expanding our sales into new markets. This meant we would have to compete with the increasing number of superpremium ice cream brands.

Reuben Mattus is universally acknowledged as the person who created the superpremium ice cream market with the introduction of Häagen-Dazs in 1960. Reuben started out in a small kitchen in the Bronx in the 1920s, making ice cream pops and lemon ices, which he delivered to local candy stores and luncheonettes from a horse-drawn wagon.

Although extremely innovative, Reuben, like all the small, independent ice cream manufacturers in New York, was at a decided disadvantage to the two large companies that dominated the market. It was the ice cream marketed by Breyers and Borden that the retailers and consumers wanted, and all the independents struggled to carve out a viable business by selling their product lines to mom-and-pop grocery stores and restaurants.

Beyond the built-in disadvantage of selling brands that were less recognized, Reuben was also faced with stiff price competition from the larger manufacturers, who were able to work on lower margins and offer financial incentives to the retailers that he couldn't match. By the 1950s, price had become the consumer's overriding consideration in choosing ice cream, and manufacturers responded with half-gallon containers that retailed for under fifty cents. To cut their costs, the ice cream companies began using cheaper, lower-quality ingredients, including artificial colorings and flavorings. They also reduced the amount of butterfat to the mandated federal minimum of 10 percent, and increased the amount of air, or overrun, to 100 percent, the maximum allowed by the regulations. It was cold and it was sweet, and beyond that, no one seemed to care what it tasted like.

In the late fifties, sensing that a niche might exist for a higher-quality product, Reuben began experimenting with different formulas. By increasing the butterfat to 16 percent, decreasing the overrun to 20 percent, and using only all-natural ingredients of the highest quality, he created an ice cream that was richer, heavier, and more flavorful than anything else on the market.

Reuben thought his target market of well-educated, middle- and upper-income consumers would be favorably disposed to a product with a foreign-sounding name, so he called the ice cream Häagen-Dazs. The package prominently featured a map of Scandinavia on the lid, with a star indicating the Danish capital city of Copenhagen. "I figured there were people who hated the Irish, there were people who hated the Italians, there were people who hated the Poles, there were people who hated the Jews," Reuben has said. "But nobody hated the Danes."

In fact, the words "Häagen-Dazs" have no meaning, and the umlaut that Reuben used for effect isn't part of the Danish written language. The ice cream itself, far from being imported, was being made in Reuben's shoebox-sized plant in the Bronx.

When it was first introduced, Häagen-Dazs was only available in three flavors, vanilla, chocolate, and coffee. The pints sold for around sixty-nine cents, which was much more expensive than any other product. As a result, sales built very slowly, and the ice cream still hadn't made much of a dent in the marketplace ten years after it was introduced.

In the early seventies, higher-quality "imported" products began to find favor with consumers, and the brand started to take off. Reuben had three guys working the streets, selling the ice cream to the upscale mom-and-pop groceries in Manhattan and the more affluent suburbs. The salesmen would fill the trunks of their cars with ice cream kept frozen on dry ice, and when they sold an account, they'd immediately fill up the freezer with pints of Häagen-Dazs.

The key to persuading the supermarkets to carry the product was getting the ice cream into the mouths of the buyers and their supervisors. If necessary, Reuben's salesmen would bring the product right to the buyers' homes. One by one, the chains started to take the product, putting it in a couple of stores in their best neighborhoods to start. As an introductory deal, Reuben offered the retailer a fairly standard trade allowance of one free sleeve for every five purchased on the initial order. (A "sleeve" of pints contains eight cartons, a total of a gallon.) Outside of that, he never discounted the product, concerned that any degradation of its retail price would detract from the image of the brand.

Sales grew steadily through the seventies, benefiting from strong word-of-mouth advertising and a growing cult following. As Häagen-Dazs addicts from New York traveled throughout the country, they began to ask for the ice cream, and Reuben began to sell to distributors outside of New York to meet the demand. By 1980, Häagen-Dazs was available in all but three states.

Reuben's increasing success with Häagen-Dazs didn't go unnoticed in the fiercely competitive New York City market. One person who noticed was Richie Smith, who manufactured several brands of ice cream that he distributed out of Calip Dairies, on Jamaica Avenue in Queens. Richie had taken over an ice cream business that his father, Lester, a lawyer by trade, had put together by acquisition. In the early seventies, Lester picked up the rights to the Dolly Madison brand, and it was that product line that was the mainstay of Richie's business.

In addition to his own brands, Richie was also distributing Häagen-Dazs to the small grocery stores on his routes. Intent on growing his business, Richie approached Reuben Mattus and told him he wanted to take over the distribution of Häagen-Dazs at all the supermarkets. Reuben, who delivered to the chain stores with his own trucks, had no incentive to turn over control of his most important retail accounts to another distributor, and he turned Richie down.

When he realized that he wasn't going to get Häagen-Dazs for the supermarkets, Richie tried to go Reuben one better, by creating Frusen Glädjé.

In Sweden, its purported country of origin, Frusen Glädjé translates as "Frozen Delight." Like Häagen-Dazs, it was a 16-percent-butterfat, 20-percent-overrun product, with all-natural ingredients. In an effort to create an aura of authenticity, Richie set up a shell corporation in Sweden, and put a Stockholm address on the package. He also included the requisite map of Scandinavia and had much of the information printed on the container in both Swedish and English. Meanwhile, the ice cream was made in a Dairylea plant in Utica, New York.

Reuben reacted to Frusen Glädjé as one might expect. He sued, claiming that Richie had ripped him off, all the way down to his umlauts. Reuben was of a mind that he had proprietary rights to high-quality ice creams with funny, foreign-sounding names. The court decided he didn't. The only consequence of the suit was that Richie had to remove the Swedish address and identify the product as being made in America.

Richie Smith was not the only one jumping on the faux-foreign bandwagon. Abe Kroll, like Reuben Mattus, was a European Jewish immigrant; he had gotten into the ice cream business in the early forties, with his brothers Jack and Mickey. About the same time that Richie came out with Frusen Glädjé, Abe's company, Gold Seal Riviera Ice Cream, introduced Alpen Zauber. With unspoken-for Scandinavian countries at a premium, Abe turned to central Europe, and touted a "Swiss Commitment to Excellence" on the pints he cranked out of his factory on 921 East New York Avenue. In short order, virtually every ice cream manufacturer, both large and small, was after a piece of the superpremium ice cream pie, with brands like Très Chocolat; Perche No!; 'Ja; Le Glace de Paris; Geláre; Godiva; and Strasels. Häagen-Dazs, which had created the category, portrayed itself as a brand of sophisticated elegance. The clones all assumed Häagen-Dazs's image was as essential to marketing superpremium ice cream as raising the butterfat and lowering the overrun, and copied it slavishly. They all took foreign-sounding names, and tried to create slick and snobbish marketing images.

The TV spots for the introduction of Frusen Glädjé epitomized the trend. In the ads, a Rolls-Royce pulled up to an expensive restaurant and beautiful people in fur coats walked through the night. In the closing scene, a comely blond woman was seated on a couch in her bedroom that had a man's suit jacket casually thrown over the back. While she held a pint of Frusen Glädjé like a marital aid, a voice-over proclaimed, "When you taste unbelievably delicious Frusen Glädjé, you may never want anything else." Richie's advertising agency was trying to convince the American consumer that a good ice cream cone was better than sex.

With all the new brands, it wasn't surprising that the superpremium market segment was booming despite the fact that overall ice cream sales experienced only modest, single-digit growth between 1980 and 1982. In 1982 alone, with Häagen-Dazs leading the way, sales of the high-priced pints jumped 70 percent, and they now accounted for 20 percent of the total ice cream market, up from only 11 percent just one year earlier.

That expensive ice creams came of age during a recession seemed counterintuitive to some. The most readily offered explanation was that the product was an affordable luxury. While consumers were forced to put off major purchases of cars, houses, and vacations, nearly all could afford to indulge themselves with ice cream. The boom in the superpremium category was also part of an overall trend in the eighties toward higher-quality products. People wanted the best, and were willing to pay for it.

(The diet and health trends that became prominent at the very end of the decade had limited impact during this period of rapid growth, even though the negative consequences of foods high in fat and cholesterol were known at the time. Weight Watchers had studies that showed that ice cream was the number-one food people gave up their diets for. It was America's favorite dessert, and people seemed more inclined to make an exception for ice cream than for anything else.)

By 1980, Reuben Mattus had built Häagen-Dazs into a $30-million business. Over the next two years, sales would double and then almost double again, to $115 million. In June of 1983, Reuben sold the business to the Pillsbury Corporation, for a reported $80 million.

Ben & Jerry's image and marketing approach was exactly the opposite of everyone else's. If Häagen-Dazs and the clones were worldly and elegant, we were funky and unpretentious. If they were slick and sophisticated, Ben & Jerry's was down-home and genuine. "We're the only superpremium whose name you can pronounce," Ben would point out, as brand after foreign-sounding brand was introduced.

Our flavors also set us apart from the competition. Over the years, Häagen-Dazs had increased the number of flavors they offered, but they were all either "straight" flavors, without any chunks added in, or relatively traditional combinations, like Chocolate Chocolate Chip. Our best-sellers were Heath Bar Crunch; Dastardly Mash, a combination of pecans, walnuts, chocolate chunks, and raisins in a deep chocolate base; and Mint with Oreo Cookies. (Formerly Mint Oreo, the flavor's name had been changed at the request of Nabisco's legal department.)

Ben eventually synthesized our core marketing proposition down to the following: "Two real guys, Ben & Jerry, who live in Vermont, the land of green grass, blue sky, and black-and-white cows, where they make world-class ice cream in some really unusual flavors." That marketing image hadn't come from a calculated attempt to run counter to the crowd. It had been forged in the early days at the gas station, when a lack of money dictated that the company be what the company was.

The name of the business, having the pictures of the principals on the lid, the slogan "Vermont's Finest All Natural Ice Cream," the funky flavors, and the handmade graphics on the pint were a natural extension of a business that had started out as a homemade ice cream parlor. It was no accident that our image was so distinct from Häagen-Dazs and the clones, which all had their roots in the packaged ice cream industry. What was remarkable, however, was that, with little thought of the consequences, Ben and Jerry had perfectly positioned the company with a unique identity in the suddenly overcrowded superpremium market.

Having a marketing image and a flavor assortment different from those of our competitors gave us an opening with the retailers that we might not otherwise have enjoyed. With limited shelf space, most supermarkets weren't going to carry more than three superpremium brands. Everyone was going to stock Häagen-Dazs, the clear market leader. We were competing with the clones to be the second or possibly the third superpremium in the store.

It was our hypothesis that the clones cannibalized each other, dividing up a limited amount of business among themselves. Retailers gained little by offering Alpen Zauber if they already carried Häagen-Dazs and Frusen Glädjé. The flavors offered by all three brands were nearly identical, and while one of the product lines might develop a following, more than likely it would come at the expense of the other two. Overall, the store was unlikely to see a net increase in sales.

Our flavors and funky brand image appealed to a different group of consumers, many of whom had not previously been drawn to the high-end ice creams. In essence, we created a niche within a niche, and in so doing, we expanded the overall size of the market. Though some of our sales certainly came at the expense of Häagen-Dazs or Frusen Glädjé, others would come from new customers who were trading up to superpremium ice cream for the first time from regular or premium brands. That translated into increased total sales for the higher-margin superpremium category, which was what retailers were looking for.

Ben & Jerry's was not the only "American-style" superpremium ice cream. Double Rainbow, a West Coast brand widely available in

San Francisco, had begun to move into Southern California. Bart's, a homemade ice cream parlor in Northampton, Massachusetts, was also starting to package its product in pints for the retail trade. Two more established ice creams, Bassetts of Philadelphia and Bud's in San Francisco, were growing beyond their traditional markets. Both of these brands had 80-percent overruns, and thus were not technically superpremiums, but they were packaged in pints and competed with Häagen-Dazs and the clones for shelf space.

Ben and I had no long-term strategic plan for the business. Decisions were made incrementally, from month to month and summer to summer, as opportunities and problems presented themselves.

Through the fall of 1983, the largest market in which Ben & Jerry's had successfully sold its ice cream was Albany, New York. Both of us figured that we should enter Boston next, thinking that it would be a true test of whether we could compete in a major urban market against Häagen-Dazs and the other superpremiums. Our assumption was that if we could enter Boston and gain a respectable market share, we could then duplicate that feat in other large metropolitan areas across the country, should we want to.

Ben & Jerry's had actually started selling some ice cream in the Boston market two years earlier. The owner of the Waban Market, an upscale grocery store in the suburb of Newton, had read about the company in *Time* and tasted the ice cream at the gas station while visiting his daughter, who was a student at UVM. In November of 1981, Ben and Jerry drove to Newton and personally delivered two hundred sleeves of pints—enough, they figured, to hold over their one account for a while.

To mark the event, Ben sent out a press release titled "Two Crazy Vermont Hippies Invade Boston with Their Ice Cream," in which he wrote, "While the invasion of Boston by way of the Waban Market might not be termed a full-scale attack, Ben and Jerry figure that it will at least pay for the gas."

Servicing one account in a market two hundred miles from their factory in Vermont made no sense, and in the summer of 1982, Ben hooked up with Bernie Reitman, who had a company called Alternative Distributor. Alternative's main product lines were specialty breads. Unfortunately, since bread was fresh and the ice cream frozen, there was no synergy between the two products from a distribution standpoint. Bernie would simply put the ice cream into a cloth-sided, wheel-around laundry basket, toss some dry ice onto it, cover the load with a blanket, and roll it into the back of a bread truck.

Bernie took over deliveries to the Waban Market and added about thirty more accounts. While Ben was happy to have the added sales in Boston, Bernie's shoestring approach to the ice cream business began to create problems with the quality of the product. (If ice cream gets too warm and then refreezes, it tends to develop texture defects.) In an effort to help, Ben sold Bernie the company's original delivery truck, which by now was pushing 300,000 miles. The problems in Boston persisted, however, and in July the decision was made to try to service the accounts ourselves, from Vermont. We figured it was a stopgap measure to maintain our toehold in the market until we could arrange for another local distributor.

We had only one delivery truck, which was fully booked, six days a week. Instead, we used the special-events van, just back from Chicago and its maiden voyage to the ice cream festival at the Hyatt. The driver would set out for Boston at around five in the morning, trying to get to his first stop before nine, returning to Vermont late the next night.

In the meantime, Ben was making regular trips into Boston, trying to line up a new distributor. Jim O'Donnell from Sweetheart Paper, who was selling us our pint cups, went around with Ben, and introduced him to all the players. O'Donnell was a middle-aged Boston Irishman, dressed casually but conservatively in a sport coat and slacks. Ben, with his bushy beard, and wearing an old shirt and a pair of jeans with holes in the knees, looked as though he'd just come in from milking fifty head of Holsteins.

The first distributor they approached was Hendries, a $30-million-plus ice cream manufacturer that was based in Milton, Massachusetts. When O'Donnell brought Ben in to see Graham West, the director of marketing of Hendries, West's eyes just about popped out.

Ben always brought ice cream with him on his sales calls. On overnights to Boston, he'd keep the samples in the walk-in freezer of the Denny's restaurant next door to his motel. At Hendries, Ben passed out the pints and gave his sales pitch while West ate the ice cream. When Ben was through, West gave him an education in how things worked in the big city.

"You know, kid," West said, "you're gonna have to come up with a little up-front money if you want to get into the supermarkets."

"What do you mean?" Ben said.

"You have to give them a deal, a little incentive," West responded.

"I couldn't do that," Ben said with a straight face. "I don't do it for my other customers, why would I do it for them?"

"Then you've got to give 'em some ice cream, say for every gallon they buy, give them one for free," West persisted.

"Oh, no, I couldn't do that," Ben repeated. "I can't afford it."

Ben's unwillingness to bend to the rules of the game drove West to frustration. That night he called up Jim O'Donnell, laughing hysterically. "Is this guy for real?" West asked. Most of Hendries's business was selling products they manufactured, and West ultimately decided not to take on the new line.

"Go see the guy in Canton," West told Ben, "he buys all kinds of things."

The guy in Canton was Paul Tosi, of Paul's Distributors. Paul's had started in 1969 as a one-truck operation delivering Hood, the dominant brand of ice cream and dairy products in New England. By 1981, Tosi's business was already up to four trucks, when he was the low bidder on a contract to deliver Hood ice cream to all the supermarkets in the Boston area. Tosi gradually added more and more product lines, including Häagen-Dazs, so he could offer the stores one-stop shopping. Eight more trucks were added to handle the supermarket business, and Paul's became the largest independent ice cream distributor in the market.

By November of 1983, Ben had met with both Tosi and Chuck Green, his general manager, and been turned down twice. They had tried the ice cream and thought it was a good product, but Häagen-Dazs was clearly the brand to have, and they weren't convinced that there was a market for an "unsophisticated" superpremium. Ben talked with other, smaller distributors, but he had his mind set on getting Paul's. He set up one more appointment with Chuck Green, and drove into Boston the night before, arriving well after midnight. Rather than get a hotel for a few hours' sleep, Ben drove right over to Canton, and slept in his car. He was fast asleep in the front seat when Chuck Green got to work at five in the morning. Ben's persistence paid off. Paul's agreed to take on the product.

Tosi and Green, like Graham West at Hendries, told Ben he'd have to buy his way into the chains. Ben still wasn't ready to cave in, but he agreed to give a dollar off a sleeve as an intro allowance on the initial order, if Paul's would match it. Ben figured that if the distributor was tied into the same deal he was, there would be some incentive to keep it from getting out of hand. Two dollars off per gallon wasn't as rich as the deals now being routinely offered by national consumer product companies like Kraft, but it was enough for a small business like Ben & Jerry's, which was just starting out in the big leagues.

A few hours after they made the deal, Ben and Tosi pitched their first account, and sold Purity Supreme, a sixty-store supermarket chain. The real invasion of the Boston market was about to begin.

To ensure the success of the Boston intro, we decided to hire a full-time salesperson. Paul's carried literally hundreds of products; as good a distributor as they were, we needed someone in the market making sure our brand was being aggressively introduced to all of their accounts.

Up to that point, Ben had singlehandedly done all the sales and marketing for what was, by then, a $1.5-million wholesale business. The person we hired was Wayne Bernard, who had been working in Albany, New York, as a sales manager for Heluva Good Cheese. Wayne got Ben's used Scirocco for a company car, and was sent into the market to sign up retail accounts.

To beef up the initial sales effort, we sent Mark Belcher and Paul Stephens, two long-term employees, to work with Wayne. Ben, who was spending virtually all of his time on the road, had taken a short-term rental on a two-bedroom apartment in Waltham, and everyone stayed there. At night, usually over pizza and beer, working with an account list from Paul's and the Yellow Pages listings of grocery stores, Wayne and the others would map out the twenty or so stores that each of them were going to hit the next day. They went into the accounts intent on taking orders; at the end of the day, they'd have a stack of them from the retailers who had agreed to take our ice cream. Within a day or two, Paul's trucks made the initial delivery and "cut the product" into the case. Selling the retail accounts in Boston was relatively easy, and with Wayne leading the way, it wasn't unusual for the sales team to sign up ten to fifteen new stores a day.

Getting the ice cream onto the grocery-store shelves was one challenge; getting consumers to buy it was another. We had a $30,000 marketing budget for the Boston campaign. Thirty thousand dollars dwarfed anything we had ever spent before, but for launching a new consumer product into a major metropolitan market, it was a laughably small sum.

Most of the money was earmarked for TV. Altman & Manley, a small Boston ad agency, was hired to produce some ten-second spots.

They featured a life-size reproduction of the pint lid, with an opening in the middle so that Ben and Jerry would be "live on the lid." After shooting the four ads that the agency had written, Ben said he had one more that he wanted to shoot. He called the spot "Cheap." It went like this:

"Hi, I'm Ben."

"And I'm Jerry."

"We may not have enough money for a thirty-second TV spot, but we sure make some of the best ice cream you ever tasted."

And that was it. Ben decided that of all the spots, he liked "Cheap" the best, and that was the only one he was going to use. The ad was scheduled to run exactly 132 times over a two-month period, an average of just over two times per day. (By way of comparison, McDonald's typically runs thirty full- or half-minute TV spots every day, in every major market in the country.) The buy was too small to have any impact on product sales, but the supermarket buyers insisted on a TV schedule for any new product launch, and it was done exclusively for their benefit. Each buyer was sent a copy of the schedule, which listed the date, station, time, and program for each of the 132 times that the ad was going to run. Most were on the local UHF station during reruns of "Star Trek," "The Fugitive," and "Leave It to Beaver." To beef up the listing, we ran a few on "Saturday Night Live" and "Late Night with David Letterman," which at the time was new and reasonably affordable.

In an effort to make the buy seem more substantial, each week's schedule was printed on a separate sheet, so that the buyers had a stack of papers in their hands. In reality, the buy was so inconsequential that if we hadn't told the buyers exactly when and where the ads were running, they probably wouldn't have believed that we were actually running them. The odds of someone flipping on his TV and seeing one of our spots, let alone listening closely enough to comprehend the message and remember what product we were pushing, were remote.

There was also some radio, a few print ads in the *Phoenix*, the alternative weekly paper, and two ads in *Boston Magazine*, one of which listed all the stores where the ice cream was available.

Which meant that we were still left with the problem of creating enough interest in the product so that consumers would buy it. Ben figured that the most effective way to promote the ice cream was to get as many people as possible to taste it.

Although paid media coverage was extremely expensive in a major market like Boston, we could sample our ice cream almost as cheaply in a big city as we could in Vermont. We decided to shut down the second shift in our plant temporarily, and send the four-person production crew to Boston to pass out pints. Hell, they could stay with the sales guys at the apartment in Waltham.

Once again, the special-events van was called into service. The crew left Vermont in darkness, arriving in Boston just as the sun was coming up. They met up with Ben at the apartment, picked up some ice cream over at Paul's, and then set out on their mission. "There's a good place, go down there," Ben would shout out to the driver from the passenger seat. When he found a spot to his liking, Ben would tell the driver to pull over, the doors in the back of the van would swing open, and Ben and the crew would go charging into whatever office building they happened to have parked in front of. They had cloth bags slung over their shoulders, like those used by paper boys, that were loaded up with pints, plastic spoons, and twenty-five-cents-off coupons. On the back of the coupons we'd printed an updated list of all the stores in Boston where the ice cream was available. Splitting up into two teams of two, they'd wander through the building, passing out ice cream to startled workers.

According to Wendy Yoder, who went on two of the trips, the reactions were varied. "Some people wouldn't take it, sort of a 'don't take candy from strangers' thing. Some people wouldn't say anything, but they'd look at you like you were on drugs. Some people would take it reluctantly and hold the pint like it was going to explode, until they saw other people taking off the lids and eating it, and then it was okay. And then we had some people who would come back and ask for more. They wanted a couple of pints to take home."

The Prudential Center was the only place where they ran into trouble. Ben and the crew managed to get up the elevators, but the security guards caught up with them and escorted them out of the building. In addition to the random stops, there were preplanned visits to the offices of newspapers and TV and radio stations in the area.

The crew made six trips in all, each one lasting four days. If the sales guys were in town, there would be as many as seven people camped out in the apartment. This could sometimes create confusion, especially in the apartment's one bathroom. The most memorable incident involved Ellyn Ladd, who was between living spaces back in Burlington at the time. She elected to make all the trips, which helped solve her problem of where to crash. One night Ellyn, who had a toothbrush the same color as Ben's, went into the bathroom to brush her teeth, after which she went back into the bedroom to get out a change of clothes. She almost passed out when she came across a toothbrush in her suitcase. We were all fond of Ben, but given all the stuff that went into his mouth, no one wanted to sample any microbes from it.

Between the sampling and the sales effort, the business in Boston built up steadily. At first, Paul's was selling three to four pallets of ice cream a week (each pallet held 250 sleeves of pints). One by one, the supermarket and convenience-store chains took the product in, and within a few months, Paul's was buying a full trailer load of twenty pallets every other week.

At the same time that Paul's had come on, Ben had also signed up Dari-Farms, another large independent distributor, based in Tolland, Connecticut. Although we had no money for advertising in the Connecticut market, Dari-Farms, like Paul's, was able to sell our ice cream into most of its accounts.

With successful market entries into Boston and Connecticut under way, it was apparent that we had to increase our production capacity significantly. We were projecting almost a 100 percent increase in sales in 1984—over 2.5 million pints, generating revenues of almost $3 million. In 1985, we expected sales of over $4 million.

We could double our capacity at the factory on Green Mountain Drive one more time by adding a second production freezer, which would enable us to fill our orders during the summer of 1984, but beyond that, there was no room to expand. A new plant was going to be needed by the following year.

For the new plant to be on line by spring of 1985, it would have to be under construction by late summer 1984. That left us approximately ten months to locate a site, design the plant, secure the necessary permits, and raise the money to build it. Which is what we set out to do at the end of 1983.

CHAPTER EIGHT

A Scoop of the Action

ur original estimate was that it would cost between two and two and a half million dollars to build and equip a new factory. We decided to try to raise three and a half million, which would give us some extra working capital to finance the increased inventory we'd be carrying, and a margin for error if our estimates were too low.

Most of the funds would be borrowed, but in order to have any chance of raising that kind of money, we needed to come up with about $750,000 in equity. Typically, when a business needs its first large infusion of cash, it does a private placement among a few wealthy investors, or turns to a venture capitalist who finances emerging companies.

The biggest drawback of soliciting venture capital was the potential for losing control of the business. As a precondition of their investment, most venture capitalists have input into how the business is managed, and they're apt to take over if things start going poorly. On the other hand, their expertise, particularly in the area of financial controls, can sometimes be the salvation of an entrepreneur who's overwhelmed by the changes brought by rapid growth.

Selling a large chunk of the business to a venture capitalist didn't appeal to Ben at all. For almost a year he had been casually mentioning the idea of doing an in-state stock offering—one that would be available only to Vermonters—whenever he, Jeff, and I talked about future fund-raising options. His conviction was that we were holding the business in trust, and that we should give the people who had supported the company from its earliest days the first opportunity to profit from our success.

Ben had gotten the idea for the stock offering sometime in 1983, when he'd stopped in unannounced to see Harry Lantz, the securities administrator for the State of Vermont Department of Banking and Insurance. Harry, who was as far from a typical bureaucrat as they come, gave Ben a copy of the Vermont Securities Act, a thirty-three-page booklet that listed all the statutes.

"There's something in there that might pertain to your situation," he told Ben.

"Can you tell me what page it's on?" Ben asked.

"Read the book," Harry said. "Read the book."

Ben came out of the meeting convinced that he had come up with an obscure state law that exempted us from everything and allowed us to just go out and start selling stock.

The idea of an in-state stock offering was a natural extension of the philosophy that Ben had espoused on the poster announcing the very first Free Cone Day—"Business has a responsibility to give back to the community from which it draws its support." Ben's idea was for the company to be owned by the same people who had lined up for scoops of ice cream at the gas station.

Beginning in the fall of 1983, Ben, Jeff, and I began to meet with investment bankers at the national and regional brokerage houses that had offices in Burlington. Typically, one of these firms would handle a company's initial stock offering and oversee the entire process of taking a privately held company public. The message we heard was consistent and discouraging. The size of the company, the condition of our balance sheet, and the small amount of money we were trying to raise (by Wall Street standards) all led the bankers to the conclusion that a public stock offering made no sense. They considered the minimum feasible offering to be somewhere between five and ten million dollars. Fees for all the lawyers and accountants who'd be involved, they argued, would eat up too large a percentage of the money that was raised in any offering smaller than that.

The bankers said Ben's proposal to sell stock only to Vermonters was "naïve and impractical." To make the offering as widely affordable as possible, Ben was suggesting that the minimum investment be kept very low, somewhere in the neighborhood of a hundred dollars. "You can't raise three quarters of a million dollars in hundred-dollar increments," one banker told us. Everyone politely suggested that venture capital was the way to go.

Our inability to interest a brokerage firm in underwriting the offering didn't dissuade Ben. If anything, it strengthened his resolve not to use venture capital.

On January 31, 1984, Ben, Jeff, and I met with Skip Allen, who had taken over our account at the Merchants Bank. We gave him an update on the lack of progress in our fund-raising efforts, and he voiced his agreement with the prevailing view that a Vermont-only stock offering couldn't succeed. After an hour or so of going back and forth, the three of us left Skip's office and walked down College Street toward the site of the original gas station. Had we been scripting a photo opportunity, we couldn't have chosen a more appropriate location for the conversation that was about to take place.

"We're going to do the Vermont offering," Ben said as we walked down the street. His voice didn't leave the impression that the subject was open to further debate.

"Okay, let's do it," Jeff said.

His response caught me off guard. Like me, he had often tempered Ben's enthusiasm for the Vermont offering with doses of reality. Both Jeff and I were concerned with the consequences of pursuing the in-state stock offering unsuccessfully. If it failed, it would be all but impossible for us to regroup, raise the money some other way, and still start construction that year. Without the new factory, capacity constraints would limit our sales growth to next to nothing between '84 and '85, regardless of the demands for the product in the marketplace. Jeff thought the odds of raising the money with the stock offering were about one in twenty, but he knew it was time to make a decision, one way or the other, and take our best shot.

Ben and Jeff both waited for my reaction.

"O-k-kay," I stammered, "I guess we're gonna do it."

Ben smiled. The debate was over. We were now all committed to making it work.

The next day we went to see Allen Martin, the managing attorney of Downs, Rachlin & Martin, one of the largest law firms in the state. After losing the Country Business Services lawsuit, we'd decided to shop around for new legal counsel, and Allen had been recommended to me by a friend.

At the meeting, we described the company's need to raise capital and updated Allen on our efforts to date. Ben outlined his idea for a Vermont-only stock offering, seeking confirmation that it could in fact be done. While Allen acknowledged that there was a federal securities law that provided for stock offerings within a single state, he suggested that we take a few weeks to reconsider all the alternatives. He wasn't convinced that we could raise the money without the assistance of an underwriter, and he offered to contact several investment bankers with whom he had done deals previously.

Ben left the meeting convinced that he had set his plan in motion. The next day, February 2, he circulated a brief memo to Jeff, Allen Martin, and me, titled "Financing Flow Chart." Item number three called for the stock offering to begin on April 15.

Over the next month and a half, Allen pursued various underwriters. The responses he received were no different from those we'd been hearing all along. By mid-March there had been no tangible progress on putting the stock offering in place. In frustration, Ben wrote Allen Martin a direct, one-page letter, attempting to get the project back on track. "As you know, when I first approached you, my request was for you to file an intrastate offering on our behalf which would enable us to sell stock in Vermont by April 15, 1984," Ben wrote. "Time is running out. I would like you to proceed with this course of action now."

Upon receiving a copy of Ben's letter, Kim Reidinger, one of the associates at Allen Martin's firm, called Harry Lantz to discuss the offering. In fact, there was nothing in the Vermont Securities Act that was of any use to us. But there was, as Allen Martin had suggested, a federal law that exempted from full registration with the SEC any security that was sold only to residents of a single state, if the issuer of the security was incorporated and did business within that same state. That was the statute upon which the offering would be based. By not having to deal with the SEC, we'd be able to save the tens of thousands of dollars in legal and accounting fees that would have been necessary in order to comply with the stricter securities laws that applied to any offering that crossed state lines. A fully registered offering would also have required audited financial statements going back three years, which was something we didn't have.

The next week, Jeff was in town for a board meeting, during which we drove over to Allen Martin's office to review the status of the offering. Allen had outlined all the areas that would have to be covered in the prospectus, which was the document in which the company and the terms of the offering would be fully described. We agreed on who would take the first crack at drafting each of the sections. After lunch, we went back to Ben's apartment and spent most of the afternoon and evening talking about all of the other outstanding issues involved in getting the new factory designed and built.

Most of the discussion was about where it would be located. We had narrowed our list down to four potential sites, and had just taken an option on our first choice, which was in Waterbury.

The land we'd optioned was on Route 100, which was the access road from the interstate to Stowe, the self-proclaimed "Ski Capital of the East." It was among the most heavily traveled tourist roads in the state, which was one of the main criteria we had used in evaluating sites. From the outset, Ben and I had talked about designing the new plant to accommodate factory tours. What better way to reinforce the image of "Vermont's Finest" than to offer people a taste of fresh ice cream right off the production line, in the shadow of the Green Mountains? There was only one problem with this scenario. The Waterbury site, which we had come to call "the Hole," was in a deep ravine, well below the road. It didn't look out on the mountains, and its most prominent view was the back end of a Mobil station.

An article reporting our plan to move to Waterbury had appeared in the *Burlington Free Press* that morning. The publicity turned out to be a stroke of good luck. While we were meeting, a partner in a local land-development group called Ben and offered to sell us a twelve-acre parcel just a little farther up the road. It was twice the land at less than half the price. We decided to try to objectively reevaluate all the sites by coming up with a consensus rating ranging from one to four, for thirteen different criteria. When we were finished, we added the scores. Even though we had yet to see or set foot on it, the new land in Waterbury seemed like the winner.

As it turned out, we had the chance to confirm our intuitive evaluation the next day. The three of us were driving to Stowe for a meeting with VIDA, the Vermont Industrial Development Authority. As a second part of our financing package, we had applied for $2.1 million of state-issued Industrial Revenue Bonds, known in shorthand as IRBs.

After getting off the interstate, we drove slowly up Route 100. A quarter-mile from the exit, we passed the Hole on our right, and, just past that, Kilkenny's Market, then the Waterbury Alliance Church. That was our last landmark. We all looked to the left. There was the site. It was a rolling hillside with a few scattered trees—nothing at all like the nondescript tracts one normally associates with industrial development. It was perfect. We drove the ten additional miles to Stowe, congratulating ourselves on our good fortune.

The fifteen or so members of the VIDA board, all properly dressed in business suits, were seated at a series of tables that had been arranged in a large horseshoe. Ben was in jeans, but we'd gotten him to wear a clean shirt, and he was looking reasonably presentable. While Jeff and I passed out ice cream, Ben made a five-minute presentation summarizing the project, including the upcoming Vermont stock offering. Each of the board members had a copy of our formal application, which Jeff had compiled and previously submitted.

As with the very first loan application at the Merchants Bank, Ben was required to submit a personal financial statement. Although he had yet to cash in on any of his holdings, Ben's net worth, on paper, was over seven figures. In addition to a 50-percent interest in the business, which he valued at $1.4 million, Ben had $1,200 in cash and $3,000 worth of personal furnishings.

Five minutes after we left the room, a member of the VIDA staff informed us that the board had approved the issuance of the bonds. The IRBs weren't guaranteed by the state, so getting them issued was relatively easy. The hard part would be finding a bank to buy them from us, because for all intents and purposes, they carried the same risk to the bank as a direct, $2.1-million loan. The only difference was that the IRBs gave the lending institution a favorable tax treatment, which, in theory, was enough to entice them to purchase the bonds from a company, like ours, to whom they wouldn't otherwise be willing to lend big money.

That weekend, Ben drafted up a memo detailing his strategy for how the Vermont stock offering would work. "The object of the in-state offering," he began, "is to allow the average Vermonter the opportunity to invest in and hopefully profit from Ben & Jerry's—an ice cream company which the average Vermonter supported, made famous, and allowed to prosper. The premise is that the small Vermont investor should have the same opportunity to profit as the large venture capitalist."

Ben wanted the minimum investment to be $125. The investment bankers we'd talked to thought that lots of small stockholders would be an unnecessary financial burden, owing to the administrative costs. Ben saw advantages in having lots of shareholders. Like us, they could straighten out the pints in the supermarket freezers and bug the frozen-food clerk when the store didn't have Heath Bar Crunch in stock.

Ben's memo went on to outline how the stock would be marketed to the public. An in-state toll-free number would be set up so that prospective investors could have questions answered and request an offering circular. Information meetings would be held around the state, at which ice cream would be served and the prospectuses passed out.

On Thursday, April 5, Ben, Kim Reidinger, and I drove down to Montpelier and met with Harry Lantz. It was Harry's job to review registration applications for securities in Vermont and license the broker/dealers who sold them. In most instances the SEC had already passed judgment on any security that was being sold in Vermont, and Harry's clearing of the securities (they were never "approved," only "cleared") was just a formality. With an in-state offering, that wasn't the case.

Harry began the meeting by giving an overview of the respective roles of the issuer of the stock (Ben & Jerry's) and the registered broker/dealer—yet to be found—who would be responsible for selling the offering. Harry didn't approve of issuers selling their own securities, believing that it wasn't something that should be done by "amateurs." Every aspect of the selling process would have to be controlled and channeled through the dealer. Apparently that ruled out most of the strategy that Ben had outlined in his memo for promoting the offering.

More important, it meant that, despite a futile effort to date, we still needed to find an underwriter who was registered with the state for the sale of securities. The only person who had expressed even the remotest interest in doing the offering was an independent broker from Bennington by the name of Don McKenna. The only problem was that McKenna's lawyer had told him that any offering he was involved in had to comply with the regulations of NASD, the National Association of Securities Dealers. Ben argued that if the NASD rules were imposed, we would in fact be complying with the more stringent requirements of a full-blown registration. "What's the advantage of the intrastate exemption," Ben asked, "if we can only do it by going through all the red tape of a regular offering?"

Harry said he'd give it some thought, and we left the meeting cautiously optimistic that something would be worked out.

Four days later it was. In a phone call with Kim, Harry, despite his previously expressed concerns about "amateurs," said he would allow

Ben to register the company as a broker/dealer for the purpose of selling our stock directly to the public. Harry had already run the idea past his department's legal counsel, who had approved it. Once the company was registered, either Ben or I, as an executive officer of the firm, could sell the stock. Other than the registration application, the only other requirement was a dealer's bond, which we could easily pick up from our insurance agent.

With the question of the underwriter finally resolved, our focus turned to the prospectus. The document would include a summary of the company's history, our marketing and sales strategies, résumés of the principals who were managing the business, a description of what we were planning on doing with the money, and projected financial statements showing expected results for the next six years. Audited financial statements from the past year would be attached to the prospectus.

Harry, who would have to review and clear the prospectus, had given us advice on how it should be drafted. It would be his job to ensure that no material that could be considered misleading was included in the document. We were to avoid superlatives and absolute statements that couldn't be proved. Harry told us to preface our commentary with qualifiers like "It's the opinion of management . . ." The figures for future performance had to be clearly labeled as projections, and the reader informed that he/she couldn't rely on them. The prospectus would also have to include a very prominent section that listed all the risk factors associated with the offering.

That weekend, Allen and Kim worked furiously to whip the prospectus into shape. At noon on Sunday, Ben and I showed up at their offices to go over the first full-length draft, word by word, and suggest revisions.

The tone of the document was typical for stock prospectuses, especially for initial public offerings (IPOs), in that it focused much more on the risks of the investment, as opposed to the potential upside reward. Ben was horrified by the initial draft, which he thought was way too negative. "I wouldn't buy the stock if I read this thing," Ben shouted after reading a few pages, "and I don't think the average Vermonter will either."

Ben and Allen were approaching the circular from different perspectives. To the lawyers it was a disclosure document, intended to protect us from any suggestion of misleading investors in the event things didn't work out as well as we had projected. To Ben it was a selling tool that he was going to have to rely on to persuade people to buy the stock.

To help make his points, Ben had brought along copies of other prospectuses that he had picked up from the various investment bankers we'd talked to. Ben was pulling entire paragraphs verbatim from the other circulars as alternatives to the more cautious language that Allen had used.

"You can't do that, Ben," Allen would say time after time, defending his original copy.

"Why not?" Ben shot back, his face getting redder and redder. "That's what they used here."

It had been a little over six months since the Country Business Services trial, and that experience was etched in Ben's mind. In that case, Ben had deferred to his lawyer's advice. This time around, he wasn't willing to assume that the "experts" knew everything and that his input wasn't of equal value.

Most of the debate was over a section up front with the heading "Risk Factors." It included thirteen numbered paragraphs, each one listing a reason *not* to buy the stock. At Ben's insistence, the section was retitled "Investment Considerations."

The first "Investment Consideration" was "High Risk," and it went right to the point: "The common stock offered by the Company hereby is speculative and involves a high degree of risk. Prospective investors should be aware that they may lose their entire investment. (If you can't afford to lose it, don't do it.)"

It was Ben who suggested the last sentence, trying to distill all of the risks down to a simple statement of fact. A few days later, working on subsequent drafts, he tried to take it out when he realized that it hadn't had the desired effect of replacing all the other warnings, but the lawyers insisted that it remain.

When we finished going through the entire prospectus, the conversation turned toward pricing the offering. To increase the number of shares to a workable amount, the stock was split 150 to 1, after which there were 420,000 shares outstanding. Our plans were to sell 73,500 shares in the offering, which was 17.5 percent of the company. The price we agreed on was $10.50, which meant we were valuing the company at $4.4 million. If the offering sold out, we'd net approximately $700,000 after expenses. More than anything else, what determined the price was how much money we needed to raise, and how much of the company we were willing to give up for it. The rest was simple division.

Setting the price was obviously not without consequence. One of the investment considerations was called "dilution," and it was important enough to warrant a separate section in the prospectus. Dilution represented the difference between what the public paid for a share of stock in the offering, and the net tangible book value of the stock immediately after the deal was closed.

In our offering, the dilution was huge, because the stock was priced really high relative to our company's book value. The worth of our business wasn't the physical assets in our plant, most of which were charming antiques. We had valued the business based on our projections and the potential to grow both our sales and profits, the top and bottom lines, exponentially.

It seemed unlikely that "average Vermonters" were going to understand the concept of dilution, let alone work through the financial statements. The minimum purchase for the offering was set at twelve shares. Ben's assumption was that someone who was risking only a small amount of money would be less likely to scrutinize the prospectus than would a more sophisticated investor who was putting up a couple of grand. Just about everyone, Ben figured, had an extra hundred twenty-six bucks they'd be willing to take a flyer on.

It was well into the early evening when we finished, but there was no doubt in any of our minds that we had gotten most of the work on the prospectus behind us. Allen broke a bottle of scotch out of his desk and poured a round of drinks. Ben got some pints he had brought with him that morning, and scooped everyone a bowl of cream. Allen, who smoked, offered a cigarette to Ben, who didn't. "Ben took it, lit up, and sat back in his chair," Allen recalls, "a glass of scotch in one hand, a cigarette in the other, a bowl of ice cream on the table in front of him, and an exhausted but contented look across his face."

Late the following week, Kim and Ben met again with Harry in Montpelier. They reviewed the most recent copy of the prospectus, which had gone through five additional drafts since Sunday night. They also reviewed how the offering would be marketed. Harry approved the use of an in-state toll-free telephone number and a script for the temps who would answer the phones. All the operators could do was take down a person's name and address, and tell them that we'd send out a prospectus. No information on the offering could be given over the phone.

Harry also looked over all the advertising Ben had prepared. Traditional financial ads, which are commonly referred to as "tombstones," contain a minimal amount of information, all of which is presented in rows of small type. At an earlier meeting, Ben had proposed the idea of running small teaser ads in the paper, with the headline, "Get a Scoop of the Action!" At first, Harry had thought the idea a bit too radical for a securities offering, and had nixed it. But Harry was starting to get into the spirit and he agreed to let us use the phrase in the tombstones, provided it was in quotes and the lettering was no more than twice the size of the surrounding print.

Most stock offerings are advertised to the general public only after they're sold out. This struck Ben and me as rather strange. Why would you advertise something after you'd sold it? Why not skip the ad and pocket the money?

The ad was just a formality to let everyone know that the underwriting syndicate had once again done good. Brokers had called their customers and recommended the new issue, the orders had been placed and the stock had been sold. So-called unsophisticated investors, who were not tied into the Wall Street network via a broker, were left out of the process completely. Once they read the tombstone, it was too late to do anything other than buy the stock in the aftermarket, often at a higher price.

Our offering was directed at people who had never invested in stocks before. Most tombstones appear in the financial section. We were placing ours with the movie and TV listings.

Over the next week the lawyers kept making minute revisions to the prospectus, circulating an updated draft every day. Ben and I were unaccustomed to this degree of refinement, and were getting increasingly numb from reading and rereading the same thing over and over. At the time we didn't have any word-processing capability in our office, and our enthusiasm for redrafting anything we wrote was dampened by having to use our self-correcting typewriter, which only remembered ten spaces back.

On the morning of April 26, the final copy of the prospectus, draft number fourteen, was hand-delivered to Harry, along with our application to register as a securities dealer. Harry cleared the document that afternoon. As far as the State of Vermont was concerned, the offering could proceed.

At four o'clock that same day, Ben and I hosted an informational meeting at the Sheraton in South Burlington for local stockbrokers and financial advisers. Ben started the meeting by describing how the offering had been structured, and logistically how it would work. The offering was scheduled to last just a month. At our option, it could be extended for an additional thirty days, until the end of June. Two months wasn't much time to sell 73,500 shares, but Ben reasoned that most people wouldn't make up their minds until the last possible moment. By having an option to extend it, we created two deadlines instead of one, which we hoped would create a flurry of activity.

The offering was contingent on raising at least half a million dollars. If we didn't raise that amount, we'd give back whatever money had come in and pursue other options, most likely venture capital.

Unlike most prospectuses, which are typeset, printed on glossy stock, and neatly bound, ours had been run off at a quick-copy offset house that afternoon, and was held together with a single corner staple. There was a subscription form on the back of every prospectus, along with an affidavit to certify Vermont residency. The first hundred copies had been delivered to us at the hotel five minutes before we began our presentation.

Ben and I took turns, briefly going through the prospectus. We highlighted our sales record over the past three years, during which our wholesale business had grown from $135,000 in 1980 to just under $1.5 million in 1983.

Everyone listened politely and a few asked questions, but no one seemed overly enthusiastic. Although we offered to pay the brokers a 5-percent commission on any shares they sold to their customers, our direct-sales effort was at odds with how they were accustomed to operating.

A press release announcing the offering was sent to all Vermont media on April 30. The tombstone, and ads announcing informational meetings that were scheduled throughout the state, started running the next day.

The meetings were held in hotel conference rooms, set up with rows of chairs facing a podium. A full-color rendering of the new factory stood off to the side on an easel. The drawing was actually out of date, going back to when we had an option on the Hole, but it reaffirmed the notion that the shareholders' money would be invested in something tangible.

The meetings would run about two hours, beginning with presentations from Ben and me and ending with a question-and-answer period during which we scooped ice cream. The ice cream freezer that

101

we hauled around with us for the meetings was always prominently placed in the front of the room, to entice those who came to stay to the end.

Most of the meetings were uneventful, with the notable exception of the night Jerry flew in from Arizona and Ben got excited by his partner's return; he concluded the proceedings by standing in a corner and mooing. Fortunately, by then, most of the potential investors had gone home. We were all glad to see Jerry come home, no one more so than Ben.

There were ten meetings scheduled between May 7 and May 23. It was like touring with a rock-and-roll band, only we had to go back to work the next morning instead of sleeping in. Around four in the afternoon, Ben and I would set out in the special-events van to that night's gig. When the meeting was over, we'd throw the freezer in the van and drive back to Burlington, pulling into the plant somewhere between ten at night and one in the morning. We'd be later than that if Ben managed to talk me into to stopping for food on the way home.

At the end of each day, I'd call the Chittenden Bank, which was acting as our transfer agent, to get an update on how much money had come in that day. All the money that was sent in was being deposited in an escrow account until the offering was closed. I kept track of our progress informally, on a hand-drawn bar chart in the shape of an ice cream sundae that I posted on the wall over my desk.

By May 9 we'd sent out more than 2,500 prospectuses and taken in over $100,000. One week later we were over $200,000. Things slowed down in the second half of the month, and we began to get nervous, but Ben's prediction about people waiting until the last minute proved true. As the end of the month approached, the money poured in. By May 31, when we announced that we were extending the offering to June 30, we had raised just under $450,000. Five days later we hit half a million, and the offering was no longer contingent.

Ben and I went back on the road for seven more informational meetings in the middle of June, but we were still almost $200,000 short of our goal heading into the last week. But June ended the same way May had—every day there was more money than the day before. The last day of June was a Saturday, and we wouldn't know for sure how we had done until after the weekend. On Monday morning, July 2, the bank called and said we'd gone over the top. In fact the offering was oversubscribed, and money had to be returned to more than one hundred people.

Just under eighteen hundred households purchased stock in the offering, which was roughly equivalent to one in every hundred Vermont families. The largest individual investment was $21,000. About a third of the investors purchased the minimum amount. A large number of shares had been bought by people in trust for their children or grandchildren.[1]

There were shouts of joy in the plant when I passed along the news that the offering had sold out. Ben and I put our arms around each other and literally gave each other pats on the back. Within two minutes, though, the "celebration" was over and we were back at our desks. As impressive as putting together and selling out the offering had been, the sense of accomplishment would be short-lived if we didn't secure the rest of the financing.

There were actually two more pieces that had to fall into place. The first was the VIDA-issued IRBs, for which we still hadn't secured a commitment from a bank. The last piece was a $650,000 Urban Development Action Grant (UDAG). UDAGs were given by the Department of Housing and Urban Development to a city or town, who in turn lent the money at a favorable rate to a local business. The business was obligated to pay back the loan, but the community, in this instance the Village of Waterbury, got to keep all the money, both principal and interest, without having to repay the federal government. The town could in turn relend the money to another business, or use it in any other way it saw fit. It was a good deal for both businesses and local governments, but unfortunately it didn't survive the Reagan Revolution.

The grant applications were completed jointly by the town and the business, and reviewed on a quarterly basis in competition with applications from around the country. The relative needs of the community, and the potential economic impact of the project, particularly in terms of creating new jobs, were the largest criteria in determining

---

1. One person who showed up on the new shareholder list was Jerry, who subscribed for the minimum amount as a token of support. The only problem was that he was no longer a Vermont resident, having moved to Arizona two years earlier. Allen Martin caught the mistake, and Jerry's purchase was rescinded. The lawyers were particularly sensitive because on June 13 the SEC had informed us that they were conducting an informal inquiry into the offering. The sale of even a single share of stock to a nonresident would have voided the intrastate exemption and could have queered the whole deal. Copies of every piece of documentation on the offering, including all fourteen drafts of the prospectus, were sent to the regional SEC office in Boston. It's not known whether they read them all, but on August 20 they called to say that the inquiry had been terminated.

which applications received funding. UDAGs were targeted for companies with limited ability to raise capital on their own, and intended to finance projects that wouldn't happen without the grant.

Grants for the second quarter of 1984 were scheduled to be announced in early August, right around the time we hoped to be breaking ground. We had sent in our application, and it was determined to be complete, with the exception of the not-too-minor detail of where the rest of the money for the project was coming from. To get the grant, we needed to sell the bonds, and we had less than two weeks to do it. Unless we had a firm commitment from a bank for the IRBs in HUD's Washington office by 4:00 P.M. on July 13, the application would be ineligible for the second quarter. Although we could always reapply, third-quarter grants wouldn't be awarded until November, which was well beyond the time when we had to start construction in order for the factory to be operating by the spring of 1985.

It had been our expectation all along that the Merchants Bank would buy the bonds. It was, after all, the bank that had loaned Ben and Jerry the money for the gas station, and given Jeff a shopping bag stuffed with $90,000 in small bills. Still, Skip Allen had yet to make a firm commitment despite our repeated requests.

Our last meeting with Skip was on June 13, over lunch at Sweetwaters, a restaurant directly across the street from the bank. He had spent the morning at a bankruptcy auction for one of his other customers, and probably wasn't in the frame of mind you want your banker to be in when you're trying to ease $2.1 million out of his pockets. We told Skip we needed an answer, one way or the other, by the end of the week. Two days after the meeting, he called with the decision of the Merchants' board of directors. They weren't going to do the deal. It was doubtful they had acted against his recommendation.

The response from other Vermont banks was uniform and lukewarm at best; $2.1 million turned out to be a large amount of money for a Vermont bank to lend to any one customer, especially one as small and unproven as Ben & Jerry's.

A lot of the banks didn't believe we could achieve the sales growth we'd projected, or that we had the management skills to run a four-to-ten-million-dollar business. The closest any Vermont bank came to doing the deal was an offer for $1.2 million, which they later increased to $1.5 million. "Can't you build a smaller plant?" they asked.

With Jeff Furman taking the lead, we started to approach banks in Boston and New York City. One by one, they all said no. We were running out of options when Ben and Jeff, in a last attempt, approached Ken Cartledge in the Albany office of Marine Midland Bank. Ben & Jerry's ice cream was widely available in the Albany market, and Ken knew of our company and had tasted our ice cream. After a positive initial meeting at his office, Ben told me to expect Ken's call with some follow-up questions about the business.

Ken did call, asking for current financial information to supplement the now dated numbers in the prospectus. For the first six months of 1984 the company had posted a profit of $134,000 on sales of $1.6 million, an increase of over 100 percent from a year earlier. We were now expecting to hit $4 million in sales by the end of 1984—the number we had originally projected in the offering circular for 1985!

Finally, after many more calls, Ben, Jerry, and Jeff met in Albany with Ken on Friday, July 13, the day the commitment letter from the bank had to be in the hands of HUD. They were still negotiating the final points of the loan when Ken drafted the letter and sent it out by teletype. Only it didn't go through. They tried again, and again, and it still didn't go through. Ken suggested they get a bite to eat, and try again after lunch, but Ben, Jeff, and Jerry weren't so nonchalant.

Ben hadn't come this far to be thwarted by a busy signal. The backup plan was for Jerry to fly to Washington and hand-deliver the letter. The next flight out, and the only one that would get him there before the deadline, was leaving in a half hour. While Ken kept trying to wire the letter, Ben and Jerry took off in a mad rush for the airport. Even under more casual circumstances, driving with Ben was an invigorating experience. "He made a left turn on a red light at this very major intersection," Jerry recalls. "I just sat back and enjoyed the ride."

Fortunately they made it to the airport, where Jerry waited by the gate while Ben called Ken to see if the fax had made it. It never did, and just before they shut the doors, Jerry got on the plane, flew to D.C., took a cab over to HUD's offices, and delivered the crucial letter. It was a full hour before the deadline. Two weeks later we got a call from our congressman's office telling us we got the grant.

We had never tried to figure out what the odds of raising $3.5 million in six months actually were. That we were able to do it was even more amazing in light of what had been going on in Boston at the same time.

CHAPTER NINE

What's the Doughboy Afraid Of?

n March 29, 1984, just as we were starting to put the Vermont stock offering together, Ben got a phone call from Paul Tosi, of Paul's Distributors.

"I've got something really important that I need to talk with you about, Ben," Tosi said. "You've got to come down here tomorrow."

"What's it about?" Ben asked.

"I can't tell you on the phone," Tosi responded, "but it's serious." Despite Ben's prodding, Tosi wouldn't say any more.

"Okay," Ben finally said, "I'll be down tomorrow morning."

Ben hung up the phone, made a couple of calls to cancel the few appointments he had scheduled for the next day, and pondered what could be so important that he had to drive down to Boston, with no advance notice, to see what was by now our largest customer.

"We've been getting calls from Häagen-Dazs," Tosi told Ben the next morning when he was seated in their conference room, "and they're telling me that if I continue to sell your product, they're going to cut me off." Paul's wife, Leona, who ran the financial end of the business, and Chuck Green, their general manager, waited for Ben's reaction to the news.

Slowly, a smile came over Ben's face. He didn't say anything while Tosi kept talking.

"Ben, I really like you, I like the product, and I think we're doing really well with it, but Häagen-Dazs is far and away the number-one seller, my customers require it, and if I don't carry it, my competition is going to come in and steal all my accounts."

By this point, Ben was laughing out loud. "I don't see how they can do that," he finally said. Ben couldn't quite get over the fact that Häagen-Dazs actually considered Ben & Jerry's viable competition, and thought it quite a feather in our cap that they did.

The Tosis and Green couldn't figure out what Ben found so funny. He'd just been informed that his largest competitor had told his largest customer to stop selling his ice cream. Where exactly was the humor in that?

"We're not sure, but we think it may be illegal," Tosi went on. "You may want to talk with your lawyer." Tosi said he would try to carry the product as long as he could, and talked about buying a couple of tractor-trailers right before the deadline.

Ben knew how important Häagen-Dazs was to Tosi's business, so he understood his concern. But he kept coming back to a simple, commonsense argument: "They just can't do this to us." Ben said it over and over again, and urged Tosi to stand firm.

There was no doubt that the Tosis, given a choice, preferred the status quo, delivering both our ice cream and Häagen-Dazs. Not only were they making good money on both product lines, but the idea that a manufacturer could dictate what products they could or couldn't carry didn't sit right with them.

Still, it was clear that there was no way Paul's could afford to lose Häagen-Dazs. The brand had 100-percent penetration, which meant that every supermarket in Massachusetts and Connecticut carried it. Typically, the large chains purchased most of their frozen desserts from a single distributor in order to reduce truck traffic at their stores and the amount of paperwork they had to process. Without Häagen-Dazs, Paul's risked losing its largest accounts to other distributors who could offer the retailers a full line of products.

The implications of Häagen-Dazs's actions, Ben realized, went far beyond whether Paul's was going to carry our ice cream. Just about any independent ice cream distributor of significant size and stature carried Häagen-Dazs. If, by virtue of Häagen-Dazs's "us or them" edict, we were precluded from using any of those distributors, we'd be relegated to using small, one-truck operators who had little clout with the retailers. The only other alternative would be to set up company-owned distribution, something we had neither the financial nor the managerial resources to do.

Ben left Paul's for the drive back to Vermont with a clear understanding of where he stood. If there was going to be a fight with Häagen-Dazs, it was going to be *our* fight. Paul's might want us to win, but there was no way they could get directly involved without putting their relationship with Häagen-Dazs at risk, something they weren't prepared to do.

Ben spoke that afternoon to Dennis Silva at Dari-Farms, our Connecticut distributor, who confirmed that Häagen-Dazs's actions hadn't been limited to a single distributor. Like Paul Tosi, Dennis had been getting phone calls about our ice cream for the past couple of months from Jim Richards, Häagen-Dazs's sales manager. At first Richards had just asked a lot of questions about us: "What's happening with it? How's it doing?" It was typical for a manufacturer to pump its distributors for information about the competition, and neither Dennis nor Paul had paid much attention to it.

Eventually, Richards had started to press a little harder. "You know," he'd tell the distributors, "you're going to have to make a decision, one way or the other, who you're going to be loyal to."

The calls kept coming, and Richards kept getting more and more insistent. Eventually he laid it out in plain English. Paul's and Dari-Farms would lose access to Häagen-Dazs unless they signed an agreement that would preclude them from selling any other superpremium brands, including Ben & Jerry's.

I was scheduled to meet with Ben and an architect to review potential sites for the new factory on Saturday, March 31, the day after Ben went down to Boston. When I got to the plant, Ben pulled me aside and told me that he'd been in Boston the day before, meeting with Paul's.

"Häagen-Dazs is telling Paul's that if they don't drop us, they're gonna get cut off," Ben said.

I shook my head in disbelief, while the news sank in.

"It's a compliment," Ben said with a grin. "We should be flattered."

Flattered, well, yes, and maybe flattened too. Häagen-Dazs was a subsidiary of the Pillsbury Corporation, a $4-billion conglomerate that owned Burger King, Bennigan's, and Steak and Ale restaurants, as well as marketing hundreds of food products under the brand names of Green Giant and Pillsbury.

When I got home after the meeting, I dug out my old marketing textbooks and researched the issue of restrictive distribution arrangements. What Häagen-Dazs was doing was referred to as exclusive dealing, which could be, but wasn't always, illegal. An agreement with a manufacturer that limited the competing products a distributor or retailer could sell only violated the Clayton Antitrust Act if the effect was "to substantially lessen competition or tend to create a monopoly in any line of commerce."

In determining whether an action substantially reduced competition, the courts considered two criteria. First, how dominant, in terms of market share, was the manufacturer who was trying to enforce the agreement? The greater the market share controlled by the manufacturer, the more likely it was that their actions would inhibit competition. Second, how much market share was controlled by the distributors who were restricted by the exclusive dealing agreement? Again, the larger the market share controlled by these distributors, the less likely it was that a competitor would have access to the market through alternative means.

We thought this case met both criteria. Häagen-Dazs had a market share in excess of 70 percent, and almost all the independent distributors in New England sold their ice cream. If every distributor who carried Häagen-Dazs was precluded from carrying Ben & Jerry's, we were effectively barred from the market.[1]

The problems with Häagen-Dazs couldn't have come at a worse time. We were desperately trying to put together the financial package for the new plant, and we now faced the immediate risk of losing our two largest customers, Paul's and Dari-Farms. More important, Häagen-Dazs's threat, if carried out, would make it increasingly difficult for us to add distribution in new markets. All the assumptions and projections upon which we had based plans for the new factory would have to be tossed out the window.

In the offering circular, we had to disclose Pillsbury's actions and their potential consequences as one of the thirteen "Investment Considerations." They were also a big concern of the bankers we were trying to interest in our IRBs. "Why are you picking a fight with Pillsbury?" Skip Allen asked us the last time we met with him. "Don't

---

1. Häagen-Dazs would ultimately argue that although they dominated the superpremium ice cream category, they were a bit player in the overall frozen dessert market. But Häagen-Dazs's restriction on the sale of competing products only covered Ben & Jerry's and the other superpremium brands. All the other product lines carried by their distributors weren't affected by the exclusive dealing contract. In effect, Häagen-Dazs was trying to argue one point both ways. On the one hand, they claimed that their small share of the overall frozen dessert market negated any claims that they were attempting to monopolize that market. But on the other hand, when they placed restrictions on which products constituted competition and were therefore off limits to their distributors, they very narrowly defined the market they did business in. The inherent conflict in this approach would be an important part of our legal case against them.

you think you might provoke a reaction on their part that will adversely affect your business?"

The next week, on Wednesday, April 4, Ben was back in Boston with Jeff, for a meeting at the Logan Hilton with Paul Tosi and Chuck Green from Paul's, Dennis Silva and his father, Dave, from Dari-Farms, and lawyers representing both distributors. There was discussion regarding whether or not Häagen-Dazs's actions were illegal, and, if they were, how likely it was that we could prevail in court against Pillsbury. The message coming out of the meeting was clear, and it was consistent with Ben's conversation with Tosi the previous Friday. Neither distributor wanted to succumb to Häagen-Dazs's directive and drop our product, but it was up to Ben & Jerry's to carry the fight.

It was decided at the meeting that we would hire a Vermont law firm, Salmon & Nostrand, to fire off an angry letter to Pillsbury that would go out under the signature of Thomas Salmon, a former governor of Vermont. Jeff had already written one letter to Pillsbury over the weekend, but it had yet to elicit a response.

There were seventeen lawyers listed on the letterhead of the in-house law department of the Pillsbury Company. The last one on the list, Richard Wegener, responded to Salmon's letter. Citing a precedent involving a ball-bearing manufacturer, Wegener dismissed Salmon's complaint that Häagen-Dazs's actions would be a violation of the Clayton and Sherman antitrust laws. "Häagen-Dazs has acted and will continue to act in nothing more than healthy competition with Ben & Jerry's," Wegener stated in his letter. "If your client wishes to test his concerns in the courts," he concluded, "we will respond in whatever manner appropriate."

The very first time Ben and I discussed what Häagen-Dazs was up to, we both agreed that our response was going to be a loud one, and we weren't going to wait three years for a lawyer to deliver it in a courtroom. Even before we determined that what they were doing was illegal, we knew it was immoral. If we could get the word out, we felt confident that other people would react the same way we had—with disbelief, followed quickly by a sense of outrage.

We also knew that in the courts, Pillsbury's financial resources and staying power gave them terrific leverage over us. In the media, the advantage was ours.

We decided up front to cast ourselves in a fight against Pillsbury, not Häagen-Dazs. Häagen-Dazs versus Ben & Jerry's was one ice cream company against another. Pillsbury versus Ben & Jerry's was the *Fortune* 500 against two hippies.

The week after the meeting in Boston with the distributors, Ben and I flew to Ithaca for a board meeting with Jeff. Sitting around Jeff's kitchen table, we talked about how to respond to Pillsbury, and what the implications were for our efforts to raise the money to build the new factory.

We took a break at around 6:00 P.M., and while Jeff went out for a run, Ben and I sat around the living room and tried to come up with a slogan for our campaign. Ben was really hung up on the word "strangle," as in "Pillsbury, Don't Strangle Us." After a half hour or so of randomly tossing ideas back and forth, I blurted out, "What's the Doughboy Afraid Of?" We both knew immediately that was it. Who better to focus our counterattack on than Poppin' Fresh, Pillsbury's pudgy animated spokesperson?

When we got back to Burlington, we sent out a press release announcing our intent to seek a restraining order in federal district court to prevent Häagen-Dazs from following through with its threats to cut off our distributors. "This is a cut-and-dried case," the release stated, "of a huge conglomerate, Pillsbury, acting through a subsidiary, Häagen-Dazs, to choke off competition." The release also noted that Häagen-Dazs was outselling us in the affected markets by better than four to one. "We don't see ourselves as much of a threat to Häagen-Dazs or Pillsbury," we concluded. "Our total sales last year were a little more than what Pillsbury gave its president and chairman of the board in compensation."

On Monday, April 23, Ben and I held two press conferences. The first, at our scoop shop in Burlington, was attended by one reporter from a local radio station. Immediately afterwards, we flew to Boston, where the second conference was scheduled for 1:00 P.M. in a meeting room at the Sheraton hotel at the Prudential Center. This time three reporters showed up. Fortunately, one was from the Associated Press. A few local papers picked up the story off the AP wire and ran it the next day.

I flew back to Burlington after the press conference. Ben stayed in Boston, and met the next morning with Bob Schroeder, a lawyer in the regional office of the Federal Trade Commission. At the same time that we were writing letters to Pillsbury, we had also corresponded with all of our elected officials and had written the FTC requesting that they investigate Pillsbury's actions. We did this even though we had been told by knowledgeable sources that the antitrust laws of the United States, for all practical purposes, had ceased to exist in the Reagan administration. Schroeder was personally sympathetic and willing to go through the motions. The usual pattern, he explained, was for the local office to recommend a case and send it down to the national office in Washington, where it would get shot down without any action being taken. That, he told Ben, what was he could expect from the FTC.

While Ben met with Schroeder in Boston, a much more productive activity was taking place two thousand miles away, in Minneapolis. Jerry had started a one-man picket in front of Pillsbury's world headquarters, holding a hand-lettered sign that read, "What's the Doughboy Afraid Of?"

Ben had called Jerry in Arizona, asking if he'd be willing to come out of retirement temporarily for the assignment. In addition to his sign, Jerry was carrying a canvas bag with a shoulder strap in which he had a stack of leaflets that we'd sent him from Vermont via Federal Express.

"Pillsbury Corporation and its subsidiary Häagen-Dazs are attempting to limit the distribution of Ben & Jerry's Ice Cream," the flyers stated in boldface type. It described the Doughboy as a huge conglomerate, with sales of $3,948,100,000. We wrote out the number instead of saying "just under $4 billion," because we thought the former looked larger. Under the subheading "The American Dream," we wrote of Ben & Jerry's humble beginnings, our entry into the Boston market, and Häagen-Dazs's threat to cut off our distributors. "They are not content to compete with us based on product, price, or marketing," we charged. "They want us off the supermarket shelves, depriving consumers of their choice of products."

"Now that you know the facts, what do you think?" the leaflet asked. "Do you think the Doughboy is afraid of two guys working with twenty-three people in four thousand square feet of rented space? Do you think the Doughboy is afraid he's only going to make $185.3 million in profits this year instead of $185.4 million? Do you think that maybe the Doughboy is afraid of the American Dream? We only want to make our ice cream in Vermont and let the people of Boston and New England make their choice in the supermarket, where guys like us can compete with guys like the Doughboy. Next time you're in your local market, pick up a pint of Ben & Jerry's and give it a taste. Because to tell you the truth, *that's* what the Doughboy is really afraid of."

On the back of the flyer was a coupon that gave people the option of getting a Doughboy write-in kit. The kit included letters of protest to the FTC and William Spoor, the chairman of the board of Pillsbury. The letter to Spoor berated him for the lack of ethics that his company was displaying, and included the postscript, "Why don't you pick on someone your own size?" In the hand-signed cover letter that accompanied the kits, Ben urged people to add a personal comment in their letter to Spoor, perhaps mentioning that they had stopped eating at Burger King or purchasing Pillsbury products at the supermarket. Preaddressed envelopes were included with the kit, along with a "What's the Doughboy Afraid Of?" bumper sticker.

There was a second coupon on the flyer, with which people could order a Doughboy T-shirt. It had the slogan on the front, and "Ben & Jerry's Legal Defense Fund Major Contributor" on the back. The T-shirts and bumper stickers, like the issue itself, were black and white.

Jerry spent a week in Minneapolis, handing out the leaflets from eight in the morning until around six at night every day. The response was supportive, even from most of Pillsbury's employees, with the notable exception of one very senior-level executive who told Jerry that he didn't know what he was talking about. "He was pretty pissed off," Jerry says, "but I stood my ground."

As we had hoped, the press took the story and ran with it. Minneapolis public radio ran an interview with Jerry, and there were articles in the Minneapolis and St. Paul dailies and the *Twin City Reader*, a news and arts weekly. The number of clippings went through the roof when a photo of Jerry, wearing a Doughboy T-shirt and holding his sign in front of Pillsbury's headquarters, was sent out on the AP wire.

One of our goals was to generate as many letters to Pillsbury and the FTC as possible. To get the message out, we decided to print the Doughboy slogan on our pint containers, along with an 800 phone number. There was a six-week lead time to get new plates made, so in the interim we printed up stickers that were applied to each pint.

Calls to the "Doughboy Hotline" started coming in immediately. After listening to a recorded message from Jerry, callers could leave their names and addresses. The tapes were transcribed the next day and the kits went out in that night's mail. At the end of the day, all work in the office would come to a halt as everyone dropped what they were doing in a mad dash to help collate the contents and stamp, label, lick, and seal the one hundred or so envelopes that had to be at the post office by 5:00 P.M. The calls starting come in with such frequency that on weekends the office staff, including Ben and I, took turns coming in twice a day to pull the completed tapes out of the answering machine and put in blanks.

By putting the stickers on the pints, we were able to appeal directly to our customers, who, other than ourselves, had the most to lose if our ice cream suddenly disappeared from the supermarket shelves. They were a natural ally and their response proved it. The stickers were also noticed by the media, which helped feed the story.

On the legal front, Pillsbury's response to Tom Salmon's letter indicated that we still hadn't gotten their attention. Poking our finger in Poppin' Fresh's eye was bound to be a whole lot of fun, but beyond whatever positive public-relations benefit we might reap, we also hoped it might give Pillsbury an incentive to settle the case amicably. To make that happen, however, we'd need to have a strong legal advocate on our side.

While Ben and I began to tweak the Doughboy campaign, Jeff went off in search of an attorney with experience in antitrust litigation. After interviewing more than twenty lawyers, he wound up at Ropes & Gray, a very large and well-established Boston firm.

While Ropes & Gray itself was very buttoned-down, our contact at the firm was anything but. Howie Fuguet's shirttail was prone to hang out the back of his pants, and when he sat back in his chair and put his feet up on his desk, you could see the holes in the bottom of his shoes. His office looked like a controlled disaster, with file folders piled on every surface, including most of the floor. This, it appeared, was a lawyer that even Ben could love.

At his first meeting, Jeff met with both Howie, who handled all aspects of corporate law, and Bill Patton, one of the firm's antitrust litigators. It was apparent to Jeff right away that these guys were in command of the legal issues of the case. They were also excited about the prospect of representing a small plaintiff in an antitrust case. Traditionally, the firm had defended the Pillsburys of the world.

It was also clear they were incredibly expensive. Jeff was amazed at the number of urinals they had in their men's room, probably more than a dozen. "At two hundred bucks an hour, I guess you can't keep people waiting," he speculated. Howie would not take the case on contingency, and was hesitant to commit himself to how much it

Bennett, better known as Ben (left), and Jerry in their formative years.

Ben, Jerry, and Malcolm in their East Village apartment in 1973, prior to Malcolm's chicken-eating escapades at Highland Community.

Vinny Vito, Jerry, and Ben prior to the opening of the gas station in 1978.

The original gas station shop, circa 1979.

Ben and Jerry scooping on the first free cone day, June 23, 1979.

Jerry and Lyn Severance, who created the company's graphic
identity, meeting at the gas station during POPCDBZWE,
the Penny Off Per Celsius Degree Below Zero Winter
Extravaganza.

Elizabeth Skarie,
Jerry's girlfriend
(now his wife).

Don Rose, who earned a charter membership in the Ice Cream for Life Club with his piano playing.

The famous pint lid photo. Note the ice cream melting down the side of the cone. *(Marion Ettlinger)*

A promotion poster for Fall Down 1978, the first Burlington appearance of Habeeni Ben Coheeni, the noted Indian mystic.

Habeeni Ben Coheeni at the company's tenth anniversary celebration in Burlington's City Hall Park. A brass plaque was placed on the sidewalk at the corner of St. Paul and College Streets, the site of the original gas station shop, to commemorate the event.

(Glenn Russell)

FALL DOWN 78

A FESTIVAL of FUN and GAMES

— TO BE HELD —
AT OR NEAR ST. PAUL & COLLEGE STREETS

SATURDAY SEPT. 30 2:00 TO 5:00 PM

☞ FEATURING ☜

CRISPIN LEATHER
ROUND·THE·BLOCK·STILT WALKING·CONTEST
GRAND PRIZE · A FREE PAIR OF FRYE BOOTS

ALL YOU CAN EAT ▼▼▼ THE BEN & JERRY'S ▼▼▼ ALL YOU CAN EAT
ICE CREAM EATING CONTEST
AN ATTEMPT AT THE WORLD'S RECORD
GRAND PRIZE ▼▼▼ YOUR NAME IN THE GUINESS BOOK ▼ ENTRY FEE $1

THE DRAMATIC!
SLEDGEHAMMER SMASHING OF A CINDERBLOCK ON THE BARE
STOMACH OF HABEENI BEN COHEEN, THE NOTED INDIAN MYSTIC.

THE GREAT APPLE PEELING CONTEST
THE LONGEST UNBROKEN PEEL WINS A DINNER FOR TWO (2) AT CARBUR'S

THE MARK TWAIN MEMORIAL
FROG JUMPING CONTEST PRIZE: GIFT CERTIFICATE
EMERALD CITY OF OZ

JUGGLERS AND UNICYCLISTS EXTRAORDINAIRE
HOMEBAKED GOODS · SINGERS, CROONERS, STRUMMERS,
PIANO PLAYERS (NOT TO MENTION PLAYER PIANOS) **CIRCUS ACTS & FIRE EATING!**

~ PROSPECTIVE CONTESTANTS ~
MUST SIGN UP IN ADVANCE AT BEN & JERRY'S OR CRISPIN LEATHER

The poster that appeared in Boston as a billboard and on the back of Boston buses.

Jerry picketing in front of Pillsbury's Minneapolis headquarters in April, 1984. (© 1984 *Star Tribune/Minn.-St. Paul, David Brewster*)

Whoppers in hand, the staff celebrated outside the local Burger King after Pillsbury signed the settlement agreement. (*Michael McDermott*)

Hand-filling pints at the Green Mountain Drive plant.

3,478,219

The production line at the Waterbury factory. The number on the wall indicates how many pounds of cookie dough went into the company's best-selling flavor, Chocolate Chip Cookie Dough, in 1992.
(*John Williams*)

Gary Samuels in his inflatable fat-man suit.
(*Jon Reis/Photolink*)

The Steve's pint—the sincerest form of flattery.
(San Francisco Examiner/Steve Essaff)

Marc Posner and Jane Williamson, the Deadheads who suggested we name a flavor after Jerry Garcia. *(Glenn Russell)*

The board of directors during a midsummer 1988 meeting at Ben's house.
(Merritt Chandler)

Cowmobile II at a Muscular Dystrophy Walkathon in Washington, D.C.

The Waterbury factory, Vermont's most popular tourist attraction. *(Lee Holden)*

The board of directors at the retreat on Cape Cod in the fall of 1987. Left to right: Phil Mirvis, Jerry, Ben, Chico, Jeff Furman (holding his son Zachary), Henry Morgan, and Merritt Chandler. *(Yvette Pigeon)*

Ben and Jerry receiving the 1988 award for National Small Business Persons of the Year from President Reagan and then Vice President Bush. *(U.S. Small Business Administration)*

Peter Lind, Ben & Jerry's Primal Ice Cream Therapist. *(Copyright © 1994 by Seth Resnick)*

Elvis (aka Chico Lager) and Norma King during the Joy Gang's Elvis Day celebration. *(Sarah Forbes)*

Sarah Forbes's "Gimme S'more Mashed Potatoes'n'Gravy" Elvis. *(Maureen Martin)*

Alice "Hound Dog" Blatchley on Elvis Day. *(Maureen Martin)*

Rick Brown, our then Director of Sales, and Mr. T. (*Arnold Carbone*)

Don Moxley, known to millions as Mr. Clean, with Gail Mayville.

The board of directors and the operating committee of the management group, at a planning retreat in the fall of 1988. Left to right: Merritt Chandler, Henry Morgan, Chico, Jim Miller, Jeff Furman, Chuck Lacy, Ben, Allan Kaufman, Dave Barash, and Jerry. (*Phil Mirvis*)

Chuck Lacy, Ben & Jerry's current president, in costume for Halloween, 1991.

Wavy Gravy at the 1992 One World, One Heart festival in San Francisco.
(Arnold Carbone)

Into the lagoons . . . my last official act as CEO. *(Arnold Carbone)*

With Jim Miller after he unwillingly joined me for a couple of laps, courtesy of his staff. *(Arnold Carbone)*

The Traveling Light circus bus at the 1992 One World, One Heart festival. (*Arnold Carbone*)

Ben and Jeff Furman in Moscow on one of their many trips leading to the opening of our scoop shop in Petrozavodsk, Russia.

Ben & Jerry's Partnershop on 125th Street in Harlem. Profits from the store help a nearby drug-counseling center and homeless shelter that were founded by the store's owner, Joe Holland. (*Gene Steinfeld*)

would cost if the case went to trial. Jeff kept pressing, trying to nail down an upper limit. "It's going to be at least $50,000," Howie finally admitted, which was hardly reassuring. It was almost as much as the $57,000 in total net income we'd made the previous year.

Jeff had been hesitant to use a big firm, not just because of the expense, but also out of concern that as a small client, we wouldn't be important to them. He finally decided to go with Ropes & Gray, however, mostly because he felt comfortable with Howie, who assured Jeff that the case would get the attention it deserved. As it turned out, we got extremely effective representation from Ropes & Gray, and Howie was so responsive to our needs that it seemed, at times, as if we were the only client of a sole practitioner.

On May 21, Howie wrote Pillsbury yet another letter, this one addressed to Edward Stringer, the company's general counsel. A copy was sitting on my desk when Ben and I got back to the plant just before midnight after one of the informational stock meetings. I grabbed it, along with some other mail and messages, and drove home. Standing in my kitchen, I started to read it, coming close to yelling out loud at the really good parts. When I was finished, I sat down and read it again.

"It is evident that the exclusionary, *if not predatory*, course of conduct that has been engaged in by Häagen-Dazs has already violated the Massachusetts and federal antitrust laws," Howie wrote. "Injury has already been suffered by Ben & Jerry's as a result of this illegal course of conduct."

Over ten single-spaced, heavily footnoted pages, Howie dismissed the arguments Richard Wegener had made in his response to Tom Salmon's letter as factually inapplicable, dissecting the cases Wegener had cited as precedents and leaving his argument a hollow carcass. Howie went on to state clearly that a refusal by Häagen-Dazs to terminate its course of conduct would give Ben & Jerry's no choice but to file an antitrust action.

In the closing paragraphs Howie admonished Stringer to pass along word to Pillsbury's top management that "it would be wishful thinking on the part of your subsidiary's officers to imagine that it can bully Ben & Jerry's, stifle its growth, and cause it to roll over. Ben & Jerry's is a classic entrepreneurial success, and its owners are aggressive. They like the taste of success and will fight for it. Häagen-Dazs will have to learn to compete on the merits in the marketplace. That is the American way, and that is what competition is all about. That is why we have antitrust laws, and it will not be difficult to present this case to a court."

Howie's letter finally got Pillsbury's attention, convincing them we had retained substantive legal counsel that would litigate the case if necessary. Though a series of phone calls in late June, Howie discussed the case with Richard Wegener, and as a courtesy he sent the Pillsbury attorney a copy of the complaint he was going to file in U.S. District Court in Boston, alleging Pillsbury's violation of the Clayton Antitrust Act.

But while the lawyers talked and faxed back and forth, Jim Richards was still telling our distributors that they were jeopardizing their access to Häagen-Dazs by selling our ice cream. He finally said that July 9 was the date by which the distributors had to drop all other superpremium brands.

With the clock now ticking toward a deadline, Howie responded by filing the complaint on July 2. He then called Pillsbury and told them that he was going back into court on July 5 with a motion for a temporary restraining order. "It's going to be granted," Howie told Wegener flatly. "Pillsbury would be better off signing an out-of-court stipulation that gave us the relief we're seeking, instead of having the court order it." With a stipulation, neither side admitted any violation of law. A court-ordered restraining order implied otherwise, and Howie knew that Pillsbury's attorneys would want to avoid that if at all possible.

Howie and Wegener were still negotiating at the end of the day on July 3. Howie agreed to come into the office on the Fourth of July, but told Wegener he was taking his son to the Red Sox game and was leaving at 11:00 A.M., no matter what. Early the next morning, Pillsbury agreed to the stipulation, and authorized Howie to sign Wegener's name to it. It would turn out to be the death knell for Pillsbury.

The stipulation used virtually the same wording we were asking for in our motion for a TRO. Until the case was ultimately decided by a trial or settled by the parties out of court, Häagen-Dazs had agreed not to prevent their distributors from selling Ben & Jerry's ice cream. The legal issue that was in dispute, whether or not Häagen-Dazs's actions violated the antitrust laws, hadn't yet been addressed, but we were assured that our distribution wouldn't be at risk while the case worked its way through to some sort of final resolution.

Although there was no admission of guilt on the part of Häagen-

Dazs, it was a great victory for us. Without having to argue our case in a courtroom, the immediate threat to our distributors had been eliminated, and with minimal expense. Even if we had gotten the TRO, we would have had to follow up within ten days by seeking a preliminary injunction, and the court costs for that hearing would have been substantial.

Even more impressive was the fact that we had given up nothing in return. There were no restrictions in the stipulation that prevented us from continuing to hammer Pillsbury with the Doughboy campaign while the legal case proceeded. Which is exactly what we did.

In July, at a cost of $250, we ran a small classified ad in *Rolling Stone* magazine under the heading of "Bumper Stickers."

WHAT'S THE DOUGHBOY AFRAID OF? Help two Vermont hippies fight the giant Pillsbury Corporation. Send $1.00 for the facts and a bumper sticker. Ben & Jerry's Ice Cream, 40 Green Mountain Drive, South Burlington, VT 05401.

In August we put up a billboard on Route 128, the main arterial road around Boston. It featured a pint of our ice cream being squeezed by two white, pudgy hands that were seemingly bursting through the billboard from behind. Howie warned us off the original headline, "Don't Let Pillsbury's $$$ Strangle Ben & Jerry's," and we settled instead on "Don't Let Pillsbury Put the Squeeze on Ben & Jerry's." Howie also told us we'd be pushing our luck if we put extensions on the billboard so the Doughboy's pudgy little feet extended out the bottom and his white chef's hat extended over the top. Howie had bought into the Doughboy campaign as an integral part of our overall legal strategy, and he rarely took issue with any of our antics. When he said we had gone too far, we knew we were over the line, and not just getting conservative legal advice from someone intent on covering his ass.

At the same time that the billboard was up, we ran the same ad copy on the back of the mass transit buses in Boston. And in one of Ben's grander strokes, he hired a plane to tow the "What's the Doughboy Afraid Of?" message, along with the 800 number, over Foxboro Stadium during a Boston College football game.

The ad in *Rolling Stone*, the billboard, and the airplane all helped keep the media interested in the story. While they did successfully carry our message to the general public, their real value was in the free publicity they helped generate.

117

Feature articles on our plight appeared in *The New York Times*, *The Wall Street Journal*, and the *San Francisco Chronicle*. The Sunday *Boston Globe* did a cover story in its magazine section entitled "New England's Own Cold War." All of these articles were sent out on the wire services and picked up by other major daily newspapers throughout the country. Even the trade publication for the imprinted novelty business wrote a major piece attributing our campaign's success to the buttons, T-shirts, and bumper stickers we were using.

About four hundred Doughboy kits were going out every week, and we regularly received copies of letters that our customers had sent to Pillsbury. One kid organized his friends into Doughboy Busters, who canvassed their neighborhood and signed up supporters. I sent William Spoor a copy of that letter, along with a note informing him that he was alienating the youth of America. "Why not think it over and repent?" I suggested.

We also received a copy of a letter that Charlie Pillsbury had sent to his father, George, who happened to be a member of Pillsbury's board of directors. Charlie had already written on our behalf to the FTC and Bill Spoor, but told his dad that he was looking forward to hearing the company's side of the story when he was home for Christmas.

After we filed our complaint, Häagen-Dazs, as might have been expected, countersued, alleging abuse of process. By fall, a schedule that called for discovery to take place through mid-December and the trial to begin in January of 1985 had been agreed to by both parties and the court.

Both sides traded requests for production of documents. Pillsbury's seemed a bit onerous. One of the thirty-eight items required us to provide copies of all documents "which constitute, mention, refer to, or . . . in any way directly or indirectly relate to the amount of any product sold, manufactured or produced by Ben & Jerry's." That covered just about every piece of paper in our office.

Our request was equally long. Howie copied their best questions and added a few of his own.

As the case moved closer to trial, both sides became motivated to try to settle out of court. In November, Howie and Bill Patton, the litigator he was working with, met in Boston with John French, Pillsbury's outside counsel from Minneapolis, Ron Lund, one of their in-house lawyers, and Arnold Messing, from the Boston law firm Pillsbury had retained to try the case. Howie drafted a settlement agreement based upon the conversation, and sent it to Pillsbury to review.

Multiple drafts went back and forth over the next three months, each one a little closer to being acceptable to each side. The final agreement was signed on March 6, 1985.

The essence of the agreement was that Häagen-Dazs agreed not to adopt any policy, enter into any agreement, or take any action to coerce any distributor not to carry Ben & Jerry's products. For a two-year period, there were further restrictions on Häagen-Dazs for the states of Massachusetts and Connecticut that simply put an end to their so-called loyalty program.

Overall, we were pleased with the agreement. It gave us protection that in many ways went beyond that offered by the antitrust laws. And in the event the problem recurred, we'd only have to prove that Häagen-Dazs had breached the terms of the settlement agreement, a much easier proposition than proving they had violated the Clayton Act.

We did, in fact, wind up back in court with Pillsbury in 1987, when Häagen-Dazs again tried to enforce its loyalty policy. One Friday afternoon, Pillsbury's lawyers filed about a foot of paper with the court, asking the judge to transfer the case to California and consolidate it with similar litigation involving Double Rainbow Ice Cream. Howie and Bill Patton went into court, the following Monday morning, with an eleven-page response. Relying almost exclusively on facts that Pillsbury had admitted within the documents they had filed on Friday, Howie and Bill were able to establish to the court's satisfaction that Häagen-Dazs was embarking on a program that would violate the 1985 agreement. The judge denied all of Pillsbury's motions, and granted us a preliminary injunction. Subsequently the matter was satisfactorily settled, and we prevailed, once again without the expense of a full trial.

The settlement agreement did require us to bring the Doughboy campaign to an end. We were given two months to use up any pint containers that had the 800 number on them, and sell off our inventory of T-shirts and bumper stickers. By the time we shut down the phone lines, we'd sent out over 15,000 Doughboy kits.

There was no doubt that the campaign was the critical factor in bringing Pillsbury to the negotiating table. They had spent millions of marketing dollars creating a positive public image for their corporate emblem, which we were publicly trashing at every possible turn. At the same time, they had unwittingly handed us a public-relations bonanza that had created brand awareness for our ice cream far in excess of anything we could have generated with paid advertising.

By itself, though, the Doughboy campaign wouldn't have been enough to get Pillsbury to back down. In retrospect, the key to the case had been the decision to retain lawyers who were already completely familiar with the relevant case law, not someone who'd have to spend time in the library, researching precedents. The combination of first-class legal muscle with guerrilla marketing was extremely effective, and it threw Pillsbury for a loop. "They desperately wanted to get Ben & Jerry's off their back," Howie recalls. "You could tell in the settlement negotiations that this had hit a home run at the top level at Pillsbury."

Signing the settlement agreement was cause for celebration. We shut down the production line, locked up the office, and collectively broke our boycott by taking the entire staff to the local Burger King for lunch.

In July of 1985, a hilarious recap of the episode, entitled "Competitors," written by Calvin Trillin, appeared in *The New Yorker*. Trillin talked extensively with Reuben Mattus for the piece. "They got PR and exposure they couldn't buy for millions," Reuben said at the end of the article. "What they did in a couple of years took me eighteen years to do. I did it the hard way." Reuben was right. And we had his company and Pillsbury to thank for it all.

CHAPTER TEN

Five to One

At the same time we were selling the stock, trying to find a bank to buy the bonds, and dealing with the Doughboy, Ben was immersed in the details of designing and building the new plant. There were three major components to the project: the building, the equipment for manufacturing the ice cream, and the refrigeration system. One option was to go with a company who could provide a turnkey operation. A second was to hire three separate contractors, and for us to coordinate their work and make sure the end result was fully integrated. The obvious choice was the former. We chose the latter.

From that auspicious decision, the project quickly degenerated into a disaster. Of the three contractors we hired, we sued one, one sued us, and the third overbilled us $100,000 on their fixed-bid contract before they'd finished three-fourths of the work. When we pointed it out, instead of apologizing, they put our account on COD and refused to ship us spare parts for our fruit feeders. How's that for customer service?

Ideally, we would have completely engineered the process systems first and then designed a building around them. To get the factory up and running by the spring of 1985, however, we had to start construction right away. As a result, there were lots of change orders for all three of the contractors, each of which had a ripple effect on the other two.

Our original deadline for starting up the new plant was April 1, which came and went with no end to the construction in sight. Asked how long it would take to finish the job, the foreman for the general contractor would invariably state, week after week, that they were two weeks away.

By mid-May we began to get desperate. Our old plant on Green Mountain Drive had run at full capacity through the winter. Until March, we'd been producing more than we were selling, and as a result we'd managed to put an extra 150 pallets of pints into outside storage, which in the winter months was roughly a three-week supply. As sales increased with the onset of warmer weather, we rapidly drew down our inventory. When the first of June rolled around, and we still hadn't made any ice cream in Waterbury, we figured we had about two more weeks before we'd be shorting orders.

The first attempt to make ice cream in Waterbury was on June 7. What we didn't know at the time, but found out in short order, was that starting up a new factory wasn't the equivalent of flipping on a light switch. Everything was new, nothing had been tested, and half the stuff didn't work. We'd fix one problem only to get just a little further in the process before something else went wrong and forced us to shut down again.

Our employees worked literally nonstop over the next two weeks, some pulling shifts as long as twenty-four hours, as we desperately tried to get the plant fully operational. Ben and I stopped going home and were sleeping on the floor in the office or catching naps right in the production room whenever we could get away from the line for a few hours.

Although we'd started manufacturing, the new plant was far from complete and there were already $600,000 in cost overruns in dispute. For example, the system that enabled us to make our own base mix, and go back to using 100-percent Vermont dairy products, wouldn't be operational for another eight months.

There were also questions about the quality of the workmanship that needed to be resolved. The roof leaked, the concrete floors in the warehouse were starting to crack, and the tile floors in production had been given a Jackson Pollock grout job. More incredibly, they sloped away from the drains instead of toward them. But the Engineering for Excellence award went to the person who put the air intake for the HVAC system directly in front of the refrigeration power plant, which occasionally leaked ammonia. Instead of dissipating, the gas got sucked back into the building and blown over everyone in the office.

The Waterbury plant had been held out to our employees as our collective salvation, the payoff for years of making more ice cream than anyone could have expected, given the Neanderthal equipment and our shoebox plant. Moving into a partially completed structure that already lacked a "new car smell" was a bitter disappointment.

To make matters worse, it was already too small. We were now expecting sales for 1985 of $10 million, compared with $4 million the previous year. That put us two years ahead of our original projections, and we needed to add onto the building immediately if we were going to fill our orders next summer. Ben and I were actually standing in his office, watching a steamroller put down the finish coat of asphalt in the parking lot behind the plant, when we realized that within a month we'd be ripping it up. "Do you think we should stop him?" Ben asked.

In May of 1985, after the nine-month restriction on resales of our stock to nonresidents expired, it started showing up in what were known as the "pink sheets," which quoted prices on thinly traded publicly held companies that weren't listed on any exchange. It quickly hit a bid price of twenty-nine dollars, almost three times what investors in the Vermont offering had paid. The increase was not only a reflection of how fast the company had grown over the past year, but also a function of supply and demand. People were bidding but no one was asking, and in the absence of any sellers, the price kept going up. It was a perfect time to do another offering, which was fortunate since we needed the money to finish up the first round of construction and start the next.

Although we were still too small for the front-line Wall Street brokerage houses, several regional firms were interested, and we chose Tucker Anthony. Marketing the stock through an underwriter was a lot more formal than it had been on the Vermont offering, but we were still determined to put our personal stamp on it. Ben proposed using the "Get a Scoop of the Action" slogan again, this time putting it on the pints with an 800 number so that our customers could get a prospectus. The underwriters, convinced that the SEC would never allow it, didn't object, but when it somehow got approved, they started to hedge.

"You can't use that slogan," the president of Tucker Anthony finally told Ben in a conference call. "It maligns the integrity of the whole stock market and makes it seem too much like gambling."

"I thought that's what it was," Ben replied simply. The line went silent while the bankers, I imagine, got up off the floor and retook their seats.

As a compromise, we agreed to a revised slogan, "Scoop Up Our Stock." By advertising on the pints, we were trying to reach people who didn't normally invest in the stock market, just as we'd done with the Vermont offering the previous year. Lots of IPOs are bought up en masse by institutional investors, such as mutual funds or insurance companies. By selling stock "retail" to our customers, we hoped to increase the percentage of the company's ownership that was in the hands of people who were aligned, we hoped philosophically, but at a minimum gastronomically, with the company. It was our supposition that these people would take a longer-term view of the investment and not be as focused on quarterly P&Ls as would the institutional investors.

A small piece of the offering was also made available to some of the investment firms with offices in Burlington. There was more than a little satisfaction in taking calls from brokers who a year ago had predicted doom and gloom, and were complaining now about not being able to get enough stock to sell to their clients.

Prior to the offering, we split the stock three for one, and the new stock was priced at thirteen dollars. It quickly sold out and was, in fact, oversubscribed. There was none of the drama of the Vermont offering, just a single phone call two weeks after things had started to let us know we could come to New York and pick up a check for $5 million.

The stock was listed on the NASDAQ national market, and within a month of the closing, the share price had surged to twenty-one dollars, before settling back around seventeen dollars.

Ben and I found it somewhat amusing to watch our stock price go up and down with very little correlation to how things were going at the company. Most of the movement was tied to investment reports that the brokerage firms were now publishing about our stock. When an analyst recommended that people buy the stock, the price went up. When they recommended that people sell, the stock went down. Either way, of course, at least in the short term, the analyst came off looking like The Amazing Kreskin.

In addition to the analysts, there was also increased scrutiny from the financial press. I took most of the calls, but occasionally they insisted on speaking with Ben, who was officially the company's CEO. Ben's most notable interview was with the *Wall Street Transcript*. The following are among the highlights of his conversation, taken from a preliminary draft we were sent prior to publication, so we could verify its accuracy.

TWST: Do you believe you can attain a 15-percent increase in earnings each year over the next five years?

BEN: I got no idea.

TWST: Umm-hmm. What do you believe your capital spending will be each year over the next five years?

BEN: I don't have any idea as to that either.

TWST: I see. How do you react to the way the stock market has been treating you in general and vis-à-vis other companies in your line?

BEN: I think the stock market goes up and down, unrelated to how a company is doing. I never expected it to be otherwise. I anticipate that it will continue to go up and down, based solely on rumor and whatever sort of market manipulation those people who like to manipulate the market can accomplish.

TWST: What do you have for hobbies?

BEN: Hobbies. Let me think. Eating mostly. Ping-Pong.

TWST: Huh?

BEN: Ping-Pong.

I got a chance to edit Ben's comments before they were printed, and made him sound up to snuff on the financials. As to his view of what forces guide the stock market, I left the first half of his answer intact, but toned down the rest of his rhetoric just a bit. "We try and focus our energy on the company itself rather than preoccupying ourselves with what the market is doing," I had Ben quoted as saying. "Over the long run, I'm sure our stock price will reflect our performance."

In the process of preparing the prospectus for the offering, the company formalized two policies that had become a cornerstone of how we defined what a socially responsible business was. The first involved corporate donations.

From their earliest days at the gas station, Ben and Jerry had been committed to running the business in a way that gave back to the community. Strapped as they were for cash, their efforts usually took the form of free ice cream cones or low-budget celebratory events like the movie festival and Fall Down.

After the decision was made not to sell the business, and as the company became more profitable, we began to make more and more cash contributions to community groups and arts organizations. At the time, we still didn't have a formalized budget or operating plan, but we were loosely trying to earmark an amount equal to about five percent of our pretax profits for these donations. No set procedure or guidelines existed for how we gave the money away. The requests came in, and if one was something that Ben or I liked, we did it.

At the same time, we continued to give away lots of ice cream, going so far as to hire a full-time employee to handle all the requests that came in. It was our goal to give ice cream to every community group or nonprofit organization in Vermont, provided only that they requested it far enough in advance for us to work out the logistics.

The motivation for giving back had always been genuine. At the same time, it was proving to be an effective marketing strategy. There was no doubt that our customers were more inclined to buy our ice cream and support our business because of how we, in turn, supported the community.

In describing all of this, we began to talk about the concept of "linked prosperity," a term coined by Dave Barash, one of our managers. What it meant was that as the company grew and prospered, the benefits would accrue not just to the shareholders, but also to our employees and the community. Each constituency's interests were intertwined with the others'.

By doing a national stock offering, we realized that for the first time we were taking the ownership of the company beyond those who had firsthand knowledge of how we ran the business. With that came an obligation to fully disclose the company's somewhat unique operating philosophy, so that anyone who invested did so knowing our intentions.

To institutionalize the donations policy, we created the Ben & Jerry's Foundation, a nonprofit organization that was set up with an "independent" board of directors, albeit one on which Jerry, the foundation's president, and Jeff were two of the three members. Ben gave the foundation fifty thousand shares of his stock as an initial endowment. In addition, the company planned to make the foundation the primary recipient of its cash donations by giving them seven and a half percent of its pretax profits. The foundation, in turn, would give away the money via grants to nonprofit organizations.

The stated goal of the foundation was to fund projects that were models for social change, or that were infused with a spirit of generosity and hopefulness. It sought to fund proposals that approached problems in nontraditional ways, which enhanced people's quality of life, and which supported community celebrations. There was an intended bias toward weird and offbeat projects that were unlikely to get funding from traditional sources.

The decision to increase the percentage we were giving away from five to seven and a half percent was made at a company board meeting that summer. Ben, feeling that five percent wasn't significant, wanted to double it to ten. I argued that it should be kept the same.

Despite the fact that we were profitable, our cash flow, as it had always been, was virtually nonexistent. Our payables were stretched to the limits, and we were still scrambling every week to cover payroll and pay the bills. When the funds we had raised for the new plant ran out, we'd been forced to pay for construction-related expenses out of operating profits. In addition, our increased sales required us to carry a much larger inventory of raw materials and finished product. We hardly seemed to be in a position to double the amount of money we were giving away to nonprofit organizations each year. By comparison to corporate America, we were already off the charts.

I also pointed out that the company would need to reinvest its profits in order to continue to grow. The stock offering, if successful, would address our immediate cash needs, but we wouldn't be able to go back to the market year after year. Future investments would have to funded internally, and the increased bite out of our bottom line would make it more difficult to do that.

Those were all rational arguments, but Ben wasn't buying any of them. "Five percent just isn't enough," he said. An hour or so after we'd begun the discussion, we agreed to split the difference. Ben was happier with the compromise than I was.

When the underwriters heard about formalizing the policy of giving seven and a half percent of the profits to the foundation, they went through the roof. They thought we were putting the community ahead of the shareholders, to whom, they argued, the profits of the business ultimately belonged. When they realized that Ben wasn't going to compromise on the amount, they tried to persuade him to soft-pedal it in the document, wording the policy in vague language that implied a degree of flexibility that would take into consideration operating results, existing conditions in the industry, and other factors deemed relevant by the board. "It's going to affect the price you get for the stock," they warned, suggesting that we would only see the low end of their estimated range if we announced to Wall Street our intention of giving such an unheard-of percentage of our profits away.

Ben couldn't have cared less about the price the offering went out at. Even at the low end, the company was going to raise more than $4 million. Surely that would be enough for whatever it was we were going to spend it on. When the underwriters realized that Ben was willing to walk away from the deal if they pushed him on the issue, they finally relented, rationalizing it in their minds as a marketing expense by noting all the goodwill and free publicity that the donations generated. And in the end it had no impact on the price of the offering.

The foundation also wound up becoming something of an anti-takeover device, an increasing concern as we became a more widely held publicly traded company, and as the percentage ownership of the insiders decreased. Howie Fuguet, our attorney, proposed that the company issue nine hundred shares of a new class of preferred stock to the foundation, which would give it voting rights as a separate class with respect to mergers, acquisitions, or other business combinations that the company might contemplate in the future. While in many ways it offered more protection from ourselves than from an outsider intent on a hostile takeover, it was designed to perpetuate the relationship between the foundation and the company, and ensure that the donation policy survived any change in management.

The second company policy that was formalized and fully disclosed for the first time in the offering prospectus was the five-to-one salary ratio. Under this policy, no one in the company could make more than five times what was being paid to our entry-level staff.

The idea of a compressed salary structure had been proposed by Jeff. He had come up with the concept after reading about a cooperative in Mondragón, Spain, which paid its managers no more than three times what the workers in its factories received. It was an idea that Plato had even rendered an opinion on, apparently suggesting that the highest-paid person in a community should make no more than five times the lowest.

At the time, Ben and I were each making $40,000 a year, hardly exorbitant considering that we were running a $10-million business. By comparison, someone making entry-level pay at the plant that year probably took home about $12,000, which wasn't exorbitant either.

The reality was that our entire salary structure was abysmally low, and no one working for us was getting rich.

We were committed, however, to increasing salary and benefits for all our employees. This was consistent with our view that our staff, like the community, was a stakeholder group that should share in the company's prosperity as it continued to grow. The wage for new hires had gone up in '84 and '85, and would go up again just about every year thereafter. In addition, all employees were reviewed twice a year and their salaries adjusted based on performance. Many of our employees were receiving annual increases that added up to more than 20 percent as we tried to raise the wage scale of the entire company.

Through our benefit policy, we also conveyed a commitment to all our employees. Our profit-sharing plan, which disbursed 5 percent of the company's pretax profits as cash bonuses at year end, was based on length of service, not on title or rank within the organization. And we were a perkless company. Everyone got the same benefit package, including the infamous three pints a day. There were no country-club memberships, and except for Norma, who carried in the mail, no reserved parking spaces. Even gifts that our managers received from business associates (the cheese wheels, pen and pencil sets, Arthur Young Tax Guides, etc.), went into a "graft box" in my office and were used to reward employees throughout the company.

Ben, as you might have guessed, was enamored with the idea of the ratio. It was one more way to send a message that his company wasn't going to operate by the same set of rules that governed more traditional businesses.

I argued against it. "The only way senior management compensation is going to become excessive," I said, "is if we give ourselves excessive pay raises." At the time, my personal goal was to make as much money as a UPS truck driver. My biggest concern with the ratio was that by tying the top salary so rigidly to the entry-level wage, we might not be able to recruit the management talent we needed to run the company as it continued to grow.

We never took votes at board meetings because it was all too clear, once the discussion had taken place, what the decision was going to be. The only concession I extracted from Ben and Jeff was that the policy be informal and that it wouldn't be announced.

That was in March. Ben managed to contain himself for about a month, before announcing at an all-staff meeting that our goal was to pay entry-level workers $20,000 and our top dogs a hundred grand. Realizing after he'd said it that he might have created some unrealistic expectations, Ben did caution that it might take a few years to get there. Unfortunately, that proviso was quickly forgotten. The $20,000 figure, however, had been burnished into everyone's mind.

As they had when we told them about the donations policy, the underwriters shook their heads in disbelief when we talked about the five-to-one ratio. How, they asked us, were we going to attract senior-level managers with a salary structure that wasn't competitive and limited pay so severely? "There's no limit at all on what the upper managers can get paid," Ben countered. "All they have to do is make sure they raise the bottom first."

Recruiting managers was something we had never excelled at, even before the ratio was put into place. Our pay scale was part of the problem. Even if we paid senior managers the same salary Ben and I were making, which we did, we were still paying less than market rates.

The biggest obstacle to hiring wasn't money, however; it was the amount of time it took. One of the biggest mistakes we made was not hiring a recruiter or human resource manager who could screen the hundreds of résumés that we'd receive in response to any help-wanted ad. Ben or I would try to sift through them, fitting that task in among everything else we were doing.

It became a chicken-and-egg proposition. Do you spend your time trying to hire someone, or doing the work that the person you need to hire should be doing? With key positions vacant, Ben and I were each doing two or three jobs, working seventy-to-eighty-hour weeks, including nights and weekends. Ben, who seemed to have no limits (and no family), would often put in over a hundred.

Recruiting was all the more time-consuming because the management positions needed to be filled with people from outside the company. While developing staff and training people for positions of greater responsibility were noble goals, the fact was that neither Ben nor I had the time necessary to do that. Nor did we have the skills. All of our knowledge about making ice cream, for example, was home-grown, a culmination of what we'd taught ourselves over the years. No one in our company had ever run a dairy processing plant comparable to the one we now found ourselves operating. We needed to bring in people whose expertise exceeded ours, and who could teach us what they had learned elsewhere.

I strongly agreed with the premise of the five-to-one ratio, which was to recognize the contribution made to our company's success by people throughout the organization. But the company didn't operate in a vacuum and it couldn't ignore the realities that the outside business world imposed on us. Ben readily accepted and promoted the idea of "pay more, get more," but he only applied it to entry-level line staff. Why did he believe that we could recruit quality at the top of our organization by paying what was sometimes less than half the going wage rates?

One of the goals of adopting the ratio was to try to eliminate division between management and employees. Sure, it helps, but it accomplishes very little in and of itself. Treating employees with respect, fostering open two-way communication, and other common-sense, golden-rule management practices are what breaks down the barriers between managers and their staff.

The five-to-one ratio had no impact on the stock offering, and its three-line mention in the prospectus probably wasn't noticed by more than a handful of investors. As it was described, it actually wasn't that restrictive. It applied only to base salary, which meant that bonus payments, stock grants, and options weren't included. In fact, we'd just put into place a stock-option plan that was intended to overcome some of the recruiting issues that the ratio might present us with.

Had we adhered to the policy as written in the prospectus, it might not have had much of an impact on the company. Over time, though, fueled by quotes in the media and at all-staff meetings, it took on a life of its own, and came to be interpreted much more strictly. What started out as an informal policy affirming our commitment to our staff would turn out to be one of the biggest sources of conflict between Ben and me a few years down the road.

CHAPTER ELEVEN

The Fake Head

Like Dastardly Mash, New York Super Fudge Chunk was a chocolate-based ice cream with a lot of stuff in it. Although Mash was one of our best-sellers, it also generated controversy between those who liked raisins in their ice cream and those who didn't. Ben, it turns out, didn't like the raisins, and every time we got a consumer letter complaining about them, he'd tell me to cut down the number of raisins per batch, and make it up with the other three ingredients. This, of course, didn't really solve the problem. The people who liked the raisins thought we were scrimping on ingredients, and the people who didn't like them were still getting enough to irritate them.[1]

Created to coincide with our entry into the New York City market in the spring of 1985, Super Fudge Chunk was inspired by a review of our ice cream that had appeared in an article by Gael Greene in *New York* magazine. "The ice cream is pleasant enough, but not thrilling," Greene wrote, "and the chips and bits seem rather sparse." It was one of the few negative pieces of press we'd received to date, and Ben wasn't willing to assume it was simply the result of an errant pint.

He came up with a formula that called for liquid chocolate syrup to be pumped into our regular chocolate mix. The result was an ice cream that was incredibly rich, fudgy, and intensely flavorful. For add-ins, Ben settled on white and dark chocolate chunks, chocolate-covered almonds, pecans, and walnuts. In response to the gauntlet that Gael Greene had tossed down, he set the specs so that the total

---

1. The company-owned scoop shop, which still made all their ice cream on the original rock salt and ice freezer, came up with a much better solution when they created a flavor called Uncle Ben's Delight, which was Dastardly Mash without the raisins.

amount of chunks, by weight and volume, would be 40 percent more than we used in any other flavor. It was by far the most expensive product we'd ever made, but that was of absolutely no consequence to Ben, who never let concerns about cost of goods sold distract him during the creative process. If it tasted great, Ben figured we'd make money on it.

Most of the large distributors in New York weren't interested in an ice cream that competed directly against Häagen-Dazs, which was in essence the hometown brand. Instead, two smaller distributors, Joel Kremen and Steve Cooperman, started a new business, Ben & Jerry's Ice Cream Distributors of New York, that was devoted exclusively to our product. Steve had ice cream in his blood. He was a second cousin of Abe Kroll, and he had hung around the Gold Seal Riviera ice cream factory since he was five.

Joel and Steve started out by selling our ice cream into the gourmet shops and mom-and-pop grocery stores in Manhattan. As consumer demand built, they started picking up the independent supermarkets and convenience stores, and finally, one by one, the larger chains.

The thing that made the New York introduction different from our experience in Boston was the "slotting fees" that the chain store buyers would extract from the manufacturers who were trying to secure shelf space for their products. Competition to first secure and then maintain space was intense, and the retailers realized they controlled a valuable commodity that could provide a steady stream of income.

At first the fees were referred to as "introductory allowances," and were generally limited to discounts on initial orders. Some manufacturers went so far as to give "free fills," which meant they'd give the supermarket enough ice cream to fully stock the freezer at all of their stores. Over time, the introductory allowances evolved into outright cash payments, and came to be known as slotting fees, ostensibly meant to offset the cost of a chain "slotting" the product into their warehouses and getting it into their distribution systems.

Slotting fees, which went to the supermarkets, were not to be confused with payments that went directly into the buyer's pocket, called "grease." Most manufacturers and distributors spread some joy to ensure that the people deciding their fate were predisposed toward their brands. One distributor supposedly paid a buyer's alimony for two years, sending checks directly to the guy's wife in Florida.

By far the toughest nut to crack in New York was Waldbaum's, which was considered by most to be the preeminent chain in the city. It has since been sold to A&P, but at the time it was a family-run operation that was managed by Ira Waldbaum, whose mother, Julia, had founded the business. Ira's son, Arthur, though not technically the buyer for ice cream, was the man to see if you wanted to get into the chain.

On repeated trips to New York, Ben saw Arthur and tried to persuade him to carry our ice cream. Arthur refused, each time asking for what we considered to be exorbitant slotting fees. Ben argued that the money would be better spent marketing the ice cream to the consumer.

"Arthur," an exasperated Ben said at one of their meetings, "it's my job to pull the ice cream off of the shelf."

"Well, Ben," Arthur shot back, "it's my job to pull the money out of your pocket."

Ben had the two quotes engraved on a brass plaque, which he sent to Arthur, who proudly displayed it in his office where no salesman could miss it. Despite his affection for the hardware, it was another year before Arthur put the product in his stores. Slotting fees were a way of life in New York for every manufacturer, and we played the game along with everyone else.

The New York introduction was also the first time that we used Vermont artist Woody Jackson's black-and-white Holstein cow image, which would eventually be placed on all of our trucks and featured prominently in our franchised scoop shops. Posters with Woody's cows were placed on bus shelters, but unfortunately they were so beautiful that most were ripped off within twenty-four hours.

Largely as a result of Joel and Steve's efforts, the New York entry went extremely well. As for Gael Greene, Ben left some New York Super Fudge Chunk pints with her doorman, along with a note, but we never heard whether or not she found the "chips and bits" up to her expectations.

Shortly after entering the New York market, we began to hear rumors that Steve's, one of the legendary names in homemade ice cream, was once again for sale. The business had been started in 1972 by Steve Herrell, whose scoop shop in Somerville, Massachusetts, became a mecca for ice cream devotees. Besides the hand-cranked ice cream, his drawing card was a technique in which the scooper, using two spades, smooshed an endless variety of "mix-ins" into the ice cream.

Ben and Jerry had made multiple trips to the original Steve's when they were formulating plans for their business in 1977, and for a short time at the gas station, they even attempted to do mix-ins the same way Herrell did. They never mastered the technique and quickly decided it would be easier if Jerry put the chunks in while the ice cream was still being cranked.

Herrell sold his business in 1977 for $80,000 to Joey and Nino Crugnale, who owned a rival ice cream shop down the street. Over the next five years, Joey and Nino opened nineteen more stores, including sixteen franchises. In 1983, Steve's was sold again, this time to Integrated Resources, a New York Stock Exchange–listed company whose annual revenues of $176 million came from limited partnerships in a variety of businesses, including fast-food franchising. Integrated's plans were to open five hundred more stores.

Over the next two years the size of the chain doubled, but Integrated never came close to the aggressive rate of growth they'd set out to achieve. In the fall of 1985, Steve's was once again shopped around, and this time it fell into the hands of Richie Smith. Richie, as you may recall, ran the largest distribution business in the New York metropolitan area and had created Frusen Glädjé. Sensing that Frusen had reached its potential and would never approach Häagen-Dazs's dominant market share, Richie had just sold the brand to Kraft.

Right around the time we heard about the latest disposition of Steve's, Richie called Ben and asked to meet with him. Ben was hesitant at first, but when Jeff and Jerry said they'd go along, Ben finally agreed.

The meeting was held over breakfast at the Howard Johnson's in South Burlington. Richie began by telling stories of distributing ice cream in New York. "Nowadays," Richie said, "if someone bootlegs into your accounts, you put nails in their tires. In my father's day, they shot the horse."

They were illustrative tales, not told in a malicious way, but intended to drive home a not-too-subtle point. No one, it seemed, went up against Richie and won. Even when he lost in the marketplace, as had happened when he was unable to wrest the superpremium crown from Reuben Mattus, he won in the backroom when he bagged Kraft for a reported $30 million for what was already a declining brand.

Eventually, Richie got to the point of the meeting. He confirmed that he had in fact negotiated a deal to buy Steve's, and that he was going to package the brand in pints for national supermarket distribution. Just as he had created Frusen to go after Häagen-Dazs, Richie was now going to use Steve's to come after us.

But there was an alternative. "We can fight each other or we can work together," Richie said. He called it a merger, and told Ben he could still be president. Richie, however, would own fifty-one percent.

Richie's pitch was very smooth. Like all great salespeople, he could look you right in the eye and tell you the biggest crock of shit in a manner that didn't seem disingenuous at all. When he finished, Richie pushed Ben for a response. "I've been living with my girlfriend for years," Ben said. "We've been here thirty minutes and you want to get married?"

We never seriously considered selling out to Richie, but we had no illusions about the potential impact of a Steve's pint on our business. For openers, we'd no longer have all to ourselves the niche we'd been exploiting, as the down-home, funky-flavored, superpremium ice cream. That obsoleted our existing marketing strategy of methodically entering one large urban market after another, a game plan based on the assumption that whenever we arrived in a new trading area, we could take market share away from Häagen-Dazs and the clones, based on clearly discernible points of difference between our brand and the others.

Of even more concern were the implications of Richie rolling out Steve's nationally ahead of us. In the markets we'd yet to enter, which included everywhere outside of New York and New England, Ben & Jerry's would be perceived as a knock-off of Steve's. As Frusen Glädjé had proved, the second brand in faced a huge uphill battle, not just with the ultimate consumer, but with distributors and retailers who would question the need for a "me too" product.

Ben, determined to take advantage of what little head start we had over Richie, proposed that we immediately enter as many new markets as possible. He wanted to start selling in Philadelphia, Atlanta, Washington, D.C., and Florida by the end of January, take a month off ("to regroup, vacation, whatever . . ."), and then launch in Chicago, San Francisco, L.A., and Dallas. Where we had previously entered one new market a year, Ben was now proposing to enter one a month.

We debated back and forth the likelihood of successfully entering so many areas at once. "Wouldn't it make more sense," I argued, "to focus our efforts on fewer markets, and make sure we establish ourselves wherever we enter?"

Ben recognized that we'd probably fail in a few of the new markets, but he was convinced that going after all eight was the best way to wind up with at least five. And he wasn't willing to concede anything to Richie without a fight. "I really don't see this as being all that complex," Ben said reassuringly.

Strictly from a marketing perspective, Ben's plan made sense. But when you factored in the resources of our organization, it didn't seem realistic to think we could pull it off. For openers, our only salesperson had quit in July. We'd been looking for a national sales manager for six months, but had yet to identify any viable candidates for the position. The consequences of not being able to recruit senior managers within a reasonable time frame were all too apparent now that we were confronted by a need to move the company quickly in a new direction.

At the November board meeting, Ben outlined a game plan for getting around the fact that he was the only person we had working on sales. The first step was to get a copy of the Yellow Pages and generate a list of all the grocery stores in each city. Each one would be sent a promo kit and a copy of the proposed media buy for their market. Two weeks later, someone in our office would call and try to pinpoint the store's location on a huge, wall-sized street map.

"And then," Ben concluded, "our four-person flying sales force can go into the market and sell all the accounts in about two weeks, before moving onto the next market, where they'll do the same thing."

I was laughing when Ben finished. "Exactly what 'four-person flying sales force' were you referring to?" I asked.

"That's the only part I haven't figured out yet," Ben admitted. "You got any ideas?"

"How about Gary Samuels?" Jeff asked.

"Great, I'll take him, who else can we get?"

Gary Samuels had been one of the first agenda items earlier that day. "He's a guy I know in Ithaca," Jeff had said. "He wants to work for us, but I don't think we should hire him." Gary was a nice enough person, Jeff explained, but he didn't think his background matched up with any of our current or projected job openings.

That, of course, was in the morning, when we weren't quite so desperate. By four in the afternoon, when all you needed to get a sales job with the company was a pulse and a plane ticket, Gary was gainfully employed.

Our recruiting skills being what they were, we never came up with the other three members of the flying sales force. Gary Samuels was it. He was in his early thirties, short, and had a full dark beard. Most of his work experience consisted of writing grant applications and developing programs for social service organizations.

I told Gary that the job was relatively unstructured, as we had never tried to sell ice cream this way before. "That's okay," he replied, "I can live on the cosmic edge." To prove his point, he produced a photo of himself standing on a bed, dressed in an inflatable fat-man suit that made him look like Bib, the Michelin man. Did he travel with that thing? I wondered. I could only hope that he did, and that the time might come when he shared a motel room with Ben.

We sent Gary to Atlanta in December to follow up on a mailing we'd done a few weeks earlier. He took the giant wall map that had little blue dots indicating all the groceries we'd contacted by phone. At every store the conversation was pretty much the same.

"Hi. I'm from Ben & Jerry's Ice Cream. We sent you a mailing with some promotional material in it a few weeks ago."

"Huh?"

It didn't help that a lot of the stores were in neighborhoods that demographically didn't lend themselves to selling a product with two white Jewish boys on the lid.

Gary actually did a reasonably good job for us, given what he had to work with. He sold a few accounts and managed to hold things together for us until the end of January, when we finally hired Rick Brown, a director of sales from California. Rick was in his late twenties and had started in the ice cream business by selling Chipwiches off a cart on Venice Beach.

By the time we hired Rick, advertising was already starting to run in the first four new markets, even though we hadn't yet sold the product into any of the major chains. In some markets we hadn't even lined up distributors. That wasn't as ridiculous as it seems, because most large retailers won't even consider carrying a new product unless there's advertising behind the launch to "pull" the product off the shelves. What Ben didn't realize at the time, though, was that while we had to have a media plan that showed our intent, we didn't have to make the actual buy until after we'd gotten the product into enough stores to warrant mass-market advertising.

For the next two months, Rick worked the four markets, trying to catch up. Having gotten off to such a rocky start in Atlanta, Florida,

D.C., and Philadelphia, Ben and I once again debated the wisdom of going ahead immediately in the next four markets. With Rick on board, Ben was more intent than ever on carrying out the original plan.

While looking for distributors on the West Coast, Rick called on Dreyer's, the region's leading manufacturer of premium ice cream. (Sold mostly in half gallons, premium ice cream is one grade below superpremium.) Dreyer's had its own distribution system and was in the process of introducing its product on the East Coast, where it was marketed under the name of Edy's. After several months of negotiations, we signed an agreement with Dreyer's by which it became our distributor in most areas of the country outside of the Northeast. With one deal, we secured distribution not just in the next four major markets, but in lots of smaller cities throughout the country as well. It would turn out to be one of the key decisions in the company's history.

Even though we knew it was coming, we were still taken aback the first time we set eyes on a pint of Steve's. Not only had Richie taken our best-selling flavors, including Heath Bar Crunch and New York Super Fudge Chunk, but he was packaging them in a container that looked remarkably like ours, all the way down to the typeface, the print borders, and the colors he chose to differentiate between the flavors. Our boast of being "Vermont's Finest" was matched by Steve's claim to be "Boston's Best."

On the lid was a picture of a bearded guy, purportedly Steve. He came to be known as "the fake head."

"He's too skinny," Ben said upon seeing the fake head for the first time. "I don't think he's eating much product. You can't really trust a skinny ice cream man."

A trivia question on a blackboard had been a fixture in Steve's retail stores since Herrell's days behind the counter. There was a trivia question on the pint, too: "What New England ice cream maker copied Steve's mix-in idea?"

Whoever said imitation was the sincerest form of flattery probably wasn't fighting for shelf space with the guy who stole his chops. We were a lot of things, including the apparent answer to the trivia question. Flattered wasn't one of them.

Our first inclination when we saw the container was to sue for trade dress infringement, a law that prevents a competitor from duplicating the "look and feel" of a product to the point where the consumer is confused about which is which. Ultimately we decided against taking any legal action, figuring that Richie would be happy to capitalize on the publicity.

Given how similar our packaging and flavors were, it became even more important for us to identify tangible points of difference between us and Steve's. What we came up with was summed up in the slogan "More Chunks, Less Bunk," which was used mostly to rally the company internally and in advertising to the trade.

We were convinced that we could make better ice cream than Richie, who had a reputation for putting out a good product initially, but then gradually, over time, boosting his bottom line by pumping in more air and putting in fewer chunks. "It's Frusen Glädjé with nuts," Frank Stracuzza, the salesman for Ben & Jerry's of New York said derisively, noting that the clone had never consistently matched the quality of Häagen-Dazs once the hoopla surrounding its initial introduction died down.

There was no Steve's factory. All the brands Richie owned were produced under contract by co-packers, which were typically huge, full-line dairies that made everything from milk to cottage cheese. As a result, there would be no pride of ownership on the part of the people making Steve's.

Ben often spoke of the competitive advantage that came from producing a product that was so difficult to make that no one else would put themselves through it. We'd spent years modifying our equipment and production techniques so we could get huge chunks in the ice cream. Even in our plant, the larger chunks, just as they had at the spool-and-bobbin mill, inevitably led to shutdowns, which cut into the plant's efficiency. Most large manufacturers evaluated their production staff by the number of gallons produced per hour, which meant there was a built-in incentive to grind up the chunks into small, uniform-sized pieces. Ben didn't care about efficiencies, and, more important, neither did the consumer.

Our biggest advantage, though, was that there was a Ben and Jerry, and the fake head on the Steve's pint wasn't Steve. Our company had what Faith Popcorn, a consultant on consumer trends, had come to describe as "real sell," which she defined as "delivering a real message in a real way," much as Lee Iacocca was doing for Chrysler.

Unlike Iacocca, we couldn't buy air time to make our pitch, so Ben and Jerry came up with the idea of driving a converted motor home, which they dubbed the Cowmobile, on a cross-country scoopathon during the summer of 1986. For Ben, who had been drawn out of the gas station with the lure of a good tape deck, the idea of spending the summer driving around the country with Jerry was too good to be true.

Jerry had moved back to Vermont from Arizona with Elizabeth in 1985, after she had completed her doctoral program. At first he only came to the plant a couple of times a week, occasionally showing up in the middle of the night to work production with the third shift. Eventually, he was back on the payroll as a full-time employee and an ex officio member of the board of directors.

Jerry spent most of his time working with Ben on projects, representing the company at events, visiting franchises, and acting as an unofficial ombudsman for the employees. Because he made himself so accessible to everyone in the company and was so down-to-earth, Jerry was particularly effective in this latter role. In his typical self-deprecating style, Jerry would often joke that it was his job to take credit for the work that everyone else was doing. In fact, he was once again an integral part of the company, contributing to its success on many levels.

After a nationwide search for the right rig to renovate into a rolling scoop shop, Jerry eventually settled on a 1977 Travco, which a computer data base for used RVs located in Massachusetts. A serving window was cut into one of the sides, and two dip cases were installed. The outside was painted with the Woody Jackson cow mural, which looked particularly hip on the curved contours of the cowmobile's body.

As Jerry had predicted in the press release announcing the trip, life on the Cowmobile was mostly driving and scooping, scooping and driving. Neither was an easy task.

"The steering was a little loose, and the Cowmobile wandered a little bit," Jerry explains, "which is why it was so draining to drive. You had to pay attention all the time. Ben didn't like that. It was also a really wide vehicle, and it had these sideview mirrors that really stuck out. Ben and I had this running bet from the first day out about who was going to hit something first. We'd been driving for weeks and weeks, and then I finally just nicked something with my mirror, and the instant I hit it, Ben yelled out, 'IT WAS YOU!' "

Their goal was to scoop about a thousand cones a day, which meant they each had to average about one a minute over an eight-hour day. At night they'd pull into a campground, real or imagined, exhausted and ready to go to sleep. "Ben slept out back, and I had a mattress that pulled down over the freezer in the front," Jerry recalls. "When it was time to crash, I'd yell back to Ben, 'Send me up my sheets,' and he'd go, 'Here's your shrimp,' cause they were shrimp-colored sheets. We'd drag ourselves into bed, and in the morning I'd be lying there, kind of going through in my mind all the things that could go wrong during the course of the day, and Ben would hop out of bed, fresh as a daisy, and yell, 'I FEEL GOOD!' It became our mantra."

Some of the more eventful parts of the trip took place in California. On U.S. 1, the two-lane coastal highway, long lines of cars stacked up behind the Cowmobile, and as a gesture of goodwill, they put a sign in the rear window announcing they'd be scooping free ice cream at the next rest area.

L.A. was notable for their drive-by scooping. "We got stuck in traffic on the San Diego Freeway, and Ben started tossing dishes of ice cream out the window to the cars in the next lane. We were at a standstill at the time, but when we started to move, he still wanted to do it."

It was also on the Cowmobile that Ben and Jerry first discovered the difficulty of ending a free scooping event in an urban environment and perfected the getaway, in which one of them started up the rig, and the other, at just the right moment, tossed a couple of half-full tubs and some spoons into the crowd and shouted, "Work it out for yourselves."

In early September, Ben and Jerry flew home from the West Coast while two employees drove the Cowmobile back to Vermont. While driving through Cleveland—where else?—in the middle of the night, white and then black smoke started pouring out of the engine, and within minutes the fiberglass structure of the vehicle was consumed by flames.

Notwithstanding the publicity that its demise generated, the vehicle was a total loss. Jerry, who, with a bit of clairvoyance, had already purchased another motor home that was even funkier and more road-weary than the original, was actually salivating at the prospect of a big insurance settlement and the chance to do the whole thing over again. "This time," he figured, "we can really do it right."

CHAPTER TWELVE

Ben Is Ben

We may have had one or two all-staff meetings at Green Mountain Drive, but they didn't become a regular occurrence until we moved to Waterbury. At the old plant, information flowed freely around the crammed office and production room, and everybody knew what everyone was working on.

In Waterbury we were suddenly separated. The production and warehouse crews were in one part of the plant, the office workers in another. Instead of sitting at desks that butted up against each other, we had doors and cubicles that walled out distractions, but also kept our co-workers at a distance.

At the same time, we started getting departmentalized. Huge chunks of the business were being carved out of Ben's and my job descriptions and passed on to managers who had recently been hired. There was now a director of retail operations to oversee our franchise program, a controller to supervise the accounting and finance functions, and a director of manufacturing. The up side was that more work was getting done. The down side was that as people became more task-oriented, they began to lose their connection to the whole of the organization.

In an attempt to compensate, once a month we'd shut down production and get together with all the employees. The two-hour meetings served several purposes. First, they enabled us to communicate what was going on with the company. Jerry would usually start the meetings by telling a story about what he and Ben had been up to lately. Ben and I would then take turns updating everyone on current events and future plans. It was a chance to share information on how our pints were selling in the new markets, what flavors we were working on, and whether or not we were making any money.

The meetings were also a forum for discussing issues that were raised by the staff. About a week in advance, a sign-up sheet was posted in the lunchroom on which the employees could list anything they wanted brought up at the next meeting. The issues ranged from serious concerns, such as burnout from overscheduling or safety issues to more innocuous subjects such as switching from Coke to Pepsi in the lunchroom or getting a new mop for the warehouse.

A far more effective way of fostering two-way communication at the staff meetings was to break up into small groups and problem-solve on a specific issue. Each group would comprise about five to eight people, representing a cross-section of employees from all areas of the organization. After about a half hour or so, everyone would come back together and Ben would write down the feedback on a big pad of paper.

The small groups enabled line-level employees to participate in the decision-making process and to contribute their thoughts on how we could improve the business. We used small groups to generate ideas on how to cut operating expenses, how to enhance our factory tours, and to develop a consensus on which new benefits to add as we became more profitable.

Staff meetings were also the means through which we preserved and passed on the company's culture, values, and operating philosophy.

One aspect of that culture was a work ethic that could be traced back to the days at the gas station when the business was struggling to survive. It hadn't been unusual for Jerry and Ben to put in seven-day, one-hundred-hour work weeks. "The business," Ben recalls of the early days, "was running us. We weren't running the business."

Although the company's survival was no longer a day-to-day concern, there was still a "whatever it takes" attitude among the staff. In current parlance, we talked about giving 110 percent, and told stories of how our employees came through whenever we needed them. The start-up of the Waterbury plant, which had required a herculean effort on everyone's part, had been an example of this. Our staff had worked round the clock as we desperately tried to get ice cream out of the new factory before we ran out of inventory and started shorting orders.

A more recent example had been the production runs of Fresh Georgia Peach. In an effort to produce a truly outstanding product, we had purchased three truckloads of fresh peaches direct from a farm at the height of their ripeness. They were immediately sent to a processor where they were defuzzed, pitted, and then shipped to the company. Starting at midnight on Sunday night, we made nothing but peach ice cream for a solid week, finishing the run at 5:00 A.M. the following Sunday. The syrup was so thick, our employees were literally sticking to the floor.

Another part of our culture was that Ben & Jerry's was a company where you could be yourself. We embraced diverse lifestyles, people could dress the way they wanted, and you could personalize your workspace however you saw fit. My office was filled with windup toys and autographed pictures of J.R. Ewing and Mr. T, my personal cultural icons.

My affection for "The A Team" as a mindless release from work had led Ben's assistant, Diane Cadieux, to give me a small rubber stamp with Mr. T's face on it. I had begun to use it on memos, much as the political cartoonist Oliphant uses the tiny bird character in his cartoons. One of the most coveted acknowledgments an employee could receive was for me to stamp four and a half Mr. T's on a performance review. It was, I noted, our highest rating.

The concept of linked prosperity whereby the company shared its rewards with the community and its employees, and an irreverent attitude that questioned traditional assumptions about how things had to be done, were other parts of the culture we sought to pass on.

Some of what transpired at the staff meetings took on an air of tribal celebration. On the first anniversary of the date they were hired, employees would be called to the front of the room, to the cheers of their peers, and given a company baseball hat by Ben and Jerry. Every year thereafter, they received a small appliqué ice cream cone that would get sewn onto the hats to signify another year of service. Handing out the hats and cones was a simple way of making sure everyone in the company was recognized individually at least once a year.

Staff meetings were also where we announced the "Fred of the Month," an award that recognized those who had figured out a way to save money or ferret our waste. Like our factory-second ice cream, which was sold under the name "Fred's Famous," I had named the award after the most frugal person I knew—me (aka Cheapo). The "Fred-like" thing to do was for an employee to nominate himself or herself, using a piece of scrap paper to explain why he or she was deserving of recognition. (Anyone who used virgin office supplies was automatically disqualified.)

One person in our accounting department received a Fred's for talking our auditors into leaving behind all their red pencils when they left the plant. Someone in production figured out that we could use the plastic liners that our pint containers were wrapped in as trash bags, thereby saving over one hundred dollars a week. Another employee, who was traveling on business and flying back to Vermont at six in the morning slept in a rental car at the airport instead of getting a hotel room.

The Fred award inspired my "Just Say No" memo, in which I implored department heads to cut discretionary spending. Every dollar not spent, it was pointed out, fell right to the bottom line. As part of the campaign I permanently banned the purchase of Post-it notes and put the pens and pencils from the supply room under lock and key. Replacements were only given out if you turned in a spent Bic or a lead stub.

From the day the SBA-guaranteed loan for the renovations at the gas station fell through, the company had been undercapitalized and had scrimped by with less money than it needed. That wasn't readily apparent to new hires who started work in a well-equipped modern factory. While the dollar impact of a lot of the suggestions was negligible, the "Just Say No" campaign and the Fred awards were an effective way to encourage a cost-cutting mentality that kept everyone focused on the impact our individual and collective actions had on the bottom line. And since the employees split up 5 percent of the pre-tax profits each year, they had a personal incentive to approach their jobs with an owner's perspective.

Some staff meetings featured spectator sports. At one, Ben and Rick Brown, the director of sales, dressed like Sumo wrestlers in loincloths fashioned out of sheets, and "belly bounced" in an effort to determine who had the more substantial stomach.

At another, we staged a contest that was inspired by problems we were having with our waste water. When we moved into the new factory, we were given an allocation that limited how much we could discharge into the municipal treatment plant. As our sales and production increased, so did the amount of dairy waste we were generating. As a result, we were having problems staying within our permitted limits.

One solution was to suck up any ice cream that fell on the floor with a wet-vac and give it to a pig farmer to use as slop. Vacuuming melted ice cream off the floor wasn't nearly as much fun as hosing it down the drain, so I decided to hold what came to be known as the "Reclaim to Fame" contest to increase the staff's awareness of the problem. "Reclaim" is the milky rinse water that gets flushed out of the pipes prior to cleaning them, so called because it's reworked into the next day's production.

The rules of the contest were simple. Each employee who entered had to drink one shot of reclaim per minute. Whoever was left standing at the end got a paid day off and a pizza lunch for everyone in their department.

We started with ten brave souls, including Ben. Half of the contestants quickly dropped out, but the others looked as if they could go at it for the better part of a day. Jim Miller, the director of manufacturing, who was anxious to get the meeting over with and restart production, decided to take matters into his own hands. Instead of refilling the pitcher with reclaim, he decided to use the pig slop.

Whereas the reclaim has the consistency of a consommé, the pig slop was more akin to chunky oatmeal. "This oughta separate the men from the boys," Jim said as he poured out the next set of shots. The smell alone drove two more from the table, and within a couple of rounds it was down to Wilbur Wright, from production, and Ben. Ben, who has always considered Cool Hand Luke a role model, maintains to this day that he dropped out only because there was something in it for the other guy, but nothing in it for him. Wilbur got the rest of the day off to recover. Ben, who had a lunch appointment right after the meeting, wasn't quite as fortunate.

Eventually our crew was doing such a good job of sucking up the ice cream that we were generating more pig slop then we knew what to do with. We decided to front a farmer in Stowe ten grand so he could buy two hundred piglets. For the most part, the pigs loved the ice cream. The only exception was the Mint With Oreo Cookies. They liked the Oreos well enough, but they couldn't stand the mint.

The ice-cream-eating pigs turned into a huge media event when a reporter came across the contract we had signed with the farmer in a file at the state environmental office. For grins, I had put in a clause that required that one of the pigs be named Ben, one Jerry, and a third Ed Stanak, after the state regulator whose office issued the permits we were trying to comply with. When the story broke, we printed up a limited-edition T-shirt, substituting black and white pigs for the trademark Holsteins on the front and the slogan "Vermont's Swinest" on the back.

*　　*　　*

Shortly after moving to Waterbury in June of 1985, Ben announced that he was burned out and looking to follow Jerry into semiretirement. He proposed that we hire a director of marketing to take his place, and for me to run the company, something he believed I was already doing. Ben would remain on the board, continue to represent the company in a public-relations capacity, and consult on product and marketing issues as requested.

"Getting Ben Out" became a regular agenda item at board meetings, but nothing happened as we got caught up in responding to the intro of Steve's. When he got back to Vermont in September of 1986, after the summer on the Cowmobile, Ben reiterated his intention to leave, and set the end of the year as a deadline.

Despite his professed desire to remove himself from the day-to-day management of the business, there was significant debate among Ben, Jerry, Jeff, and myself about whether or not Ben was actually willing to give up control of the company. No one we could hire for the marketing position would make the same decisions Ben would. Nor would I, working alone without Ben, run the company exactly the same way the two of us might have done together. "If you give up responsibility, Ben," Jerry pointed out, "you give up authority." Ben assured us he was ready to cede authority to others, and we advertised the marketing position.

The prospect of Ben taking a less active role in the business was both encouraging and disconcerting. There was no doubt that Ben had been the driving force who was most responsible for the company's success. In some areas he was such a pervasive presence that it seemed hard to believe we could find someone to take his place.

It was Ben, for example, who had imprinted the company's culture with his fanatical commitment to producing a high-quality product. His standards were uncompromising and beyond those of anybody else in the company.

There was no quality issue on which Ben was more obsessed than getting the right amount of chunks into every pint. We knew from our consumer mail that some deficient ice cream was getting through. The problem was that, short of melting down every pint, we had no way of knowing which ones they were.

Most of the company, myself included, were willing to accept the number of complaints we were receiving as inevitable. As a percentage of the total number of pints we were producing, we'd argue, they were irrelevant. Ben, however, wasn't satisfied, and he cited studies that indicated that for every person who actually complained, there were many more who had the same problem but didn't take the time to write. The recourse they chose, Ben reminded us, was simply to stop buying our ice cream. The same studies indicated that every person who wasn't satisfied with a product was likely to tell at least ten other people about his or her unfavorable experience, multiplying the consequences of each errant pint.

We had modified the fruit feeder so that it would inject large chunks into the ice cream, but still hadn't figured out a way to get a consistent quantity into every pint. Ben was currently proposing that we invent a densitometer that would scan each container and somehow reject the ones that didn't have the right amount of chunks. As part of the research, he had us send pints through airport X-ray machines and a hospital's MRI scanner.

Directly related to quality control was R&D. Ben's ability to eat massive quantities of ice cream and render constructive opinions was legendary within the company. Developing new flavors is not to be confused with recreational ice cream eating. Once, Ben asked for 144 variations on a product, each with slightly different chunk sizes and proportions of one ingredient to another.

"Are you really going to eat all of these?" I asked him incredulously.

"No," he replied, "I'm going to start eating them, find out which ones I like, and then eat some more in that direction."

It was a tough job, but somebody had to do it. And at least up to then, that body had been Ben's.

No matter how many variations of a product Ben tasted, and how many times he changed the formula, he was always convinced he could further improve what he was working on. That tended to drive the people who had to keep making up the test batches nuts. From time to time Jim Miller would get even by giving Ben three bowls of an identical product and sadistically watch him squirm as he tried to figure out which one he preferred.

In addition to the product itself, Ben was the creative force behind the company's marketing. He had great instincts about what would and wouldn't work, and we relied almost exclusively on them. We never did any demographic studies or test marketing of a product before we rolled it out. If Ben thought it was a good idea and I didn't raise any insurmountable financial or operational objections, we'd do it. We were daunted by the prospect of turning our marketing and image over to a total stranger in the hopes that he or she could duplicate Ben's success.

Still, there was something really appealing to the idea of Ben stepping aside. For all that he brought to the company, working with Ben was, in plain English, a pain in the ass.

To begin with, contrary to his laid-back public image, Ben was a taskmaster and a perfectionist who held everyone to incredibly high standards. He rarely passed out praise and was always focused on what was wrong or had fallen through the cracks.

Sales in 1986, for example, had doubled to $20 million, and on the whole we were holding our own against Steve's. In some markets, though, Richie Smith had secured better distribution than we had, and our sales were lagging. Typically, those were the only markets Ben ever talked about. It was legitimate feedback, but there was good news, too, that warranted mention.

Ben was usually so singlemindedly convinced that he was right about something that he often didn't even acknowledge the legitimacy of alternative points of view. In his mind he was being forthright and honest, but the impact of criticism from Ben, particularly given his role in the company, was powerful and demoralizing.

One reason Ben was so confident in his opinions was that he had firsthand experience with most jobs within the company, going back to when he had worked the counter in the gas station and driven the delivery truck. He was also an incredibly quick study who was able to contribute meaningfully to a discussion on just about any subject that affected the business. Prior to and during the construction of the Waterbury plant, for example, he had become fully versed in complex refrigeration systems and all the other manufacturing processes that went into a large dairy plant.

Still, overall, Ben's management style was at odds with how he wanted the company to treat its employees. His intent was that Ben & Jerry's would be a business that conveyed love, support, and respect to those who worked there.

It would have been easy to label Ben a hypocrite for failing to behave personally as he was apt to preach. Some people did, but it wasn't quite that simple. For one thing, Ben was as hard on himself as he was on anybody else. For another, he readily acknowledged his shortcomings as a manager, and was remorseful that he couldn't improve. "I don't work well in groups," he'd say. After all, he had never aspired to be the leader of a publicly held corporation with 150 employees, and there was plenty in his past to indicate that it was a job for which he was ill suited.

The problem was that even though he knew he was interacting with people poorly, most of the time he just couldn't stop himself, and his pattern of behavior, although sometimes curtailed, was never changed.

Ben also had absurdly optimistic expectations about how fast we could get things done. This was particularly frustrating, since he usually put off decisions to the last possible moment, believing that the company should be able to turn on a dime and implement whatever he'd come up with overnight.

Once Ben made a decision, it was usually only a matter of time until he changed his mind. That meant we could count on a few false starts to just about every project, and plan on doing some of them two or three times. Operating in a last-minute, crisis mode was the norm if it was something in which Ben was involved, and as a result, the organization was in a constant state of turmoil.

It wasn't Ben's intention to make everyone's life so difficult. There was no mean-spiritedness involved. In his mind, he was just improving on whatever decision he'd made, all for the greater good of the business, and in fact, more often than not, he was. "Man who never changes mind never admits mistakes"—a fortune he'd pulled out of a cookie—was one of Ben's favorite sayings. One year he had it blown up on the copier, wrote "Merry Christmas" on it, and sent it out to all the managers as a greeting card.

"Ben is Ben," was the saying most managers used to explain the phenomena, which essentially meant that you should just expect him to change his mind or come up with some seemingly whacked-out idea, and not be surprised when he did.

Of course, a lot of Ben's seemingly whacked-out ideas weren't so wacky, once they were implemented. Nobody other than Ben, for example, thought that we could roll out the product nationally ahead of Steve's, yet that decision would turn out to be one of the most important in the company's history. Ben's entrepreneurial drive pushed the organization beyond its perceived limits, but without him, "impossible" projects that more traditional managers, including myself, were often too quick to dismiss would never have been attempted.

Beyond the sales and profits that these ideas generated, they were what gave the business its identity and made it unique compared with our more "corporate" competitors.

A large part of my job was insulating the rest of the organization from Ben, a role I'd inherited from Jerry. People who couldn't challenge Ben face to face would come into my office, leaving it to me to take their case to Ben. It was also my job to soften what Ben said to people, taking out the bite and getting them focused on the message. Someone suggested I keep a copy of Ben's schedule and show up a half hour after he did to mend fences after his interactions with others.

Although the external image of the company had been crafted by Ben, the internal culture was much more a reflection of my personality than of his. I was a regular presence in the factory and all the employees, most of whom I knew by name, considered me their boss. Ben, who traveled on business constantly, lived in fear that he'd run into a long-term employee in the plant and not know his or her name. As a result, when he was in town, he tended to limit his interactions to those people he needed to have direct contact with.

My relationship with Ben had started out extremely positive. Lately, though, it had begun to deteriorate. Increasingly, it seemed to me, Ben was in the habit of randomly showing up at the eleventh hour to offer his opinion, even after he'd announced up front that he wasn't going to participate in a particular decision. I would have welcomed Ben's input on just about anything, but it was frustrating to put time and energy into a project, often working with outside parties such as lawyers, architects, and engineers, only to have Ben show up at the end of the process with a "suggestion" that put us back to square one.

As a result of being second-guessed all the time, people were reluctant to proceed with anything until they had Ben's input. Since he was away from the plant so often, succumbing to that temptation would have had a paralyzing effect on the company. Given the pace at which we were growing—1986 was the fifth year in a row we'd doubled in size—we needed to be able to make decisions faster than ever.

There was also a need to be able to do things in a more organized fashion. Every decision now affected more people, and when things got changed or delayed, there was a ripple effect throughout the company.

The issue that was at the root of most of my conflicts with Ben was the great unresolved debate over growth. Ben was concerned that if the company got too big, it risked becoming just another bureaucratic corporation, no different from any other. To prevent that from happening, Ben would announce from time to time a limit on just how big we were going to be.

"What we're looking to do is reach the capacity of our equipment and stay there," Ben told the *Burlington Free Press* in March of 1980, right after the pints had been introduced. "We will not make another quantum leap."

It was only the first of many times that Ben tried to limit sales by tying them to how much ice cream we could produce. When we were at $2 million in sales, the limit was $8 million, the capacity of the plant on Green Mountain Drive. When we decided to build the new plant in Waterbury, the limit got pushed up to $15 million. Six weeks after we moved in, we decided to add onto the factory, and upped the ante again.

I think Ben used the exercise of setting limits to rationalize the upheaval all of us were feeling as a consequence of how quickly the business had grown. It was equivalent to creating a light at the end of the tunnel, and it provided reassurances, however hypothetical, that we wouldn't be working perpetually at that pace.

The limits were also consistent with the very conservative approach to the company's finances that the entire board—Ben, Jeff Furman, and I—endorsed. At many high-growth entrepreneurial companies, there's a tendency to get intoxicated by success and assume that the sales curve will go up exponentially forever. We were always amazed at the company's success and, despite being confident in our abilities, didn't believe that we could sustain our existing rate of growth for very long, even if we wanted to. One of the good things about the limits was that they made sure that we kept our heads straight and didn't start running our $20-million business as if it were a $100-million company. Had we done that, we probably would have screwed things up.

But at the same time, the limits skewered our long-range planning by putting up a mythic horizon, beyond which we never looked. As a result, the addition of production capacity and management talent lagged behind our growth, which placed an incredible and unintended burden on our staff.

Even when confronted with what seemed to me to be irrefutable evidence that we needed to further expand the plant to meet demand, Ben was reluctant to do so. Since I was the person who had responsibility for making sure we had enough ice cream to fill our orders, that drove me crazy. It was all I could do to get Ben to go along with construction projects that would get us through the next season. Come the following fall, we would once again be in the position of not having enough capacity for the subsequent year and again be scrambling to add onto the plant.

Even when Ben agreed to a project, it was always subject to last-minute revisions. After an addition to the storage freezer had been designed and engineered, Ben decided it was too big, and lopped off one-third of it. He had only agreed to the most recent expansion, which would increase the capacity of the plant to around $50 million, after a series of heated arguments over what we should build and how we should build it. Fifty million dollars, not so coincidentally, was Ben's newest limit on how big the company was going to be.

Despite a lot of talk on the subject, we rarely made decisions that were consistent with the idea of limiting our growth. Having the two founders hyping our company coast-to-coast in the Cowmobile, for example, certainly wasn't going to help slow things down any. And in fact, whenever our sales approached whatever limit we'd set, we simply pushed it back another $10 million or so, then worked like hell to hit the new number.

The only thing we ever did in an attempt to reduce our rate of growth was to decide not to expand sales into new geographic areas, but instead focus our efforts on New England and the eight markets we'd entered in response to Steve's. In retrospect, instead of slowing down our sales, over the long run it probably had the opposite effect. By going "deep" before we went "wide," we were actually ensuring our success in the biggest and most important markets in the country.

Beyond the fact that our slow-growth strategy wasn't one, there were other contradictions to any self-imposed limits. Foremost among these was Ben. Like most highly creative people, he was forever fascinated by what was new and different about the business, which, in turn, was what had fueled our growth. It had been Ben's frustration behind the crepe griddle in the gas station, after all, that had led to the start of the wholesale operation. Even as he withdrew from day-to-day operations, Ben showed no inclination to limit the number of new projects he wanted us to pursue.

For example, even though he was advocating that we limit our sales, he was also proposing that we expand our novelty business. Novelties are the single-portion ice cream items that are usually sold at convenience and mom-and-pop grocery stores. Häagen-Dazs had

154

just come out with a chocolate-covered stick novelty that had the look of a winner, and Ben was worried that if we didn't offer consumers an alternative, we'd be forcing them to buy our competitor's product.

Novelties couldn't be produced on the same equipment we used for the pints, and the only way to get into the business quickly was to find someone to manufacture the product for us. We did, and in July of 1986 we introduced the Ben & Jerry's Deluxe Chocolate Covered Bar, a full five ounces of chocolate-covered ice cream on a stick. After eating a few, most people in the company came to the conclusion that the product was way too big.

"It's not too big for me," Ben countered. Of course, as a rule, no amount of food looked too big to Ben. Eventually he came around to the idea that a smaller portion might work, especially if we lowered the price. Unfortunately, we had already printed up tens of thousands of cartons on which the declared weight was five ounces.

"No problem," Ben announced after he'd pondered the dilemma for a couple of minutes. "We'll put a sticker on the boxes that says 'Now Smaller and Cheaper.'" Ben wanted to kick off the promotion by immediately dropping the price on our existing inventory of five-ounce bars. He suggested we put another sticker on those boxes, this one proclaiming, "We Goofed, You Gain," explaining to customers that the extra ounce of ice cream was a short-term windfall. That way, he reasoned, they wouldn't feel ripped off when they picked up a smaller product at the same price in a couple of weeks.

Before we could follow up on that brainstorm, the company that was making the product for us went out of business. Despite having lost our supplier, Ben was adamant about not giving up on the new product line, and he proposed that we install the equipment to make novelties in the Waterbury plant. How hard, after all, could that be? "It's a damn machine," Ben reasoned. "You plug it in."

Actually, it was about five or six machines, set up sequentially. If we doubled the size of the production room, upgraded the refrigeration and electrical systems, and accepted the fact that we'd forever have an inefficiently laid out manufacturing facility, we could have done it. Ben ultimately agreed that it would make more sense to find another co-packer.

The novelty machine was just one of the ideas that Ben was urging us to pursue at the same time he was preaching the "slow growth" gospel. Within one month of a board meeting at which we agreed to introduce one new product in 1987, Ben had proposed half a dozen.

That was in addition to the Ben & Jerry's "Zippy," a carbonated milk drink for which Ben suggested we put together a joint venture and build another factory across the street.

But Ben's most provocative idea came in a memo titled "Recent Revelation," in which he unveiled calculations that he and Jerry had made as to what would happen to our sales if we sold the national 7-Eleven account. Seven thousand stores times seven gallons per store per week, times eight dollars per gallon. In round numbers, $20 million in additional sales. "Incredible," Ben concluded, noting that this amount of sales, added to the $28 million we were projecting to sell elsewhere in 1987, "brings us darn close to that fifty-to-sixty-million-dollar plateau (goal? target? end?) of which I am so fond." Did you notice how Ben slipped in that next ten million?

In other words, nine months after pushing us into a national roll-out in response to Steve's, Ben still says he's trying to limit how big the company's going to be. At the same time he gets the company about a million dollars' worth of free publicity while driving cross-country in the Cowmobile with Jerry, and proposes that we buy a $650,000 novelty machine on which we can make a half-dozen more new products, not including the Zippys we're going make across the street. And, just so we don't let any unused pint capacity sit by idly, we sell 7-Eleven $20 million of ice cream next year so we can reach our fifty-million-(excuse me, fifty-to-sixty-million-) dollar goal.

As the saying goes, Ben is Ben.

CHAPTER THIRTEEN

The Freezer Door

The idea of naming a flavor "Cherry Garcia" in honor of Jerry Garcia, the lead guitarist of the Grateful Dead, came by way of an anonymous postcard from two Dead heads in Portland, Maine. "You know it will sell," they wrote, "because Dead paraphernalia *always* sells. We are talking good business sense here, plus it will be a real hoot for the fans."

Ben's original idea for the flavor was to duplicate the taste sensation of chocolate-covered cherry cordials. After experimenting with all kinds of cherries, some chocolate-covered, some bare, he came up with a recipe that called for whole Bing cherries and smaller-than-normal chocolate chunks, referred to by our supplier appropriately enough as "Green Mountain Flakes."

The flavor was launched on Washington's birthday, 1987, and promoted with ads in *Rolling Stone* and *Golden Road*, the Grateful Dead fan magazine. We also printed posters that featured Ben and Jerry in tie-dyed T-shirts, under the heading "Euphoria Again." Just so there would be no missing the connection, the words "Cherry Garcia" on the pint lid were written in the psychedelic script associated with the band. Press releases heralded the flavor as the first ever named after a musical legend. (At the time we didn't know that a Bing Crosby ice cream had been sold in the fifties. It was vanilla flavored, of course.)

Eight of the first pints we produced were sent via Federal Express to Garcia. His publicist and his wife both called to pass on word that he'd enjoyed the ice cream. "As long as they don't name a motor oil after me, it's fine with me," his publicist quoted Garcia as saying.

Not everyone in the Dead organization, however, was amused.

Within a few weeks of the product's introduction, Ben received a phone call from Hal Kant, the band's longtime attorney. He informed Ben that Garcia didn't normally permit people to use his name or likeness to promote products, but would consider it in this instance, in light of the fact that the product was already in the marketplace, if an appropriate royalty was paid. Kant asked Ben to get back to him with a proposal.

Instead of following up with Kant, Ben thought it would make more sense to talk directly with Garcia, and he wrote him in care of the Dead's offices. "I would much prefer to work together with you," Ben wrote, "in the good spirit of both our organizations, as opposed to participating in the sickness of lawyers and the legal system."

Ben's letter may or may not have been passed on to Garcia, but it was most certainly passed on to Hal Kant. Kant demanded that we cease using the name, and said he was passing a copy of Ben's letter on to *his* attorney "for advice with regard to the defamation contained therein."

Although we hadn't contacted Garcia directly prior to introducing the flavor, we had made some attempt to figure out what the Dead might think about the whole thing. While they'd been in San Francisco on the Cowmobile, Ben and Jerry ran into one of the editors of the Dead fan magazine and floated the idea past her.

She made some calls and then told Ben he should just go ahead and do it. "This kind of stuff is fine with Jerry," she said, "but if you ask, the lawyers will get involved."

Faced now with the prospects of not only being sued by the Grateful Dead, but also by the Grateful Dead's lawyer, we pulled Ben out of the negotiations and inserted Jeff Furman, who, with his beard and longish gray hair, looked a little like how Jerry Garcia might if he had been put in a dryer and shrunk. Jeff called Hal Kant and arranged to fly out to California to meet with him.

Jeff made it clear that the last thing we wanted to do was litigate a lawsuit with the Grateful Dead. If Garcia wanted us to pull the flavor, he told Kant, we would. He eventually negotiated a licensing agreement that allowed us to use the name in exchange for an ongoing royalty payment. For the first year, part of the money went to the Rex Foundation, a charitable organization that the Dead had established, which had been named after one of their roadies.

With the legal issues resolved, we sent out word via notices in the underground Grateful Dead network that we were looking for the person who had suggested the flavor. A month or so later we received a note on the back of a Cherry Garcia lid from Jane Williamson. "I hear that you're looking for me," she wrote. The handwriting matched, and when Jane correctly identified what had been on the other side of the original postcard (a drawing of Ronnie Reggae), we knew we'd found the one.

Jane and Marc Posner, her boyfriend and co-conspirator, were our guests of honor at the next annual shareholders' meeting, and although they didn't make out as well as Garcia, they did get a year's supply of ice cream and newly minted Cherry Garcia tie-dyed T-shirts. The slogan on the back said it all: "What a long, strange dip it's been."

Cherry Garcia was an immediate hit. It became one of our top three best-selling flavors, and it generated incredible publicity for the company. And since it was licensed by contract, it also gave us a point of difference with Steve's that Richie Smith couldn't appropriate.

Meanwhile, things were not going quite so well with the director of marketing whom we'd hired in January to take Ben's place. We probably should have taken it as an omen when he asked Ben, "Who's this Jerry Garcia guy?" Unfortunately, that conversation hadn't taken place until after he'd been offered the job. More recently, he'd proposed that we open our scoop shops for breakfast and serve scrambled eggs in waffle cones, an item he wanted to call "Cone Egg, the Breakfast Barbarian."

By the end of the summer, I came to the conclusion that we'd hired the wrong person, and eight months after he'd retired, Ben was back. It was, he reminded me, just a temporary measure until we could find someone else to take his place.

There's a certain implied priority to fixing the freezer doors in an ice cream plant. Still, ours never worked quite right. They were supposed to respond to a pull cord that hung down on either side, parting in half like the doors Maxwell Smart walked though on his way into Control Headquarters.

The problem with the doors originated with the architect or engineer who specified the size of the opening to the box. It was barely big enough for the forklift to fit through, and if the mast of the truck was raised just slightly . . . CRUNCH. After a few run-ins, the doors didn't seal completely, and before long only one side opened automatically.

This forced the forklift driver to dismount and manually open the other side. The driver actually had to get off the truck twice, once to get into the box and a second time to close the doors after driving through. The preferred solution was to leave the doors open all the time, using the plastic strip curtain that hung just inside the doors as a token insulating barrier.

The curtain was intended to reduce the amount of air exchanged for the few seconds the doors were supposed to be open. But with the doors left open for extended periods, warm air poured into the box, and frost built up everywhere. When the circulating fans in the freezer rumbled on and the air started whipping around, the frost would blow loose and it would appear to be snowing. It was as if you'd been placed inside one of those plastic snow globes sold at tourist attractions like Niagara Falls. "Greetings from the Ben & Jerry's Freezer, Wish You Were Here."

One day while walking around the plant, Ben happened upon the freezer doors. He was livid. How, Ben wondered, could an organization that claimed to be committed to quality ignore a problem that directly affected its product?

Of even more concern to Ben was the fact that it had fallen on him to point out a problem that needed to be fixed. His walks through the plant were now a random event. We were failing as an organization, he reasoned, if we were still relying on him to be the watchdog for product quality.

As he was apt to do when he came across a problem in the plant, Ben came to my office to get me. I followed him out to the loading dock, where he showed me the doors and then took me into the box to point out how it was playing havoc with the refrigeration.

The thing that was most memorable about a freezer tour with Ben was that you never got to put on a jacket before going into the box. I sometimes thought it was part of his negotiating strategy. He'd position himself between you and the door and methodically start making his points. All you could think was "I got to get out of here," but Ben, standing alongside you in short sleeves, never let on that the minus-twenty-degree temperature was affecting him in the least. Within minutes he had easily extracted commitments to whatever it was he wanted you to do.

The term "freezer door" became a metaphor within the company for anything that wasn't working and was being ignored despite a painfully obvious need for attention. It referred not just to physical

160

things, but to managers, systems, and procedures that our rapid rate of growth had laid waste to.

At the end of the summer of 1987 there were "freezer doors" everywhere. A lot of our problems stemmed from a decision earlier that year to automate the pint lines. Up to that point, we were still filling and capping each pint by hand, the same way we'd done it at Green Mountain Drive. Working with our suppliers, Jim Miller had finally come up with a modification to the standard filling machines that would allow us to get large chunks into the pints.

Installing any new piece of equipment was always more disruptive than anticipated. Our problems were exacerbated by the fact that at the same time we put the automatic fillers in, we also installed machines to put a tamper-evident plastic band on every pint. Trying to get one of the two machines up and running would have been a realistic challenge. Attempting both changes at once was a disaster.

Our down time went through the roof and our inventory went through the floor. Actually, it went *onto* the floor, and pig slop hit an all-time high. After about three weeks we were all but out of ice cream and shorting orders left and right.

In an effort to catch up, we started running "marathons." On a typical production day, there were two eight-hour shifts making ice cream, after which a cleanup crew got the plant back in shape for the next day. When we ran marathons, we'd make ice cream continuously for forty-one hours. Some weeks we'd run double marathons, which added the equivalent of a full day of production.

To run marathons, the production crew had to work twelve-hour shifts, an incredibly long time to be on your feet doing physical work. Recognizing the hardship that was being borne by part of the staff, I asked the office workers to pull shifts in production after hours so that we could increase the frequency and length of the breaks everyone received. Virtually everyone, including Ben and Jerry, pitched in. The office staff also organized potluck dinners for the production crew and Jerry hired a masseuse to give workers back rubs during their breaks.

For many, the shortfall in production was a reminder of other times in the past when the company had faced adversity and stepped up to beat it down. There was a difference, though, between this crisis and the Doughboy or the threat from Steve's. This one was self-inflicted.

Despite the marathons and a decision to give up on the banding equipment, we never quite recovered from starting out the summer with an empty freezer. In September, when the crush of the peak season was finally behind us, we had an all-company meeting that focused on the state of the organization. By now we had over 150 employees, and the assemblies were taking place in the receiving bay where the tanker trucks offloaded the dairy products we used in our ice cream.

The bay was a narrow space, just slightly wider and longer than the trucks themselves. Chairs were set up in rows, five on each side of an aisle that snaked down the middle.

The unofficial staff meeting anthem, Bruce Springsteen's "Tunnel of Love," was cranked out over a sound system as everyone filed into the room. On the way in, there was a self-service cafeteria line with fresh-squeezed orange juice, bagels, donuts, and coffee.

The goal of the meeting, Ben explained, once everyone was seated, was to break up into small groups and generate a list of everything that was screwed up at the company—an inventory of all the freezer doors, if you will. This was the first meeting in about four months in which we had used the small groups to solve problems. Ben had grown frustrated by the one-way communication that had begun to characterize the meetings, and had insisted we revive the old format, regardless of the logistical issues presented by the increased number of employees.

There were sixteen groups in all. After about an hour, everyone came back to the bay, and one by one, a spokesperson for each group stood up and read the top three items off their lists. Jerry and I sat up front and listened. Ben took notes on an overhead projector, using hash marks to indicate which problems were identified more than once.

Communication was the number-one problem, showing up in one form or another in every group's report. Our employees also took us to task for hiring people poorly (themselves excepted, one would assume), and then throwing newcomers into the fray without proper training. Maintenance, and the reliability of the equipment we'd given people to do their jobs, made the lists. So did the lack of policies, systems, and long-range planning that were needed to deal with our growth. Some groups questioned whether the company was giving back to the employees the same 110 percent it was asking of them.

Although getting all the problems out into the open had a cathartic effect, I found it somewhat disheartening to be confronted with so many organizational failures all at once. Ben, on the other hand, took the complaints in stride, and he reveled in the process by which everyone in the company was being given a chance to voice their concerns. "It's only an indictment of management if you think that a well-managed organization doesn't have problems," Ben reasoned. "This was just telling us what we had to work on and letting the employees know that we knew about it."

Ben was also enthusiastic about getting feedback that was unfiltered by supervisors and managers, the normal couriers of information. He regularly expressed the opinion that people at the bottom of the organization knew better than anyone else what problems they faced and how best to deal with them.

One of Ben's biggest concerns was avoiding a sense of alienation and apathy that grew out of the company's failure to address and resolve the problems that were brought forward repeatedly by the line-level employees. How many times, he'd ask, could you reasonably expect people to complain about a piece of equipment that was malfunctioning, before they came to the conclusion that it was a fact of life they'd better get used to. The freezer door had no doubt elicited a reaction when it first broke down. Eventually, everyone had come to accept it as a fait accompli. Ben was always trying to convince people that when things didn't get fixed, it only meant they had to shout louder or in a different direction, but that under no circumstances should they give up and accept things that weren't right.

Ben's views on management, while sincere, were not without their share of contradiction. When Ben told the staff to shout louder, he was mostly referring to people who didn't report to him. As in other companies led by strong-willed, visionary entrepreneurs, there were no areas that had been managed more from the top down than those Ben had direct responsibility for. Despite the button he'd taken to wearing, it wasn't *his* authority Ben was suggesting people question.

At the end of the meeting, Ben reaffirmed his commitment to slowing down our rate of growth so we could focus on the organizational issues, using an analogy to make his point. The employees, he said, were all surfers, paddling madly, trying to stay out in front of a huge wave that represented the growth in the superpremium ice cream industry. Ben suggested that maybe we back off the crest, stop paddling so furiously, and float around while we tried to build a boat. Then, he reasoned, we could pretty much go anywhere we wanted to.

That sounded like a great idea to a staff whose bones still ached from a summer full of double marathons, and in many ways it made perfect sense. Over the long run, it was unlikely we could continue to grow the business profitably unless we improved the efficiency and quality of our organization. With profits and sales increasing so rapidly, it was hard to acknowledge that such a fundamental problem existed. Ben was attuned to it far before anyone else, and he was essentially blowing the whistle, forcing us to pay attention to something that could only be ignored at the risk of greater consequences down the road.

Ben never bought into the argument that a business that wasn't growing was dying. He offered up instead the analogy of a bonsai tree. "There's a lot of stuff going on that proves it's alive," he'd say. "Its just not getting any bigger."

Still, there were problems with Ben's imagery. To me, a surfer epitomized what entrepreneurship was all about—someone out in front, extremely flexible, taking risks, and on the cusp between the thrill of victory and the agony of defeat. Ben's analogy ignored our customers and the competition. We were locked in a dogfight for market share with Steve's, Frusen Glädjé, and Häagen-Dazs. Our competitors certainly weren't going to sit still while we trimmed our sails. Who was to say that, once we had our act together, the super-premium wave wouldn't be a ripple?

What was even more frustrating, though, was that the board of directors was still making decisions that were inconsistent with Ben's publicly stated desire to slow down and focus our energy within. For example, we had just decided to build a second manufacturing plant in Springfield, Vermont, that would be devoted exclusively to the novelty line.

The implications of starting up a second factory were huge. Besides the one-time distractions of putting together the financing and getting the project designed and built, there was the larger issue of figuring out how to manage a multi-site organization. We were just coming to grips with the realization that we couldn't get information from one end of the Waterbury plant to the other. What made us think we could communicate effectively between two factories that were a hundred miles apart?

As it turned out, we did run into problems raising the money for the new factory. When the stock market tanked in October 1987, we were forced at the last minute to shelve plans for another stock offering. It wasn't until December that we were able to restructure the equity offering into a convertible bond and raise the money.

Not that we didn't take the bad financial news in good humor. The day after the crash, we had a truck on Wall Street scooping free cones for the investment bankers and brokers. We offered two flavors—That's Life, which was vanilla ice cream with pieces of stale apple pie (the stale pieces held up better in the ice cream), and Economic Crunch, which was actually some leftover Nutcracker Suite from the previous winter, renamed for the occasion. (I gave myself a Fred's for that one.)

Two weeks after the all-staff meeting, the board of directors held a three-day retreat devoted to long-range strategic planning. Two outside directors had been added over the past year who had begun to broaden the board's perspective significantly.

Merritt Chandler was a former Xerox executive who had stopped by the factory on Green Mountain Drive one day in 1984, and offered to consult with us, free of charge, on the construction of the new plant in Waterbury. With Ben spending most of his time that year in New York City, working on sales, Merritt had all but managed the project by himself. It was only as a result of Merritt's efforts that we had managed to get the factory built at all, and he had been consulting with us on a wide range of business issues ever since.

The other outside director was Henry Morgan, the former dean of the business school at Boston University. Henry's background included working as the head of personnel at Polaroid under Edwin Land, one of the country's most famous visionary entrepreneurs. One of the reasons Henry wanted to join our board was that he was intrigued by the challenge of helping us make the company more socially responsible, while building a profitable business at the same time.

The meeting was held in a house that we rented in Truro, a small town on the north side of Cape Cod. On Henry's recommendation, we invited Phil Mirvis, an organizational development consultant, to join us at the meeting. Phil had served on the BU faculty with Henry, who described him as one of the most antiauthoritarian people he knew. Phil had been particularly vocal in opposing a proposal to extend management school credits to ROTC students, arguing that it wasn't clear to him that the business of a university should be training a militia. That, and a few other outspoken opinions, probably cost him his tenure. He had received unanimous approval from the faculty, but was turned down by the president's office and left BU, in his own words, "fired with enthusiasm."

Phil arrived in midafternoon and observed the board in action for the rest of the day. The next morning he started the session by asking each of us to describe the culture we wanted to create and to talk about our aspirations for the company's future.

Ben spoke first. "I want our people to love their work and have positive feelings about the company," he said. "Everyone should feel taken care of and listened to. This should be a company that gives generously, and where people feel joy, warmth, support, and accomplishment."

Jerry spoke of maintaining a family feeling. "I'd like the staff to feel like it was their company," he said. "We're getting away from that."

Jeff envisioned a company that had "a spirit and energy to make a difference in the world."

I spoke of wanting us to continue to be successful going forward, noting that we'd be judged by our current performance, not by our past accomplishments. "I don't want this to be another growth company that came and went," I said.

Henry felt that to date we were "fumbling successfully," and that we needed more open communication throughout the company. "The values of the leaders aren't understood or shared below," he said.

And finally, Merritt talked of reawakening the enthusiasm that was latent within the organization. His vision for the company was of an aggressive, forward-thinking, socially conscious, and highly profitable business.

Everything everyone said was sufficiently vague so as to not seem mutually exclusive. For the most part, the board seemed reasonably aligned on where we wanted the company to go.

After presenting our individual thoughts, we worked together to generate a list of ideas that, if realized, would get us closer to achieving our vision for the future, what Phil dubbed "the paths to the Promised Land." Among the items we identified were getting our supervisors and managers to teach, listen to, and hear people without getting defensive, recognizing and celebrating achievements throughout the organization, encouraging bottom-up communication from the line level to upper management, and reconciling, once and for all, our conflicting views regarding growth.

As a next step, Phil made two trips to Vermont to meet with as many managers as possible. The members of the board had been philosophical and expansive in their vision of the future. The managers offered a perspective that was grounded a bit more in the day-to-day realities of the business. After the interviews, Phil sent us a written evaluation of the organization, identifying its strengths and areas of concern.

The managers, Phil determined, had a very high commitment to their jobs and the company, and a strong conviction that working at Ben & Jerry's was "something special." It wasn't clear what that special something was, and the term actually meant different things to different people, but there was a prevailing sense of pride and satisfaction.

The managers also had a genuine interest in getting the organization to operate more effectively. Many, however, were new, either to the company or to their positions, and taking on managerial responsibilities for the first time. Some lacked an understanding of basic management functions, such as planning and budgeting. Others had never been coached in human relations. Most had been thrown into their jobs without proper preparation, few were being properly supervised, and almost all were in it up to their eyeballs.

Nearly every manager complained about the lack of systems to handle the problems posed by our rapid growth. (That year, 1987, was the first we hadn't doubled in size, but sales had gone from $20 million to $32 million, which was still the largest dollar increase we'd ever achieved in one twelve-month period.) Examples included inadequate computing capability, loose or nonexistent financial controls, and an absence of procedures to ensure coordination between departments. A few saw progress, but for most, any improvements weren't keeping pace with the speed with which the organization was changing.

Most of the managers Phil talked with agreed that people were being stretched to the limit, but there were differing opinions concerning what to do about it. Some thought it was in the company culture to do more with less and just knuckle down and work harder. Others wanted to add staff. Working smarter, not harder, would have been an option, but no one knew how.

There was also no shared conviction about how the organization should operate. Some were content to work within their departments, while others wanted more cooperation in resolving conflicting priorities.

There was also confusion about the underlying values of the company. In his work with the board at the Cape, a broad but common set of themes in terms of where we saw the company headed had emerged. There was no such unanimity among the managers. Most took "social responsibility" to mean that we gave away a lot of ice cream and money. "The vision of the board," Phil wrote, "is not clear to many, and to others it is illusory."

Ben and I were seen as both strengths and weaknesses within the organization. Ben was the embodiment of the notion of social responsibility, while I was the company's operational and fiscal soul. The managers were unsure, however, regarding our respective roles. Was Ben in or out as the head of marketing? Who was really running the company?

There was also confusion about how much longer I going to stick around. At the time Ben proposed taking a less active role, I'd committed myself to stay through the end of 1989. My intent, which I made known to the managers, was to leave at that time. Even as we had started to look for a replacement for Ben, we had also quietly begun to search for mine.

Although I was only thirty-three, I hoped to "retire" early in life. In 1969, when I was fifteen, my father dropped dead of a heart attack the night before Thanksgiving, a month short of his fifty-second birthday. It came with no warning and was an event I could never forget.

For the past ten years, going back to when I owned the bar, I'd been working over eighty hours a week, with limited vacations. My nights and entire weekends had been devoured by the business. Even when I wasn't working, I was. Ben & Jerry's was the last thing I thought about before I fell asleep at night, and the first thing to cross my mind in the morning. It was not a sustainable pace. My plan was to work extremely hard for a few more years, take some time off, and then pursue something that was not as totally consuming.

Ben's recent departure, which was only temporarily on hold, and my plans to leave in a couple of years raised questions about the future leadership of the organization. It didn't appear as if we were training anyone to take our places. To some it seemed like a race for the door.

Phil's proposal for working with us going forward included two projects. The first was to help the board clarify the mission and values of the company, and redefine its role as it became less active in day-to-day management. The second was to help me develop a team of managers that could assume responsibility for running the company.

Until we added Henry and Merritt as outside directors, the board and senior management had been one and the same, and almost every significant decision had been made either collectively or individually by Ben, Jeff, and me. Our monthly board meetings took up two full days, and with Jeff in Ithaca, it was usually the only time the three of us got together.

The meetings themselves were extremely informal. Most were held at Ben's house, and occasionally we had discussions while floating around in the pool. There was never an agenda sent out in advance of the meetings. At the start, we'd go around the room and each of us would offer up a list of whatever we wanted to cover, resulting in an agenda of thirty to forty items. Starting at the top, we'd work our way through the list, going from complex issues, such as distribution, to more trivial discussions, such as whether the ice cream sample on the tours was large enough.

The process of an entrepreneurial company's founders passing on the management of their business to others is one that occurs, at some point, in almost every successful venture. It's often a time of conflict as roles change and people give up control over aspects of a business that were once their exclusive province.

All of us agreed that it was the appropriate time in our company's history for the change in management to occur. None of us knew, however, just how divisive the process would be, and what stress it would put on us, individually and as a company, over the next twelve months.

No one, however, was more anxious for the transition to take place than Ben. On November 30 he sent the board his "letter of resignation," effective March 1, 1988, expressing his frustration that we had yet to hire a new director of marketing and that he was still devoting his entire life to the company, years after we had agreed to lower his involvement. "I look forward to joining Merritt and Henry as outside directors," Ben wrote.

Ben was out again. Well, sort of.

CHAPTER FOURTEEN

Ice Cream for Peace

As a jump-start to the work with the managers, Phil Mirvis proposed a three-day off-site meeting, starting on February 1, 1988. The intent was to use a combination of indoor and outdoor experiences to improve our ability to act as a team and to develop a common vision for the next few years. Eighteen people were asked to participate, including the seven department heads who reported directly to me, and some of the key managers at the next level down.

The retreat was the first day of work for two people who would play major roles in the coming year. Allan Kaufman had been hired as executive director of sales and marketing, once again absolving Ben of responsibility for those functions. Allan was in his mid-fifties, which was quite a bit older than most of the other managers, and he had worked for a host of big-time Madison Avenue advertising agencies. He was bright, opinionated, and outspoken, which would prove to be a volatile combination.

The other new manager was Chuck Lacy, who was brought in as something of a free agent to work on special projects. Chuck had an MBA from Cornell, and was working in hospital administration in Ithaca, New York, where he had served on a nonprofit board with Jeff Furman. Although he wasn't presented as an heir apparent, we had hopes that he might emerge as a viable candidate to replace me when I left.

The site we chose for the meeting was a vacant summer camp in Fairlee, Vermont, which was about a two-hour drive from Waterbury. A ropes course, which would be the focal point of many of the outdoor activities, was spread out in the surrounding woods behind the cabins.

We arrived at a little after 10:00 A.M. and, after getting settled, came together on a large open field for the first group activity, which was called "sardines." Phil divided us up into three "clusters" according to our functional areas—marketing, manufacturing, and administration—and the members of each group were roped together, then blindfolded. Our task was to locate a stack of three inner tubes that had been placed somewhere on the field.

There was no attempt within any of the groups to try to figure out a game plan before setting out randomly. People shouted out instructions to each other, most of which were ignored. Eventually, one group stumbled into the tubes and proceeded to cheer for their own success and razz the others for their incompetence. The experience, Phil suggested, provided a good representation of how the company was currently operating.

A variety of other hands-on problem-solving and decision-making activities, intended to explore new ways of working together, followed over the next two days.

The most telling event of the retreat was the meeting on the second night at which Ben and Jerry came and talked about their vision for the future of the company. By design, they had been excluded from the team-building activities, and it was their only participation over the three days. We met in the camp's dining room, the managers seated in a large semicircle with all eyes focused on the founders.

Jerry talked of the start-up of the business and why he had chosen to leave in 1982. Ben spoke of his vision for the company and of his desire to break new ground on what a socially responsible business could be. "I'd rather fail at something new than succeed at something old," Ben told the managers, urging them to take risks and innovate in terms of redefining the traditional role of a business.

The retreat had been presented to the managers as the start of the transition from a company run by Ben and the board to a company run by them. After two days of team-building, many were all too quick to dismiss Ben's vision as quaint and no longer relevant. Allan Kaufman, for example, having worked for the company all of forty-eight hours, was already challenging two of its most visible and long-standing tenets. "You didn't invent charity, Ben," Kaufman said in response to the discourse on linked prosperity and giving back to the community. As for the company's compressed salary ratio, Kaufman wanted to know if there was going to an opportunity for anyone else to get rich at Ben & Jerry's. " 'Five to one' is fine with you and Jerry," he said. "You've already got your millions."

To most of the managers, even those who had only recently been hired and knew him only by reputation, Ben was a mercurial figure who turned the organization upside down whenever he got involved in something. Few gave Ben due credit for his skills as a businessman, or recognized just how crucial a role he had played in the company's success to date. Over the three days, for example, no one ever expressed any doubts about our ability to be just as successful without Ben's direct involvement in the business, an assumption that bespoke significant bravado on our part, given his track record.

For his part, Ben came away from the meeting with concerns, most notably that the managers' goals for the business appeared to be at odds with his own. Was this group of people, he wondered, going to give life to his vision of what corporate America should be? It had never been his intention, in giving up responsibility for day-to-day management, to relinquish his vision for the business as well. The managers apparently hadn't understood that distinction, and seemed to be saying, in effect, "Thanks for sharing your thoughts with us, Ben, and everything you've done to date, but we're the pros from Dover, and we'll take it from here."

Where was I in all of this? In the middle, and more than a little confused by what Phil would come to describe as my "pronoun problem"—when to say "us" and when to say "them." I'd always felt that my values and vision for the company, though a little more grounded in fiscal and operational reality, had been aligned with Ben's. I certainly didn't see myself as a bean counter, and was comfortable with the notion that we should continue to redefine what a socially responsible business could be as the company grew and evolved, which was essentially the direction that the board had agreed to at the meeting on the Cape.

At the same time, I was being drawn closely toward the managers, who were looking to me for leadership in making the transition to a new structure. It was this group from which I was getting support and encouragement, and as their only voice on the board, I would come to see myself more and more as one of them.

The success of the retreat was that it gave us an understanding of the need to develop a broader focus in our planning and decision making. For many, it was the first time they'd ever reflected on goals and objectives beyond their own department.

For example, in the past, whenever we'd talked of the need to make more ice cream, we'd thought only of one department, production. The retreat had created an awareness that manufacturing also directly involved shipping/receiving, maintenance, and quality control, and that these four departments had to coordinate their efforts, not just amongst themselves, but also with the other two clusters, marketing and administration.

We also came away from the retreat with increased confidence in our individual abilities and those of the group collectively. Unfortunately, in many ways the new-found self-assurance was unjustified. Essentially all of the management, technical, and human-relations skills that had been collectively lacking in the group before the retreat, remained. Nor had we addressed with any substance any of the fundamental issues that the organization faced.

More than anything, the retreat created what Phil described as a " 'we' feeling," which was graphically confirmed when we repeated "sardines," right before driving home. Working together, all three groups reached the tubes in less than half the time.

An unintended consequence of the retreat, though, was that it set up a tension between the board and the management group. Perhaps it was an unavoidable part of the transition in leadership, but that tension developed into open confrontation in the next couple of weeks—ironically enough, as the company started talking about peace.

The idea of taking one percent of the annual U.S. Defense Department budget and using it to promote peace originated with Phil Snyder, a friend of Jeff Furman's from Ithaca. Snyder had written an article in 1983 titled "The One Percent Plan: A People-to-People Step Toward a Durable Peace." It was Snyder's belief that overcoming the fear and suspicion that stood between the American and Soviet people was the key to establishing a lasting peace. Relations between the two countries in the 1980s were far removed from their current state; the arms buildup of the Cold War was in full swing at the time, boosted by Reagan's "evil empire" rhetoric.

Snyder's proposal was to develop a comprehensive cultural and economic exchange program that would begin to form the basis by which a "genuine movement towards a *peace based upon understanding* could emerge." As a result, he wrote, "the rather confused, stereotyped and fearful images that both people currently hold about the other would be replaced by a knowledge based upon actual experiences and contact."

The idea was to fund the program by diverting one percent of the total Defense Department budget out of the hands of the military. "In terms of our long-term survival," Snyder concluded, "these dollars will be far more effective than a few B-1 bombers or any equivalent investment in armaments ever could be in ensuring a secure future for all of us."

Ben was immediately drawn to the idea when Jeff showed him Snyder's article and the three held a series of meetings in New York City at which the feasibility of the idea was discussed. Sometime toward the end of 1987, Ben decided that he was going to start a nonprofit organization called "1% For Peace." To promote it, he decided that Ben & Jerry's would rename its stick novelty "Peace Pops."

According to Ben, the organization would try to get Congress to pass a law allocating one percent of the annual military budget toward activities focusing on peace through understanding. The organization would be overseen by a blue-ribbon board of directors. Included on the list of potential board members were the Pope and Jerry Garcia, which makes this probably the first and only time the papal head and the Grateful Dead have been considered for the same position.

The idea of spearheading the 1% For Peace campaign was quite a leap for the previously apolitical Ben, who had tended in the past to avoid even the basics of participatory democracy like voting. He was beginning, however, to see that as the founder of Ben & Jerry's he had greater reach and influence than he had as an individual, especially as we established a reputation for being an innovative, socially responsible business.

"Peace," Ben argued at the January 1988 board meeting at which he presented his idea, "is a bipartisan issue. No one is against it." He reasoned that business could foster social change faster than government could, and urged the board to accept whatever minimal risk was involved and take a stand.

The board approved relaunching the stick novelty as Peace Pops, but had reservations about endorsing an organization they knew nothing about. The board was also reluctant to take what it considered to be a progressive political stand on its own. It urged Ben to drum up support among other businesses—Coca-Cola and McDonald's were two that were mentioned—and that together we could consider signing on to the campaign.

With the board's tentative blessing, Ben plunged straight ahead. In mid-February he sent out a five-page letter to a list of potential supporters. "I need your help," the letter began, and continued, "The Board of Directors of Ben & Jerry's has directed our company to manufacture a product called PEACE POPS. The copy on these 2 million to 8 million packages will be used to help alert the population to excessive military expenditures and to garner support for 1% For Peace."

The letter described the one-percent initiative, and listed some of the projects that might get supported. "It doesn't really matter to me what the money is used for as long as it's allocated away from death and destruction and towards cooperation and human needs," Ben wrote.

One of the keys to the campaign was getting other businesses involved by creating 1% For Peace products that would promote the initiative on their packaging and perhaps generate some revenue for the organization. By way of example, the Ben & Jerry's Foundation had agreed to donate the equivalent of one percent of the company's pretax profits to the cause.

"There is a deep frustration in the country around enormous and wasteful military expenditures," Ben concluded, "and an equally deep desire of people to have a world of real peace and mutual security."

No one on the board other than Jeff was sent a copy of Ben's letter. When it finally crossed my desk, I was furious. In my opinion, Ben had made commitments for the company that went beyond what the board had agreed to.

Coming less than ten days after the managers and I had had our heads enlarged at the retreat, the timing of Ben's letter couldn't have been worse. After a few days of carping among ourselves, we drafted a response to the letter that was sent to the board. I signed it, as did the four other members of the newly formed management Operating Committee—Jim Miller, the director of manufacturing; Dave Barash, the head of human resources; Allan Kaufman, the director of sales and marketing; and Chuck Lacy.

"The subject of Peace Pops and how they are to be marketed," we wrote, "threatens to emasculate the process of management decision making we are trying to establish and seems to deny the two-way communication—from the board to the staff and the staff to the board—the board seems to want to encourage.

"We have been told that the board voted to proceed with a product called Peace Pops. The decisions about implementation, however, seem to have been made by Ben alone. This may be the way things used to be done, but unless all the rhetoric about communication and management decision making was simply rhetoric and all this work we are doing with Phil and ultimately will do with the staff is for nothing, it is not the way we do things anymore. We are either going to be an organization run by a management team, or an organization run by Ben. Which is it to be?"

The memo also laid out our specific concerns about 1% For Peace. Like the board, the managers were reluctant to put the prestige of Ben & Jerry's behind an organization that didn't exist. We proposed, instead, using the Peace Pop to promote the concept of peace through understanding, but that it not be tied directly to a specific organization.

The day after Ben received our memo, he and Jerry met in my office with the Operating Committee. Ben acknowledged that the decision-making process and communication on the issue had been less than great, but reasoned that this was because the project had been initiated during the marketing department's period of transition from his leadership to Allan's. It was his opinion that the board had in fact taken a position in support of 1% For Peace, and that renaming the stick novelty Peace Pops was a decision that had been made appropriately at the board level.

Ben also believed that no rational person could take issue with the core idea behind the campaign. "If peace through understanding isn't the way to achieve peace," he asked, "what is?"

Ben also dismissed concerns that by taking an antimilitary stand we risked alienating customers and losing sales, quoting surveys that indicated that an overwhelming percentage of the population favored reductions in the Defense Department's budget.

We argued back, starting with our belief that it simply wasn't going to work, and that Ben had embarked on what Allan described as a "quixotic gesture."

"The feds, Ben, are not going to hand over $3 billion to you and your friends," I said.

Ben considered that a slur against the blue-ribbon board of advisers he expected to assemble. "It's not me and my friends," he shot back. "These are Nobel Prize winners and some of the greatest minds in America."

Ben viewed our argument that the credibility of 1% For Peace would be enhanced by keeping it at arm's length from Peace Pops and Ben & Jerry's as an excuse for keeping the company from getting involved. He also dismissed concerns that the 1% For Peace campaign might come off as a marketing ploy that was simply intended to sell ice cream. Ben was motivated by an honest and heartfelt desire to change the world, and he was confident that people would see his efforts the same way he did.

The managers left the meeting frustrated that their suggestions on how to go forward were ignored, and convinced that Ben was rewriting history, trying to justify the process by which he was singlehandedly making the decisions on Peace Pops.

Ben left feeling totally unsupported and, for the second time in less than two weeks, convinced he was in the process of turning over his company to a bunch of risk-averse managers whose values weren't aligned with his. In a word, Ben and Jerry wondered if the management group was "weird" enough.

At the same time that the board and managers were clashing over Peace Pops, interestingly enough, they were also at odds over "joy." Jerry's question, "If it's not fun, why do it?" had been a stated credo of the business since its inception.

Most of our employees felt working for Ben & Jerry's was by far the best job they ever had. There was a palpable energy that came from the company's success that kept everyone motivated, and most believed that the company had a genuine commitment to their welfare and that their compensation and the overall quality of their work life would continue to improve.

Our wages were, in fact, increasing well ahead of the cost of living and we were adding benefits every year as we were better able to afford them. Although, as a result of the five-to-one ratio, wages for a few people at the top of the company weren't competitive with what they might get elsewhere, for the most part we were paying our employees better-than-average wages.

Still, at this point most employees would probably not have characterized their day-to-day work as fun. In fact, for many it was mentally and physically grueling, which is what you might expect in a small business grappling with the implications of explosive growth.

177

The disparity between reality and the perception of the outside world regarding what it was like to work for the company had been raised at the "freezer door" all-staff meeting back in October of 1987. I began to refer privately to Jerry's motto as one of the "three great lies." (To which Jerry responded, "It's not a lie, it's a question.") Allan Kaufman, noting how hard everyone was working, jokingly called the company "a sweatshop in a pastoral setting."

Since returning from the retreat in February, the managers had been working with Phil on long-term strategic and one-year operating plans for the business. There was a great deal of employee involvement in the process, and the managers were now trying to sort out the conflicting priorities of the different clusters and to figure out what each department needed from the others in order to succeed at their jobs.

Through this planning process, we were just coming to grips with the fact that despite the ongoing expansion of the Waterbury plant, we would once again be short on pint capacity next year. Even without entering any new markets, we expected that our current momentum would carry us from the $32 million in sales we'd posted in 1987 to approximately $75 million in 1990.

The debate among the managers over what to do about the production shortfall, and whether we could get the board to acknowledge and deal with it, was heated. In the middle of this discussion, which was really more like an argument, Jerry, with Ben by his side, walked into the room and announced that they thought there should be more joy in the workplace, and that we should have a committee actively working on it.

To the managers, who were overwhelmed by the operational problems that the company faced, the proposal to start having more fun at work seemed like an indication that Jerry and Ben were completely out of touch with what was going on at the company. It hardly seemed coincidental to us that Ben had decided to prioritize joy following his "retirement."

To Ben and Jerry, the managers' resistance to trying to institutionalize aspects of our culture, especially something as innocuous as having more fun, was an indication that the very soul of their company was at risk.

Eventually the managers came around to the idea, and the committee was formed. One of the first proposals to come out of the Joy Gang was to buy a Syncro-Energizer, a machine that consisted of goggles that flashed patterns of colored light, best experienced while sitting in a dark room listening to New Age music. Supposedly, this synchronized the brain and helped people with problem-solving as well as giving them a sense of euphoria and improved self-esteem. Jerry at first suggested that we build a small room in the plant where people could go to get the full experience. I suggested he stop the elevator between floors and turn off the lights.

Much more successful was Elvis Day, during which employees participated in look-, sound- and sneer-alike contests. I came to work that day in a white stretch limo, dressed as the "Las Vegas Elvis" in a jumpsuit with flashy epaulets. It was only good enough for second place. Sarah Forbes, one of the artists from the marketing department, took first prize with her "Gimme s'more mashed potatoes 'n' gravy" Elvis.

Not all musical-themed Joy Gang events were as successful as Elvis Day. A celebration in honor of Barry Manilow bombed, mostly because they kept playing "Mandy" over the PA system.

The managers' reactions to the Joy Gang and 1% For Peace were symbolic of where the organization was in the spring of 1988. The roles of the board and management were changing, which created tension and stress on both sides. Routine management discussions turned into emotionally charged debates, and we'd invariably find ourselves polarized into two opposing camps on almost every issue.

One reason the transition in leadership was so difficult was that it was taking place at the same time that the company's values were being redefined. To Ben, the vision he was now espousing was a natural evolution, consistent with beliefs he'd held from the days at the gas station. To the managers, Ben's vision was a moving target that was imposing a new set of arbitrary and open-ended guidelines under which the company now had to operate. The truth was probably somewhere in between.

Further complicating the transition was the fact that Ben's vision was so atypical of how almost all of us had come to expect a business to operate. Making and selling ice cream, it seemed, was becoming almost incidental to what the business was about, rather than being its very core.

Adding to the problem was a degree of ambivalence on Ben's part. He wasn't willing, for example, to stand up before the managers and say, in effect, "Look, it's my company, I started it, I built it into what it is, and I own 40 percent of the outstanding stock. This is the direction I see us going in, and that's the way it's going to be." Had he done so, the managers would have had clear expectations about what their role was going to be, relative to Ben's.

The message Ben had actually sent the managers, intentionally or otherwise, was exactly the opposite: "I'm outta here, you run the company." It was inevitable that when Ben clarified his intent to maintain influence and control over the company's direction, and crossed the not always clearly defined line between "policy" and "operations," that conflict arose, especially when at the same time he insisted that others, not he himself, be accountable for the results.

The issues we confronted, as the company struggled to grow while remaining true to the values and vision of its founders, were publicly aired in a July 1988 *Inc.* magazine cover story titled, "The Bad Boys of American Business—Ben & Jerry's Battle to Keep Their Company Young Forever." With hindsight, it's easy to see that it would have been impossible to achieve something so unconventional without false starts, setbacks, and some degree of conflict.

"Our company will be changed, there's no doubt about that," Jerry was quoted in the article. "We just have to make it a good change."

CHAPTER FIFTEEN

We Are the Weird

The conflict between the board and the managers over 1% For Peace pointed to an obvious need to articulate to the organization exactly what our vision for the business was. Ben's view of how the company should operate had grown well beyond the two quotes—"Business has a responsibility to give back to the community," and "If it's not fun, why do it?"—that had appeared on the flyers announcing the first Free Cone Day. "It's not a question of making great ice cream, making some money, and then going and doing socially responsible things," he now argued. "Caring about the community has to be imbued throughout the organization so that it impacts every decision we make."

Ben's beliefs were driven by the realization that the Ben & Jerry's Foundation was limited in what it could do to deal with the social problems the world faced. For every ten grant applications it received, it could fund only one. He had come to the conclusion that our impact would be significantly greater if the resources and purchasing power of the business were also used to address unmet societal needs.

Ben had recently become friends with Anita and Gordon Roddick, the founders of The Body Shop. Anita's belief that a business should be a values-led organization in which more than strictly economic considerations were factored into the decision-making process was greatly influencing Ben and reinforcing his views on the direction he wanted the company to go in. The Body Shop used everything from its store windows to its trucks to promote social causes. It had struck a chord with Ben, and had confirmed to him that a consumer product company such as Ben & Jerry's could influence society through its ability to communicate with its customers.

Ben also argued for evaluating our performance based on more than the traditional measures of profitability, proposing that we "re-define the bottom line" to include both an economic and a social component. "We can't just optimize profits," he reasoned, "we need to optimize the community as well."

As an example of what he was talking about, Ben pointed to the New York subway project, which he'd proposed to the board right after returning temporarily to the marketing department in September of 1987. Ben's idea, inspired by a particularly grim ride under-ground, was to take our entire marketing budget for New York City and use the funds to renovate and maintain one subway station in pristine condition for a year. In addition to the seven full-time main-tenance people, Ben intended to provide artwork, a sound system, and a myriad of other improvements. In a letter describing the project, Ben told Ed Koch, the mayor, that he was looking forward to getting together with him to mop the platform and get the project off to a good start.

Ben and Jeff had a series of meetings with the New York City Transit Authority to follow up on the idea, getting so far as to choose a station—the express stop at Seventy-second and Broadway. As with anything Ben did, he immersed himself in the details, enthusiastically reporting back to the board on the authority's five-step gum-removal process and their method for getting the smell of urine out of con-crete. In a six-page memo in which he outlined the scope of the work, he even proposed a way to get the garbage off the tracks without shutting off power to the third rail ("cut out the floors on several cars and have a team of people with spears and vacuums").

The correspondence between Ben and the city had already gen-erated considerable media attention, even as the project got bogged down in conflicts over whether it violated the Transit Union's collective-bargaining agreement. That matter was now before an ar-bitrator, and the project was, at least for the moment, on hold.

The board discussed Ben's vision and tried to come to grips with what the impact might be on the company's profitability. Everyone agreed that we needed to make money, not just to survive, but also to create a model that other businesses might follow. Henry Morgan related his experience at Polaroid with its founder, Edwin Land, who had been one of the first business leaders to boycott South Africa in protest of its policy of apartheid. "Land would have considered the policy a flop if no one had followed him," Henry said.

No one knew what the likelihood of a reduced level of profitability might be. Although Ben foresaw a potential for a negative impact in the short term or from one or two specific projects, overall he felt that the results would be as good or maybe even better. "The goal," Ben added, "was to do things that were both socially responsible and profitable."

In that regard, I found the example of the subway project somewhat disconcerting. Ben had worked out a budget literally on a paper napkin and, by my estimate, had offered to do at least half a million dollars' worth of work against a budget he believed to be a quarter of a million dollars, but which was actually closer to $150,000.

As the person on the board with direct responsibility for the company's financial results, I was uncomfortable with the notion that we might start to accept lower profits in exchange for a social payoff. I had always argued that even as we became more socially responsible, a goal I fully supported, we should hold ourselves accountable to the same financial standards by which Wall Street evaluated any other business. Otherwise, no one would take us seriously.

The task of boiling down everything we'd said into an evocative statement was given to Henry. During a break at the May board meeting he went off to a corner of Ben's house, and returned about fifteen minutes later with a single page of copy. It was read to the board, who changed three or four words, before approving the following Statement of Mission:

> Ben & Jerry's is dedicated to the creation and demonstration of a new corporate concept of linked prosperity. Our mission consists of three interrelated parts.
>
> Product Mission: To make, distribute, and sell the finest quality all natural ice cream and related products in a wide variety of innovative flavors made from Vermont dairy products.
>
> Social Mission: To operate the company in a way that actively recognizes the central role that business plays in the structure of society by initiating innovative ways to improve the quality of life of a broad community, local, national and international.
>
> Economic Mission: To operate the company on a sound

financial basis of profitable growth, increasing value for our shareholders and creating career opportunities and financial rewards for our employees.

Underlying the mission of Ben & Jerry's is the determination to seek new and creative ways of addressing all three parts, while holding a deep respect for individuals inside and outside the company, and for the communities of which they are a part.

The mission statement, according to Phil Mirvis, was "a great conciliation that captured what had come through the board's ideological and practical debate. We're here to make money, we want to have impact on the global community, and we have a pride and craft as ice cream makers."

All we had to do now was get the rest of the organization to buy into it.

The next day, the board and the management group met together at the Waterbury Holiday Inn. To try to break the ice, each of the managers was wearing a "Ben" or "Jerry" mask and a "We Are the Weird" button when the board came into the room. The gesture was well taken as an attempt to reaffirm our connection to the founders.

A great deal of the meeting was spent discussing the working relationship between the two groups. Although both sides outwardly expressed optimism that we could begin to work together more effectively, basic questions surrounding our respective roles and the full implications of the mission statement went unresolved.

Most of Ben, Jerry, and Jeff's time during the summer of '88 was spent on 1% For Peace. Sixty or so activists, businesspeople, artists, and politicians had responded to Ben's initial letter, and showed up in New York for the organization's first meeting. Everyone thought the idea had merit, but there were almost as many ideas on how to proceed as there were people in the room. Some agreed that the most compelling peace issue confronting the global community was the relationship between what were still then the world's two superpowers. Others wanted the focus broadened to include issues such as Third World injustice or domestic problems including homelessness, racial inequality, and poverty.

Ben was named the organization's acting executive director, and a committee charged with the task of figuring out how to move the idea forward was formed.

Peace Pops were finally introduced toward the end of July 1988, packaged in a box with copy that directly confronted the basic issue of misplaced government priorities and wasteful spending on the military. With the managers' collective noses still out of joint over the process by which Peace Pops had come to pass, it probably should have come as no surprise that the product launch was a disaster.

The biggest problem was that we missed the summer season that was so crucial for novelties. By purchasing and renovating an existing building, we were able to get the Springfield plant on line less than nine months from when the board had committed the company to the project, which was a remarkable accomplishment. But even if we had hit our original July 1 deadline, it would have been too late to distribute the product effectively for the current season. With a modest three-week delay in the start-up and shakedown of the plant, Peace Pops didn't hit the retailer's freezers in most markets until mid August.

There were also problems with the product. It was still too big, even though it had been downsized to four ounces, and at a retail price of $1.99 it cost as much in most stores as a pint. There was also an unresolved adhesion problem with the chocolate coating, which kept flaking off when you bit into the bar, and the texture of the ice cream, compared to that in our pints, was "fluffy."

Ben's perception, which was reasonably accurate, was that some of the managers were indifferent to whether or not the product succeeded, and he began to speak of a phenomenon he called the "Coheeni Kiss of Death." Anything he was too closely associated with was doomed. It was hardly coincidental that Peace Pops had been introduced without a marketing strategy other than to let our distributors know that the product was available.

Ben and I had continued sparring over 1% For Peace through the summer as we tried to agree on what the organization's relationship with the business was going to be. Unfortunately, my actions had unintentionally sent a message throughout the company that I was ambivalent about how many Peace Pops we actually sold. Having just invested millions in a new plant to manufacture novelties, I was well aware that the consequences, if the new product failed, would be huge. They would certainly outweigh any momentary satisfaction from being able to go back to Ben and say "I told you so." Besides, if Peace Pops did flop, it would never be clear whether it was because the original idea had been flawed or because the company hadn't carried it out effectively.

Still, it wasn't until five or six months later, when it was painfully apparent how poor a job we had done on the introduction and were struggling to regroup, that I realized just how much the lack of alignment between Ben and me had cost the company.

Peace Pops was our first attempt to actualize the newly minted vision of the company, and by most accounts we had failed, not just on the social mission, but on the product and economic missions as well. Although the quality and pricing issues were quickly resolved, and the product line was relaunched the next summer, our initial missteps were costly.

Things went somewhat better with our next social mission initiative, which was an attempt to use the Greyston Bakery as a supplier, although here, too, there were lessons to be learned. Greyston was run by Bernie Glassman, a Jewish aerospace engineer from Brooklyn who became a Buddhist and set up a Zen community in Yonkers. The bakery hired the homeless and the hard-core unemployable to make cheesecakes and fancy torts that sold in gourmet shops and restaurants throughout the New York area. Profits from the bakery were used to provide transitional housing, counseling, and training for its employees, all intended to break the cycle of homelessness.

Ben had met Bernie through the Social Venture Network, a semi-annual conclave of socially responsible businesses. Ben wanted to use Greyston as a supplier, and asked Bernie if he could produce the thin, fudgy, chewy brownies that we used in our other novelty, the Brownie Bar ice cream sandwich.

The deal with Greyston was presented as a no-brainer. We can buy brownies from supplier A, which is a traditional business, or get the same brownies for the same price from supplier B, which is employing the homeless and doing wonderful things in its community.

The reality was that dealing with a small, socially responsible company that was attempting to do something it had never done before entailed more effort than conducting business as usual with an established supplier. That isn't to say that it wasn't worth doing, but we should have proceeded more carefully.

As a second supplier, the brownies Greyston produced had to be identical in taste and texture to what we were currently purchasing. That turned out to be a much harder proposition than either Bernie or Ben had expected. After months of trying, it became apparent that Greyston couldn't match the original product. In the attempt, however, they had dug themselves into a giant financial hole. Based on Ben's letter of intent, Bernie had gone out and borrowed $250,000 from the Chase Manhattan Bank to upgrade the bakery and buy new equipment. Without any revenue to offset the increased overhead, Greyston now had a major cash-flow problem.

Walking away from Greyston wasn't an option, so we decided to take one of our best-selling franchise bulk flavors, Chocolate Fudge Brownie, and put it into pints. The specifications for that product were much more forgiving. All Greyston had to do was cut the brownies they'd been baking into one-inch-square pieces.

But even that proved to be a problem. They didn't have enough racks in their bakery, so the brownies were packed for shipping before they had cooled. By the time we got them, instead of pouring out of the box like cornflakes, they were a solid block of chocolate.

Normally, when a product doesn't meet specs, it gets returned to the supplier for credit. Given Greyston's financial condition, it wasn't an option not to pay for the product. Had we done so, it would have put them out of business. In fact, to help them out, we'd prepaid three shipments in advance. Instead, our production crew went after the brownies with hammer and chisel, trying to salvage as much of the product as they could.

When Greyston got into financial trouble, Jeff went to see firsthand what was going on in their operation. One walk around the bakery made it apparent to Jeff that Bernie had oversold Ben on what he could deliver. Jeff started meeting with Bernie's managers on a regular basis, and worked with Bernie's banker in an attempt to get the business's debts restructured. He eventually came up with a ten-point plan that helped turn their operation around. Chocolate Fudge Brownie became a solid-selling pint flavor, and Greyston a reliable supplier of quality ingredients.

In terms of infusing the social mission throughout the organization, the initial impact of Greyston was mixed. Though most people considered using them as a supplier to be a good idea in theory, the perception on the floor of the production room from the people who were reworking the brownies was that we had sacrificed the quality of our product and the traditional bottom line in order to accomplish

187

some social good. It was an early indication that integrating all three components wouldn't always be easy, and that at times, one mission might actually be at odds with the other two.

There were two other social-mission projects that Ben and Jeff were working on in 1988. One was an attempt to open up a scoop shop in the Soviet Union. They had been to the USSR twice, trying to find an appropriate partner for the proposed joint venture, but so far they had mostly spent a great deal of time talking with what turned out to be the wrong people. The idea was to use the profits from the shop to fund cultural exchanges between the two countries, which made it a natural tie-in with the work they were doing on 1% For Peace.

Closer to home, Jeff created a program that put a profit-making business—one of our franchised scoop stores—to work with a non-profit organization. Our first "Partnershop" was opened in Ithaca, New York, by The Learning Web, a community group that matched up kids one-on-one with mentors so they could get real-world skills. The Ben & Jerry's shop, run by a Learning Web spin-off called Youth Scoops, Inc., provided job experience and business training for kids under twenty-one. The profits of the business made the program self-funding so that the organization no longer had to constantly seek grants and donations for its work.

The Ithaca store became a model for other Partnershops. For each of the stores, the company waived its normal franchise fee and provided the additional management assistance that was necessary to get the business up and running. Our Baltimore store is run by PEP, which stands for People Encouraging People. Employees in the store are part of the organization's rehabilitation program for the psychiatrically disabled. The Laraway School, which offers specialized vocational and counseling programs for youths, runs a seasonal Partnershop in Johnson, Vermont.

By the end of 1988 we had taken our first tentative steps at actualizing the company's mission. Where we had failed, however, was in crafting and carrying out a strategy to help the organization comprehend and understand what the mission statement in general, and the social component in particular, was all about.

Ben's expectation had been that he could just lay out his vision and everyone would enlist. "What's your strategy for educating the masses, Ben?" Phil Mirvis had asked him at one point. "If you're going to be revolutionary, figure out what Lenin's tactics were, and do it right."

As a belated start to that process, a meeting to introduce and explain the three-part mission to the staff was scheduled for November 11. With more than three hundred employees, we had long ago outgrown the receiving bay, and the meeting was held in the indoor sports complex at the Bolton Valley ski area. Ben started the meeting by explaining why we had created the mission statement. "As the company gets bigger," he said, "the mission will ensure that we're all moving in the same direction. It provides a framework for how everyday decisions should be made throughout the company."

Jerry, Ben, and I each then spoke about one of the three components. For the product mission, Jerry told how he and Ben had come up with their original formula, motivated by their intent on making the best ice cream possible.

For the social mission, Ben explained why the company had assumed the nontraditional role for a business of fostering social change. "Most people suspend their values about contributing to society when they go to work," Ben said, "believing that its something they're only supposed to be concerned with in their free time at home." He went on, "It's when we're at work that we're most powerful, because we're organized and we have the financial resources of the company behind us. The results we can achieve within the company, working together, are far greater than those we could accomplish working as three hundred individuals on our own."

And finally I introduced the economic mission, taking the stage to the highly amplified sound of the crashing cash registers and thumping bass line of Pink Floyd's "Money." The lecture that I gave, "Fredonomics 101," was a quick primer on where the money came from and where the money went.

After the serious work of the meeting was finished, there was a guest appearance by Don Moxley, the original Mr. Clean. After visiting Disney World and marveling at the lack of litter in the park, I'd embarked on a cleanliness campaign at work. To drive home the point, I was now using a rubber stamp of Mr. Clean's face on my memos, side by side with Mr. T's.

Through incredible luck, my assistant, Gail Mayville, tracked Don down in Las Vegas, where he was driving a cab, and, unbeknownst to me, flew him to Vermont for the meeting. He was a little paunchier than he looks on the product, but in white pants, T-shirt, sandals, and earring, he was definitely the real thing.

The all-staff meeting had an immediate payoff. Gail took the challenge from Ben to heart and proposed a broad set of initiatives intended to get the company's environmental act together. We worked out an arrangement so she could devote half of her time to getting them implemented.

Gail's ideas ranged from setting up a company-wide recycling program to putting together a consortium in which we joined with other businesses in purchasing a truckload of post-consumer recycled copier paper before it was available through local office suppliers. With Gail taking the lead, we were able to make changes on the packaging for our novelties that not only were an improvement environmentally, but also saved us money.

To leverage her individual efforts, Gail formed "Green Teams" at each location that further increased awareness of environmental issues and identified opportunities for improving our performance throughout the company.

One of Gail's most ambitious projects involved figuring out a way to keep the five-gallon white plastic buckets that our egg yolks and other ingredients came in out of the landfill. Gail set up a joint venture between a small resource recovery plant in St. Albans, Vermont, which happened also to employ some emotionally and physically disabled individuals, and Occidental Chemical, a manufacturer of the HDPE plastic from which the buckets were made. Occidental provided the funding and development of new equipment that enabled the St. Albans plant to shred the buckets into "regrind," which could be recycled into other plastic products. In addition to the environmental payoff, the net savings to the company was over $20,000 per year.

The environmental projects were the most successful actualization of the three-part mission to date. Unlike Peace Pops or the Greyston brownies, the idea had emerged from within the organization, which was exactly what we had hoped would happen. And it proved, for the first time, what we could accomplish when everyone was headed in the same direction.

CHAPTER SIXTEEN

The Jive 5

By October 1988, a year after the all-company meeting at which we had generated the list of all the freezer doors, there was no doubt that the management group had made tangible progress. Some structure had been given to the way in which the company was organized, we had begun to develop rudimentary processes for how decisions got made, our planning and budgeting had improved and was beginning to look more than one year out, and we had formalized an orientation program that welcomed new employees into the organization.

We were also doing a much better job of communicating what was going on throughout the company, largely by way of *The Daily Plant*, a monthly newsletter that was being written and produced by our employees. In addition to passing on information about current events, the *Plant* included an assortment of features and columns that illustrated the company's offbeat culture. In one issue, Bob Davison's "Hypothetically Raoul" advice column featured a "Disfigure Fred's Head" contest, in which employees were asked to do nasty things to a drawing of my face.

Our sales had also continued to increase significantly in 1988. Based on results for the first three quarters, we were projecting total sales for the year of $48 million, a 50-percent increase over 1987. For the most part, we had been successful at beating back the challenge from Steve's over the past two and a half years. One of the keys to our success had been the "Two Real Guys" radio spot, which featured the following jingle, sung a cappella, first by a doo-wop group and then by an enthusiastic opera singer.

There ain't no Häagen, there ain't no Dazs,
There ain't no Frusen, there ain't no Glädj'
There ain't nobody named Steve at Steve's,
But there's two real guys at Ben & Jerry's.

To drive home the point that the guy on the Steve's pint wasn't Steve, we had also temporarily put a "Two Real Guys" gold-leaf banner on all of our pints, underneath the founders' photo.

The campaign worked. Nationally, we were the number-three superpremium brand, and in many markets we had passed Frusen Glädjé and taken over second place. In New England we were number one, with a market share approaching 50 percent.

We had also resolved the question of how to keep up with the increased demand for our ice cream. Increasing capacity at the Waterbury plant wasn't practical for a number of reasons, including limits on our waste-water-discharge permits, which we were still having trouble meeting. There was no way we could increase the factory's output until a pretreatment system that was scheduled to be built in 1989 was operating. We also ruled out putting a pint line into the new factory in Springfield, believing that the plant would operate more efficiently if it was focused exclusively on novelties.

The idea of building a third plant was also rejected. Our management was already stretched to its limits, and couldn't deal effectively with another construction project. Until our sales and profits caught up with the recent investments we'd made in both Springfield and Waterbury, we wouldn't be in a position to raise the money for another factory anyway.

The alternative we recommended to the board was that we temporarily contract out production to a co-packer until we had the financial and managerial wherewithal to build a third plant. That would buy us the time we needed to focus on the organization without ignoring the realities of the marketplace.

This approach was not without risk. All our co-packing experiences with novelties had been disasters. Having someone else make the product for us was also at odds, in some respects, with the "Two Real Guys" campaign. Of all the alternatives, though, it was by far the best, and the board agreed, on the conditions that any co-packer would use only Vermont dairy products and that we would have our own quality-assurance staff on site.

We'd also made progress in the past year with our franchise program, which, like the rest of our business, had experienced exponential growth. By the end of 1988 there were seventy-six stores, and we were now opening them at a rate of about one every ten days. Although the franchises never represented more than 10 percent of our total sales, because of their visibility they were perceived as a much larger part of our business.

For years the franchise program had grown haphazardly. Rather than consistently following a preplanned marketing strategy, we'd largely reacted to whatever inquiries came through the door. As a result, we'd opened stores in places like Heath, Ohio, even though at the time we weren't selling our pints in that state.

We also had very loose operational standards that weren't consistently enforced, which was a crucial problem in running a franchise program, and the system suffered from the inexperience of many of the initial shop owners.

In an attempt to give us a chance to catch up operationally, we put a moratorium on signing new agreements and began to renegotiate some of the existing multi-store contracts to reduce or slow down the number of stores that were being built. It was our intention, we told our shop owners, to put our efforts into "your stores, not more stores."

A franchise advisory council, consisting of shop owners from throughout the country, was formed to improve the feedback we were getting from the field. It was an attempt to get beyond the typical adversarial relationship that exists between a franchisor and those who are essentially contractually obligated to adhere to whatever pronouncements come down from above.

Over the next few years we would also rewrite our operational standards, increasing the frequency of visits to the stores by our field reps. Additionally, in an effort to improve the profitability of our stores, we reduced the price they were paying for their ice cream.

Although some things had improved over the past year, there had been a decided lack of progress in other areas. Most of the company's systems still hadn't caught up with our growth, and the addition of a second plant in Springfield had vastly increased the complexity of our operation.

Also, we still weren't effectively addressing the lack of human-resource skills that was a pervasive shortcoming among our managers. Some "off the shelf" training programs had been set up, mostly for line-level supervisors, but we had not provided enough one-on-one mentoring through which people who had never managed before could learn how to coach and lead their employees effectively.

Of even more concern was that some of the managers, including a few at the senior level, were treating subordinates in ways that didn't live up to the company's ideals. Ben had been the company's most visible autocrat and was therefore the easiest one to take shots at, but he was by no means the only manager at the company whose interpersonal skills left something to be desired.

We were also constantly trying to fill at least half a dozen key management vacancies. The job most desperately in need of being filled was that of chief financial officer, a position we had only recently created when it became apparent that the skills of our existing accounting staff had been overtaxed by the company's increased size.

Although we were using a search firm and advertising the position aggressively, the compensation policies of the company made it difficult to find a qualified person. Under the five-to-one salary ratio, the highest salary we could pay was $81,000. According to the headhunter we were using, CFOs for companies the size of ours—$48 million in sales this year, $60 million projected for next—commanded six-figure salaries, in addition to bonuses and stock options that could easily push their total compensation to more than twice what we were offering.

More vexing was the notion that even if the person did a great job, the most he or she could look forward to was a $5,000 raise—and then only if we were able to give our scoopers another fifty cents an hour.

Ben, Jeff, and I had differing recollections about what had been intended when we adopted the five-to-one policy in 1985. I maintained that it referred strictly to salary, which was how it had been described in the prospectuses for the 1985 and 1987 stock offerings. Ben and Jeff contended that the ratio should be applied to total compensation, which was certainly how the public and our employees had come to perceive the policy, based upon the media coverage it had received.

Working with a compensation consultant, our director of human resources, Dave Barash, and I had presented numerous proposals for using stock options or grants so that we could recruit the management talent we needed to run the company and offer financial incentives to our existing staff. All of the proposals were rejected by the board or sent back for additional study, mostly because they weren't egalitarian enough to satisfy Ben or Jeff. "Just because one person's skill happens to be talking on the phone and selling ice cream and another person's skill happens to be working on a machine making ice cream doesn't mean that there should be all that big a spread in these persons' compensation," Ben argued.

The search for a CFO was also slowed down by the board's decision to try to recruit a female candidate. At the time, our senior management was all white and all male. I was all for diversity, but, given the immediate need we had for financial expertise, I resisted the idea of eliminating half of the potential applicants from what was already a very small pool.

The last pint flavor that Ben had developed before "deactivating" was Chunky Monkey, which was introduced in May of 1988. Like Cherry Garcia, it had been suggested by a customer, Susan Aprill, who wrote to us about two girls who had come up to a cafeteria serving line she was working on and suggested a new item, which was everything left over from their lunch mixed into a cup. Susan wrote to us thinking the name the girls had used to describe their concoction sounded like a good flavor of ice cream—banana (monkey) with nuts and hunks of chocolate (chunky).

Jerry came across Susan's letter while he was hanging out at Ben's house with some friends playing Ping-Pong. "We're totally sold on the 'Chunky Monkey' idea," Jerry wrote back.

Despite some misgivings that there wouldn't be much of a market for banana ice cream, Chunky Monkey made it into the top five and developed a regular following that it has maintained to this day.

Right after Chunky Monkey was developed, we hired Peter Lind as the head of our R&D department. The help wanted ad for the position stated that "playing with your food as a child" was one of the prerequisites of the job. A former chef and actor, Peter seemed well suited for the task. His lab was in full view of the factory tours, and the doors to the cabinets were given appropriate labels ("Eye of Knute," "Rest of Knute," "Secret Stuff," etc.). When the tourists passed by, Peter and his cohorts would hold up signs saying things like "We're professionals, don't try this at home."

Following Ben as the company's self-described "primal ice cream therapist" was probably a no-win situation. Unlike Ben, who could dictate increases in chunk size by fiat, Peter had to deal with the Flavor Committee, a group of seven people who got together every Tuesday afternoon to pass judgment on whatever he'd been working on. Getting the committee to agree on which dish of ice cream we liked best was all but impossible, but even when we reached a consensus it didn't necessarily mean that the product was anything to be proud of.

One of the first flavors to come out of the committee was Fred & Ginger, a flavor which never made it into pints. "I'm going to sell it to every Chinese restaurant in San Francisco," Allan Kaufman boldly predicted of the ginger-flavored ice cream with chocolate chunks in the shape of bow ties. Perhaps he did, but they all must have ordered only one tub. The flavor quickly took its place in flavor Boot Hill, alongside Honey Apple Raisin Oreo.

The first pint flavor the committee approved was Sugarplum, which was going to be available during the upcoming holiday season. It was a plum ice cream with a caramel swirl. Even with the benefit of five year's worth of hindsight, it remains, in Peter's estimation, "the worst flavor we ever had."

Other than new flavors, Peter was also spending a great deal of time trying to develop a product that was lower in fat and cholesterol than our regular ice cream; we hoped to introduce it in 1989.

Not all of the flavor suggestions we received from our customers were winners. After Cherry Garcia, we were inundated with suggestions ranging from Donny Almond to Milly Vanilla. One customer suggested we name a flavor "Scoop O' Jesus," assuring us that despite misconceptions perpetrated by the liberal media, "we Christians do get decadent sometimes, especially when it comes to food."

Flavor suggestions were only one type of mail we received from our customers. By 1988 we were getting almost a hundred letters a week, some praising the product and our company, others voicing dissatisfaction with a particular pint and requesting a refund.

In the company's early years, Jerry had answered all the mail by himself. "I was the person making the ice cream, so I figured they were writing to me personally," he says. By 1986 the volume had increased significantly, and the company hired Alice Blachly, whose only job was to respond to customer inquiries.

Alice had a literary background and was more familiar with the works of Keats and Shelley than of Garcia and Weir. At fifty-nine, she was quite a bit older than most of her co-workers, and she was, in fact, one of the original members of "Ben & Jerriatrics," a support group for employees over forty.

Lots of the mail we received was extremely creative, with some customers writing novelettes describing their passion or disappointment. Those letters were taken as a challenge by Alice, who attempted to send back an equally inspired response. Form letters were rare, and each reply was individually crafted based on the specific feedback the customer had given us.

Since returning from Arizona, Jerry had taken it upon himself to add a handwritten note to every one of Alice's letters, going so far as to have batches of mail sent to him via Federal Express while he was driving across the country with Ben in the Cowmobile. It was as a result of his reading all the consumer mail that Jerry had come across the letter suggesting Chunky Monkey. All of Jerry's comments were thoughtful and unique, and they conveyed to our customers an incredibly caring attitude.

We weren't aware of it at the time, but studies indicate that someone who has a problem with a company that the company resolves to their satisfaction is more likely to be a loyal customer in the future than a consumer who's never had a negative experience. In effect, we were converting a potential liability into an asset, just as we had done when we took the threat from Pillsbury and turned it into a promotional windfall.

Many of the letters were simply to tell us how much customers had enjoyed our ice cream, or to ask a question about the company. One woman wrote and asked for a suggestion on which flavor to serve with her Grandma Annie's apple pie.

The most frequent product complaint we received was that a particular pint didn't have enough chunks in it. Some customers went so far as to count exactly how many chunks were in a pint they'd purchased, or enclosed drawings to illustrate their insufficient size.

Many of these letters came from regular customers, who often wrote not so much to complain as to let us know, as one friend to another, that their most recent purchase hadn't been up to our usual standards.

On rare occasion we'd receive a complaint about the chunks being too big. One customer, who got an unbroken Heath Bar in a pint, told us that if she wanted a candy bar, she would have bought one.

The most passionate complaints invariably came when we discontinued a flavor. Given the limited amount of shelf space in the supermarkets, we only produced twelve flavors in pints at any one time. Whenever we introduced a new flavor, one of the less popular ones got dropped.

"People are very attached to their flavors," Alice says, and they have a hard time understanding why they should be deprived of their personal addiction just because the rest of world's taste doesn't match theirs. "Please take that Mocha Chip off your shoulder and put it back into the freezer case where it belongs," one customer wrote.

One of the strongest responses we received was when we dropped Dastardly Mash, an original pint flavor that saw its sales cannibalized after we introduced New York Super Fudge Chunk, a second chocolate-based ice cream with lots of stuff in it. One loyal customer, who returned from a five-month sabbatical in the Far East to discover that Mash was no longer available in pints, told us that he was "taking this matter to both my analyst and spiritual director, in an attempt to discern whether the fault is mine or yours." Recognizing that the loss of his purchases while he was out of the country might have been what pushed us over the edge, he concluded, "I have returned and please undo your dastardly deed and restore the Mash."

After the introduction of Peace Pops, we also began to get letters that applauded the stand we had taken as a business. Although there were a few letters that were critical, the overwhelming majority were positive, and they were the first indication that there were a large number of consumers who were willing to use their purchasing power to support those businesses whose values matched their own.

At the end of 1988 we decided to form the "Jive 5," a joint board/management committee that included Ben, Jeff, Allan, Chuck, and me. The group was charged with the task of further defining and developing the company's social mission.

In many ways, the Jive 5 was a result of Henry Morgan's increasing frustration with being in the middle whenever the social mission was discussed at board meetings. The dynamics of the board were such that on many of the issues, four votes could be counted in advance of any debate. Merritt Chandler, the other outside director, was usually supportive of my position that the company needed to be run more as a business. Jeff Furman was always aligned with Ben. The swing vote was Henry's, and we would often joke that he was the one who was running the company.

Henry believed that if the social mission was going to be an integral part of what the company did, it had to be treated the same as any other part of the business. It needed to have an operating plan and a budget, and those in charge of it had to be held accountable for results. Equally as important, the managers had to participate in the development of the initiatives. To date, the social mission had been defined piecemeal, whenever Ben and Jeff announced another new project they wanted the company to pursue. Merritt, in uncharacteristically blunt language, equated the way in which Ben and Jeff were interacting with the managers to the behavior of seagulls. "They swoop in, shit all over everybody, and then fly away."

Unfortunately, despite an agreement to try to refashion our interaction away from the win/lose, us/them dynamic we always seemed to fall into, the Jive 5 didn't do any better than the board at resolving our differences over the social mission.

The biggest point of contention was the company's marketing, which, with a three-part mission statement, was now much more than an attempt to influence consumers to purchase our ice cream. It was also how we conveyed the company's underlying values and our social and political agendas.

The disagreement between Allan and Ben over the direction that the company should be taking with its marketing had begun in the spring of 1988, when the New York subway project finally fell through. After months of negotiations and extended deadlines, an arbitrator had finally ruled in favor of the Transit Union, which had maintained that our offer to provide non-union workers to clean up the station violated their collective-bargaining agreement.

On April 4 we ran an ad in *The New York Times* with the headline, "Ben & Jerry's Wants Another Off-the-Wall Idea," soliciting suggestions of other worthwhile things we could do with our marketing funds, now reduced, we noted, by the cost of the ad. The responses, as you might expect, were many in number and diverse in opinion. One person thought we should buy giant cardboard boxes emblazoned with our logo and distribute them free of charge to the homeless. Another suggested we pay for everyone's parking at Mets games.

After sifting through all the suggestions, Allan decided to give a $150,000 endowment to the new Museum of American Folk Art that was being built across from Lincoln Center and underwrite a summer series of Shakespeare performances in the city's parks. At the same time, Allan moved most of the rest of the marketing budget into other sponsorships and underwriting. His response to a last-minute appeal literally saved the legendary Newport Folk Festival from extinction. Funds were also given to the Boston Ballet for their "Concerts on the Common," and to the Geese Theater Company, a troupe of ten actors that provided performances and workshops in the nation's prisons.

Ben was enthusiastic about some of what Allan was doing, in particular the Newport Folk Festival, which he believed attracted people who matched up to our typical customer profile. The Geese Theater, on the other hand, however noble, didn't meet that test. How many of our customers, Ben wondered, were in prison?

His biggest criticism was that there were no radical initiatives like the subway project. Although it had never come to fruition, that was now the standard by which all marketing efforts were being judged. Ben thought that most of what Allan was doing was too mainstream or "Mobil Oilish"—for example, his underwriting of broadcasts on public television of the National Ballroom Dancing Competition and a Peter, Paul and Mary holiday concert. Ben no longer wanted to sponsor the arts; he wanted to pursue projects that met basic human needs. "I'm not willing to get my picture in the paper for the ballet," was how Ben had put it.

At the Jive 5 meetings, Allan and Ben would get into what Phil Mirvis described as their "Jewish uncle/nephew" routine. Both were incredibly strong-willed and knew exactly which buttons to push to set the other one off. Neither would give an inch.

Allan saw the meetings as nothing more than Ben and Jeff attempting to dictate to him how he should do his job. He was fiercely protective of the marketing budget, and resistant to virtually every idea they brought up.

The sheer number of proposals that Jeff and Ben wanted the company to pursue was staggering. At one point there were more than thirty projects on our agenda, with new ones being added every week. Some were directly related to the core business of making and selling ice cream, such as finding alternative suppliers similar to Greyston. Others, such as helping dairy farmers in southern Vermont set up a co-op that could produce value-added products like butter, weren't.

Although Ben and Jeff had been adamant at board meetings about the need for the managers to prioritize the goals and objectives in their operating plans, they resisted attempts to focus the social mission into a more coherent, manageable agenda. As a result, even after the all-staff meeting, the social mission remained an abstract concept for most of our employees.

In an effort to eliminate some of the confusion, we decided to try to express in greater detail what the company's social mission was.

Ben, however, wanted to go one step further and use the company's values as a screen for new employees. Ben's thinking was no doubt influenced by the difficulty he'd experienced in getting the managers and the organization aligned behind 1% For Peace and some of the other social mission projects he'd been proposing. By making sure that we hired only people who believed in the company's values—"the right head" was how he put it—Ben thought that we'd be paving the way for greater acceptance of the company's more progressive initiatives down the road. "It would be silly," Ben argued, "for the company to hire people who aren't willing to support the values that express the company's social mission, just as it wouldn't make sense for us to hire people who aren't committed to making great ice cream and running the business profitably."

Jeff drafted a statement that was intended to clarify how we were defining the social mission, and circulated a copy to the rest of the board for consideration. We were taken aback. As written, it was a loyalty oath that said "our employees must adhere, support, encourage and work for the following values," after which it listed six beliefs covering everything from human rights and the environment to reducing military expenditures.

The response was immediate and, with the exception of Ben and Jeff, unanimous. Henry and Merritt went so far as to say that they'd resign from the board if we decided to use it. Jerry, among others, argued that diversity of opinion would ultimately build strength in the organization, not division.

Ben and Jeff maintained that it was a normal part of the recruiting process at every business to compare a job applicant's values with those of the company. (Buck Rogers, the former vice-president of marketing at IBM, said as much in his book, *The IBM Way*. "Since IBM operates with a well-defined value system, it's essential that the young people recruited into the company are comfortable and compatible with those values," Rogers wrote.) The only difference, Ben and Jeff contended, was that our values, by virtue of our three-part mission statement, were more progressive than other companies and went beyond our perceived short-term self-interest.

There was no disagreement among the board regarding the values themselves, and the fact that they represented legitimate positions for the company to take. After a lively discussion, we agreed that we would state what the company's values were, but that we couldn't impose those beliefs on our employees, and the idea of using them as a screen for employment was quickly shelved.

Henry had said it best: "Our employees have to adhere to the company's policies, but their beliefs are their beliefs. The only way to instill the values of the company is by example, from the top down."

CHAPTER SEVENTEEN

Pay No Attention to the Man Behind the Curtain

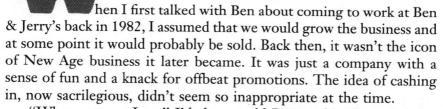hen I first talked with Ben about coming to work at Ben & Jerry's back in 1982, I assumed that we would grow the business and at some point it would probably be sold. Back then, it wasn't the icon of New Age business it later became. It was just a company with a sense of fun and a knack for offbeat promotions. The idea of cashing in, now sacrilegious, didn't seem so inappropriate at the time.

"When you go, I go," I'd always told Ben, and in fact, when we were at $2 million in sales in 1983, we started to talk about selling the company when we got up to $8 million, coining the phrase "ate and out" to cryptically describe the strategy.

Ben had, in fact, decided to get out when we got to around $8 million, but he didn't want to sell the company to do it. His proposal that he go and I stay, however, hadn't worked out the way either of us had planned. Ben never really got out, at first because we had trouble finding a director of marketing to take his place, and eventually because he didn't believe those he left behind were running the business in accordance with his evolving values. It hadn't worked out for me because, although I was given, or assumed, responsibility for the company's performance, I never had the opportunity to manage it myself.

When I accepted the offer from Ben to run the company, I made a commitment to stay only through the end of 1989. In the spring of 1988, reenergized by the work with Phil Mirvis, I had privately been reconsidering my plan to leave so soon. By the end of 1988, after suffering through a series of torturous Jive 5 meetings, I had stopped reconsidering. I decided it really was time to leave.

In my mind, Ben had lost empathy with the people who were

struggling to run the business, and some of his ideas were putting the livelihoods of our employees and the investments of our shareholders at risk. I had recently gone to hear Donald Burr, the former president of the now defunct People's Express, speak of that company's demise, which was a hard and fast reminder of how tenuous was the continued success and survival of a high-growth company such as ours.

During the week before Christmas of 1988, I called the outside directors and met with each member of the operating committee and Ben and Jerry, informing them of my decision. At the January 1989 meeting, the board discussed plans for replacing me.

My recommendation was that Chuck Lacy take my place. There was no other current employee qualified for the position, and it didn't seem likely that we could recruit a stronger candidate from outside the company, given our compensation policies.

Chuck had been with the company for a year, and had proven to be a thoughtful, intelligent manager who had handled a wide variety of assignments well. Although he didn't display the same exuberance that I did in public speaking situations, Chuck had excellent people skills in one-on-one and small group interactions. At six foot eight, he was a huge man, with a full beard and enough of a waistline to show that he was eating his share of product.

There was unanimity on the board in support of giving the job to Chuck. Ben's only request was that we withhold making a firm commitment until after he had had a chance to talk with Chuck about the social mission. On the assumption that he would pass that test, the board laid out a strategy to transfer the leadership from me to Chuck.

According to the plan, Chuck would be named the company's general manager and gradually take over responsibility for the day-to-day operations of the business over the next twelve months. As a start, the marketing cluster and the finance and accounting functions would report immediately to him.

I came out of the meeting with a promotion, having been given the titles of CEO and president. It acknowledged the role that I'd fulfilled over the past three years, but, more important, it set up the next transition. Passing the CEO title from Ben to me to Chuck would be perceived as less traumatic than a direct pass from Ben to Chuck, who had relatively little visibility as a leader within the organization, and was totally unknown to the investment community and our shareholders. Ben, who had nominally held the CEO's and president's jobs, would retain the title of chairman of the board.

I agreed to extend my employment contract, which went through the end of 1989, for an extra year. Assuming he confirmed through his performance that he was up for the job, Chuck would become the CEO and president at the end of 1990.

Within a week after the board meeting, Chuck and Ben met and agreed that the social mission would figure prominently in how the company was run. Chuck, who had a strong activist background, had no reservations at all about making the commitment. He had always been the member of the operating committee most open to integrating the social mission into our operations, and Chuck's vision for the business was very much aligned with Ben's.

Chuck was wise enough to recognize just how critical Ben and Jerry were to the future success of the business, and he believed that the social mission was the way to keep them engaged. He also had reason to be concerned about the likelihood of their continued involvement in the company. In January of 1989, Ben had decided to start up another business to manufacture a butter-crunch candy made with Brazil nuts and cashews that had been sustainably harvested from the rain forests. The candy would be sold both as a packaged product in gourmet food stores and in bulk to Ben & Jerry's for a new flavor of ice cream.

The idea had grown out of a conversation at a Grateful Dead benefit concert for the rain forest between Ben and Jason Clay, the director of Cultural Survival, a nonprofit organization working as an advocate for the world's native peoples. Jason was trying to prove that the forests were more valuable standing than when their trees were cut and burned for short-term gain. He handed Ben a small bag of nuts and asked him if he might be interested in using them as an ingredient in the ice cream.

By starting another company, Ben would be free to explore all the possibilities he envisioned for what a socially responsible business could be. There would be no restraints from being publicly held, and no objections from entrenched and unenlightened managers. His intent was to donate 60 percent of the profits of the business to environmental groups, 1% For Peace, and the employees. The added benefit of giving away such a large percentage of the company's earnings, Ben figured, was that it would automatically constrain the growth of the new business.

The press release announcing my promotion to CEO and Chuck's to general manager made no mention of my intention to leave within the next two years. The story, as reported in the press, was that Ben was turning over the management of the company to Chuck and me. Ben's decision to become less active, which was actually now over three years old, had never been formally announced, and the perception externally was that he was as involved as ever in the business.

All of our employees understood that Ben's giving up day-to-day management of the business was old news. Internally, the take on the press release was exactly the opposite of what the outside world perceived. It was I, not Ben, who was on the way out.

Chuck wasted little time in restructuring both of the areas that reported directly to him. We still hadn't hired a CFO, and our financial and accounting functions were approaching a meltdown. Adding to our problems were shortcomings with new software for our computer systems and the decision of the person who managed that department to leave the company.

One of the problems faced by all growing companies is that almost every management job gets more complex as the company gets bigger and bigger. Even without promotions, people are forced to take on more responsibility. Some are able to increase their skills and keep pace. Others can't, and as a result, there's a constant need to recruit people who are more experienced into the organization. We were never able to get far enough ahead of the growth curve to effectively train and develop senior management staff internally and fill those positions from within.

Just when he needed it most, Chuck got an incredible break when Fran Rathke, a CPA with Coopers & Lybrand, knocked on his door and applied for a job. Fran had gone to UVM and had decided to move back to Vermont from Boston. Within a week after her initial interview, Chuck offered Fran a job as the company's accounting manager, and moved the two existing managers from the department into new positions with redefined and reduced responsibilities. At the same time, he arranged for Dick Phipps, a consultant who had experience working with manufacturing companies, to provide direction and help in putting new financial systems into place, acting in essence as a temporary CFO.

The search for a full-time CFO continued through July of 1989, when we came to the conclusion that it would make more sense to let Fran try to grow into the position. She was named controller, and a year later she would in fact be promoted to the senior financial position. Despite the amount of time it took to fill the position, it would prove to be one of the best hiring decisions we ever made.

Next on Chuck's list was marketing. He had come to the conclusion that the best way to resolve the conflict over how the marketing budget should be spent was to let Allan Kaufman go, which is what he did. The Jive 5, reduced in number, became obsolete.

A couple of other long-term managers were also let go, some positions were eliminated, and in general the company went through a period of belt-tightening, increasing the expectations and accountability for each employee's performance. There was also some effort made to clarify and, in some people's minds, backtrack from some of the statements we had made about participatory management. In some ways the organizational development work with Phil had unleashed a bureaucracy with committees of people who were debating issues that should have been decided by one person or at least by much smaller groups. Even the administrative assistants, for example, had formed a committee to voice their concerns.

The notion of having groups of people from throughout the company work on specific problems made sense. Ideally, all those who needed to be involved would be. No more, no less.

Inadvertently, though, we'd created the expectation that we would solicit everyone's input before making any decision. In an article in the March 1989 *Daily Plant*, I made it clear that wasn't going to be the case. "The company is not and never has been a model of democracy," I wrote. Even on issues on which we did solicit and receive widespread input, having a voice did not equate to having a vote.

Which isn't to say that we were looking to impose an autocratic management structure on the company. There was still the belief that those in the trenches should be given the resources and discretion to solve the problems they faced without having to kick them upstairs to some higher authority.

But in some areas, having a values-led organization precluded participation in decision making. Ben's vision for the business, for example, was far ahead of the direction our staff might have chosen by consensus or head count. For the most part the social mission, in particular that portion of it which could be construed as the company's political agenda, was not really open to debate. Input might be solicited, but it was more a matter of discussing how to achieve certain objectives than of soliciting opinions on the objectives themselves.

*   *   *

In September 1989 the board was in Ogunquit, Maine, on its annual three-day retreat. Even though my decision to leave had ostensibly resolved some of the questions about the leadership and direction of the company, Ben's role and that of the board of directors still dominated the discussion.

We were able to come up with a job description of sorts for the board fairly quickly: setting policy, long-term goals, and priorities in regard to all three parts of the mission statement; making sure that the managers' annual operating plans were consistent with those objectives; and helping the managers by offering support, counsel, and assistance, while at the same time holding them accountable for their performance.

As usual, it was a little harder to nail Ben down. He was committed to helping with the transition of leadership from me to Chuck, but was increasingly frustrated that while the company was receiving increasing notoriety and acclaim outside the company for its progressive stands and two-part bottom line, he wasn't receiving strong support or reinforcement internally for those same ideas.

There were issues unrelated to the social mission that concerned Ben as well, which, despite his urging, he believed the company wasn't adequately addressing. One was the company's lack of commitment to institutionalizing a process that would lead to continuous quality improvement. Another was his concern that the organizational development work hadn't resulted in alignment around the mission, improved morale within the organization, or increased the efficiency with which the company was operating.

Ben also cited a recent major operational decision about distribution that had been made despite his vigorous objections. "In the future, I don't really know if I can tolerate the company making a decision like that, which is of such personal importance to me, and still represent the company," Ben said.

"You're holding the company hostage," Henry replied. "You're saying that the rest of the board and the managers can participate, but if we don't come up with the decision you want, then you're going to walk."

"It's okay for the company to do what it wants," Ben argued back. "All I'm saying is that my representing the company has strings attached to it. It's dependent on the company making things happen in those areas that I think are important, and making decisions that I can support."

Chuck, who was sitting through a full retreat for the first time, gently took Ben to task for being so hard on the organization. "Lots of people share the vision of the company, Ben, but don't know what to do about it. When we stumble, it's not a vicious thing. It's human frailty."

In the end we weren't much further along toward resolving anything than we'd been when we started. Ben still professed that he only wanted to be an outside director or, at most, a consultant whose opinions were valued.

"That's the same role it's been, Ben," Jerry pointed out, "only now we're saying that it's going to work."

A few weeks after the meeting in Maine, Chuck began to have second thoughts about the way in which the transition in the leadership was playing itself out. He was confident in his ability to manage the company's finances and manufacturing, but believed that the business would be much stronger if Ben once again took an active role in marketing and product development. After the meeting in Maine, he had no way of knowing how long Ben was going to stick around. His fear was that one day he'd wake up and be the only one left, which was one reason he was having trouble sleeping at night.

Chuck had also come to the conclusion that he didn't want to put himself in the same position I'd been in with regard to the company's performance. He strongly supported the idea of the company's pursuing social intervention, but wanted Ben to share in the responsibility for the financial results of the business.

In early December, Chuck went to Ben's house over a weekend and, on a walk in the woods, expressed his concerns. Chuck told him he was only willing to take the job if Ben became active in the company again and took over the marketing department. His message was clear: I need you, the company needs you, and I'll work with you, but I will not do it on my own.

Despite his misgivings, Ben acceded to Chuck's request. Chuck and Ben's relationship had grown quite strong over the past year. In some ways their future partnership had been cemented in mid-October when they had driven a truck full of Peace Pops down to Concord, New Hampshire, for an anti-Seabrook rally. Ben was one of several people who spoke at the event in opposition to the licensing of the nuclear power plant. Afterwards, he and Chuck passed out free ice cream to all the protesters.

Chuck had been really enthusiastic about making the trip, and never gave a second thought to whether or not it was an appropriate event for the company to be involved in. Ben was amazed that something that would have been such a contentious issue in the past was now so easy.

It wasn't the first time Chuck had protested against Seabrook; he'd actually been arrested for civil disobedience at a rally there in 1977. His beard, which he started growing during the two weeks he spent "locked up" in an armory "with seven hundred of the coolest people I'd ever met," is a lasting memento of his criminal record.

Ben's agreement with Chuck to take a more active role in the company omitted one minor detail: Who was going to be the CEO and president? Neither of them wanted the titles, and each was adamant that the other should take the job.

Which was why the subject of the company's leadership was at the top of the agenda for the January 1990 board meeting. That meeting was the first for Liz Bankowski, who had just been invited to join the board. Liz had been Governor Madeleine Kunin's chief of staff, and had gotten to know Ben on a trip to the Soviet Union on which several business leaders from the state had accompanied the governor.

The board met in the conference room at the Waterbury plant, with Phil Mirvis in attendance. Phil described the internal struggle that had taken place over the past two years regarding the philosophy and direction of the business. He believed that the more I had hawked the numbers, the more Ben had pushed the social mission, and vice versa. The overriding question now, Phil concluded, was how to get Chuck into a position where he could succeed.

Liz suggested that the place to start was with what Ben wanted to do.

"I feel comfortable taking responsibility for marketing and R&D in partnership with Chuck," Ben responded.

"Is it your company?" Jerry asked his partner. "Do you take responsibility for it?"

"I feel really clear that it's not my company. My preference is not to be involved in it or responsible for it. Ideally, the company would operate without me the way I would choose to operate it."

"Your goals are mutually exclusive," Henry countered. "The only way it will operate close to how you want it to is if you have a role in running it."

"Ben, you need to come back because you want to lead the company," Chuck said, "not because I need you. I can't deliver to Ben what he wants in marketing, and I'm not prepared yet to be the CEO of the company. I realize you guys need some certainty from me, and I'm just not prepared to do that." Chuck had come into the meeting extremely clear that there was no way he was going to take the CEO's job, and there was no flexibility in his position at all.

After a few more rounds of Chuck saying, "I'm not going to be the CEO," and Ben replying, "Well, *I'm* not going to be the CEO," Phil gradually started to sketch out job descriptions and titles for each of us. At year's end, when I left, Ben would take back the CEO title and oversee the company's marketing. Chuck would pick up the operations side, manage sales, and become the chief operating officer of the company. Jerry would be officially added to the board, become vice-chairman, and officially assume a much more active role in the management of the business. We didn't know it at the time, but Jerry would eventually become as much of a presence and a force within the senior management of the company as either Ben or Chuck.

"This is the most bizarre situation I've ever been in," Henry said at the end. "Usually everyone wants to take on more than he can handle."

At various times in the meeting, Phil had raised the possibility of my staying on. Whenever he did, I refused to consider it. I wouldn't leave the company in a lurch if the transition got sidetracked, but I wasn't going to be part of a long-term solution.

After the board meeting, and prior to the public announcement of the changes, I convinced Chuck that he should take the title of president, even if he was unwilling to be the CEO. It would increase his clout and credibility both within and outside of the company. I had ulterior motives as well. For the past three or four years I'd had a quote that I'd clipped out of *Forbes* magazine taped to the front of my Rolodex: "The true mark of greatness in a CEO is how well he chooses his successor."

Despite the anguish that the transition in the leadership of the company created for those of us who lived through it, everyone, including me, believed that the result we'd achieved was one that would serve all of our stakeholder groups well. With the benefit of several years' hindsight, all of us realize that the biggest mistake we made was in personalizing the conflict to the extent we did. Ben and I came to embody two extreme positions, which made it impossible for us to compromise and find middle ground, even though I was very much aligned with the company's values and Ben clearly understood that the company had to make money.

My leaving was without bitterness or regret. As a member of the company's board, I would continue to have contact with, and contribute to, what had been such an important part of my life. More than anything else, I personally felt relief, and I certainly took satisfaction in what the company had accomplished in the eight years I'd been there.

Most of my time in 1990 was spent overseeing the franchise department, filling in for a management vacancy. That gave Chuck the opportunity to establish himself as the head of the operating committee without my constantly looking over his shoulder.

My impending departure was noted and honored more than once throughout the year. At the all-company meeting in June, Rick Brown, our director of sales, greeted me dressed like Mr. T. The jewelry he was wearing was not of the costume variety. A few minutes later, I found out why. Like Mr. Clean before him, the real Mr. T had come in search of the only CEO in America who had a rubber stamp with his face on it.

At the October all-company meeting, I fulfilled my one outstanding obligation to the company. Dressed in a wet suit, I jumped into and swam a few laps in the sewage pretreatment lagoons that had finally been built behind the Waterbury plant. They would once and for all resolve the problems with our waste water that had plagued us since we'd moved to Waterbury. In trying to get the treatment plant built, we'd endured lawsuits by our neighbors challenging our zoning permits, an engineer who'd gone bust, and leaks in the liner, and had been fined by the state for delays in construction.

Phil Mirvis thought the event conveyed the perfect message—that I was willing to get down and swim in shit for the company. (Actually, it was milky water. The domestic waste was piped directly to the municipal treatment plant and never hit our lagoons.) Hell, I was only swimming in it. Ben had actually drunk the stuff.

CHAPTER EIGHTEEN

Turning Values into Value

ales in 1989 were $58 million, a 23-percent increase over the $48 million we had posted the previous year. That was the lowest percentage increase in sales in the company's history—a significant reduction from the 50-percent-plus growth in 1988 and 1987 and the five previous years, when we'd roughly doubled in size every twelve months. It might have been the best thing that could have happened, in that it finally gave our systems and people a chance to catch up.

The impact of the increase in sales was further mitigated by the decision we had made in 1988 to co-pack our pints. All of the incremental volume was being produced for the company, under contract, at the Dreyer's/Edy's ice cream plant in Fort Wayne, Indiana. A full-time quality-assurance staff was sent to Indiana to ensure that our product specs were met, and that all of the dairy products used in the ice cream were shipped from Vermont, but otherwise we didn't have to hire additional employees in order to achieve the increase in sales. For the first time since the Waterbury factory had been built in 1985, there was no ongoing construction and we weren't asking our people to produce more ice cream than they had the previous summer.

Signs that we had made meaningful progress the previous two years on the overall organizational development work were confirmed by a confidential written opinion survey given to all our employees in January 1990. Eighty-six percent had positive overall job satisfaction, and 88 percent were proud to work for the company. Two-thirds thought that there was lots of family feeling in the company.

Some of the most surprising results of the survey had to do with the company's social mission. Contrary to what most of us had assumed, 85 percent of the employees claimed to understand it, and 78 percent supported it. Asked how the social mission related to their own values, 61 percent thought it was pretty much in tune with where they were at. Only 27 percent considered it too radical. Twelve percent thought it too conservative!

The survey responses, of course, were not entirely positive, and they identified a few "freezer doors" that hadn't been fixed. Almost half of the manufacturing staff cited continuing problems with the quality and reliability of the equipment they were using, 58 percent of all employees said that departments weren't cooperating, half of the employees thought there was too much firefighting, and about the same number were concerned about the company's burgeoning bureaucracy.

In terms of communication, which had been the number-one problem that the staff identified at the October 1987 all-staff meeting, the results were favorable. Five methods of putting out information to the organization, including the *Daily Plant* and all-company meetings, were judged to be effective by a majority of our employees.

Interestingly, what in most companies was the number-one method of spreading news was only considered effective by a little more than half of our staff. "Your grapevine sucks," Phil Mirvis said when he reported back the results to us.

The improvement in morale within the organization could also be traced to our willingness to acknowledge the problems that existed. In a series of articles in the *Daily Plant* and through lots of one-on-one meetings, we had openly begun to address issues that were of concern to our employees, such as job security, how to resolve conflicts with supervisors, and whether employees needed to conform to a prescribed set of political beliefs in order to satisfy the social mission. Most of the people who worked at Ben & Jerry's were willing to accept that things were less than perfect, as long as they knew we were aware of what the problems were, and perceived that we were trying to fix them.

We'd been equally successful over the past two years in establishing our product in the marketplace. Our market share had increased to 25 percent, and we were now the number-two superpremium brand of ice cream, the only legitimate challenger to Häagen-Dazs, which still dominated with 62 percent of the category's total sales. Kraft, which had been acquired by Philip Morris, had never been able to reestablish Frusen Glädjé as a viable contender, and its market share was now less than 10 percent and still eroding.

Likewise, Steve's had taken a tumble and now accounted for less than 3 percent of the sales of superpremium ice cream. Although he had been able to sell the ice cream into the retail stores, Richie Smith had never created a marketing strategy that connected with consumers. The "Two Real Guys" campaign had successfully positioned our brand as the original, down-home, funky superpremium ice cream, and the packaged Steve's product as a clone. Recognizing that, Richie had recently redesigned the Steve's pint, taking the fake head off the container and giving it what a company spokesperson referred to as the "urban sophisticated look."

The failure of Steve's to establish itself as a viable brand in the supermarkets had little overall impact on Richie's still-growing ice cream empire. His New York distribution business was as strong as ever, and through Steve's, which he'd taken public in 1986, Richie had acquired Swensen's and an 86-percent interest in Heidi's Frogen Yozurt Shoppes. Between the three brands, Richie now controlled a retail ice cream and yogurt business with more than 450 outlets.

And he had anything but given up on Steve's. In September of 1989, trying to capitalize on the country's increasing fixation on desserts that were lower in fat and calories, he had introduced Steve's Light. Richie's move coincided with a similar one at Ben & Jerry's, and followed the launch of "light" products by most of the premium and regular ice cream manufacturers.

Our Light had been introduced at our franchised scoop shops in July 1989. At the time, the retail stores were facing stiff competition from the yogurt shops that were proliferating across the country, and our franchises desperately wanted to offer a product their customers perceived as being healthier.

Technically, Light was an ice milk that was made from a mix formula that had only a 7-percent butterfat content. That compared with the 10-percent minimum required by law in order to label a frozen dessert "ice cream," and the 15-percent butterfat content of our original product line. Still, in many ways, the notion of a superpremium light was an oxymoron. While it was true that the product had one-third less fat and 40 percent less cholesterol than our ice cream, a four-ounce portion of Ben & Jerry's Light had approximately nine grams of fats, 40 milligrams of cholesterol, and 220 calories. "It's not sprouts," I noted when I saw the nutritional breakdown.

Our initial plan was to test-market Light, first in bulk in our scoop shops, and then in pints in a few selected cities. If the tests went well, the product would be rolled out nationally for the spring of 1990, the traditional time of year when new frozen desserts are introduced in supermarkets. But once again, Richie Smith's plans changed ours. Faced with the prospect of being preempted by Steve's Light, we decided to roll out Light pints in all of our markets in the fall of 1989.

Unlike 1986, this time we had a huge advantage over Richie. Our Light was a line extension of a successful product that had a growing 25-percent market share. Steve's Light was a spinoff of a brand that for all intents and purposes had failed. There were certainly retailers who, given the right slotting fee and introductory allowance, would take in anything, but most buyers, having already tried and tossed the original Steve's out of their stores, would be less inclined to give the reincarnated product a chance.

Ben's original idea for marketing Light was to put a "skinny-ized" photo of him and Jerry on the lid, duplicating the look of a distorted mirror in a funhouse. As part of the promotion, customers could send a photo of themselves to us for similar treatment. There was also talk about a Ben & Jerry's exercise video.

Some of us thought the idea of advertising weight loss, even in what was such an obviously a tongue-in-cheek manner, bordered on deception, given that the product was hardly health food. That became even more of an issue when Ben proposed a TV spot that re-created the earlier format of him and Jerry, live, in an oversized lid. Each would be wearing Groucho Marx disguises. The proposed copy: "We got so skinny eating Ben & Jerry's Light, people don't recognize us anymore." After considerable debate, Ben agreed to change the word "skinny" to "healthy."

By far the best promotion for the new product line was the "Thousand Pints of Light" campaign. In each market, we identified a local hero who was doing something meaningful to give back to his or her community, and arranged a celebration to recognize the person's efforts. Jerry, who attended most of the events, began each with an announcement. "We've had the tape from the 1988 Republican convention analyzed," he'd say, "and it turns out that the President was misquoted. He didn't say 'a thousand *points* of light.' He said *pints.*"

One award went to Norvell Smith, a fifteen-year-old from an inner-city Chicago neighborhood who had spoken out against the gang violence that had resulted in the deaths of three of her classmates. Another went to Marianne "Mother" Wright from San Francisco, a sixty-year-old mother of twelve children who made meals out of her home to feed the homeless in a local park.

Immediately on the heels of the roll-out of Light, the company introduced Rainforest Crunch, the pint flavor made with the Brazil- and cashew-nut brittle from Ben's new venture, Community Products, Inc. Not realizing at the time that he was going to get so reinvolved at Ben & Jerry's, Ben had followed through and successfully launched the business the previous fall. The timing of the product couldn't have been better; it was released just in time for the twentieth anniversary of Earth Day, when the country's environmental consciousness was at a peak. Instead of using the standard container for the flavor, a rain- forest-themed package was designed that told consumers how they could support the efforts of those who were working to stop world- wide deforestation.

Sales in 1990 were $77 million, on which the company posted after-tax profits of $2.6 million. Not all the news was good, though. Light was in trouble. Lots of people tried it—once—then went back to our original ice cream or whatever other frozen desserts they'd been eating. Part of the problem was the quality of the product. It tasted pretty good in the factory, but without the high butterfat content to give it body, it was prone to get icy and grainy within the channels of distribution. Steve's Light fared no better, and by the end of the year it was apparent that there wasn't a market for a superpremium ice milk.

This meant that our franchised scoop shops still didn't have a product that offered their health-conscious customers a legitimate alternative to the yogurt shops. Many of our shop owners had seen their business fall off 20 percent or more as TCBY and other chains opened up nearby. They implored us to develop a truly low fat prod- uct. In response, we introduced five flavors of yogurt in bulk, exclu- sively for use in our scoop shops, during the summer of 1990.

In January of 1991, Häagen-Dazs, which had sat on the sidelines when Steve's and Ben & Jerry's came out with Light, entered the low-fat fray with a frozen yogurt that was packaged in pints. Their entry into the market followed the successful introduction by several independent manufacturers, including Élan, Columbo, Honey Hill, and Yoplait, of frozen yogurts that were now competing directly with the superpremium ice creams.

When it became apparent that Light was failing in the supermarkets, Chuck and Ben decided to package our yogurt in pints. With luck, we could exchange one product for the other without giving up any shelf space to our competitors.

The yogurt was made with a 2 percent butterfat mix and satisfied the "industry" low-fat standard, although some of the flavors, most notably Heath Bar Crunch and Coffee Almond Fudge, weren't really low-fat once the chunks were added in. The fruit flavors, though—Raspberry, Blueberry Cheesecake, and Banana Strawberry—were. A four-ounce portion had less than two grams of fat and approximately 135 calories. And they tasted great. Despite our late entry into the category, by the end of 1992 Ben & Jerry's was the number-one superpremium yogurt in the country.

The other new product that was introduced in the spring of 1991 was Chocolate Chip Cookie Dough ice cream. The flavor had actually been "invented" in the fall of 1984 in the Burlington Scoop Shop. By way of the big pad of paper that was hung in the store to solicit feedback and ideas, an anonymous customer had suggested putting raw cookie dough in ice cream. Davis Sutherland, one of the ice cream makers, or "screamers" as they called themselves, got Gene Steinfeld, the baker, to make up a batch of raw dough without salt or baking soda in it. Gene spread the dough out on a pan and put it in the hardener. When it was frozen, Davis chopped it up into cubes and tossed it into a batch of vanilla ice cream.

Cookie Dough was a huge and immediate hit in the store, so much so that the owners of the other scoop shops in the area started to complain because the flavor wasn't available to them. (The Burlington store still made on the premises almost all of the ice cream it sold, and as a result, it was able to offer a much greater variety of flavors than could our franchised scoop shops, which could get some forty flavors in bulk from our factory.) People were going into the area franchise shops, asking for Cookie Dough, and when they were told that it wasn't available, they walked out and drove into downtown Burlington to get it.

Cookie Dough became my favorite flavor, and after we moved into the Waterbury plant in the summer of 1985, I declared that getting the flavor into pints was our first and foremost R&D project. Mass-producing the flavor in our factory, however, turned out to be harder than anyone imagined. Like the cream filling in the Oreo cookies, the dough got stuck in the fruit feeder.

At first we tried to make the dough less gummy by adding milk powder and different sugars, but it dried it out so much that it no longer had that gooey, brown-sugary taste. We also tried to liquefy the dough and pump it into the ice cream, and coat the dough in chocolate in hopes that it would slip through the fruit feeder. It did, but the chocolate overpowered the dough and we never got the taste right.

More than five years after trying endless variations of countless solutions, my number-one project was still on the drawing boards. Then one day, Peter Lind, the head of R&D, was at Rhino Foods, a small Burlington-area food manufacturer, talking about the cookie and brownie batters that were baked in our franchised scoop shops. As they discussed the problems we were having getting a cookie dough to feed into the ice cream, Peter and Ted Castle, the owner of Rhino, came up with a possible solution.

An initial run showed some promise, although at first we kept getting "molecular structures" as the dough clumped together. The task was turned over to a team of employees, including line staff from production, maintenance, and quality assurance. After every run, Peter and Ted debriefed the team on what had gone right and what had gone wrong, and they made adjustments—reconfiguring the line, altering one of the procedures on how they handled the dough prior to putting it in the fruit feeder, and so on.

Finally they got it, and Chocolate Chip Cookie Dough was introduced in March. Within two months it was our best-selling flavor, the first time Heath Bar Crunch had been dislodged from the top of the list.

Other than the development of new flavors and products, the area where Ben's return was having the biggest impact was in marketing. The search for someone who could work with Ben and manage the department was completed shortly after Ben returned full-time when we hired Holly Alves, who had been the marketing director at Esprit clothing.

The company's strategy was referred to internally as "relationship marketing"—developing a connection with our customers that went beyond that achieved by traditional advertising and promotions. One of the first examples of how we'd done that successfully was the factory tours, which had begun in 1986, a year after the Waterbury plant was opened. By 1991 it was the largest tourist attraction in the state of Vermont, drawing over 225,000 paid admissions for the year.

219

The tours offered us an incredible opportunity to create what we hoped would be "customers for life." With paid advertising, we had ten seconds or a momentary scan of a page, in among the clutter of other ads and the medium's editorial content, to capture a consumer's attention and convince that person to buy our ice cream. On the tours, we had the rapt attention of our customers for over an hour, which afforded us an unparalleled opportunity to educate visitors on our company's history, products, and business philosophy.

Attempting to combine some of those same elements with a community celebration that harked back to the days of Fall Down, Ben came up with the "One World, One Heart Festival." "One of the nice things about becoming bigger is that you can throw bigger parties," the flyer for the event stated. "This festival is a time to play and celebrate together—it's also an opportunity to take the first step in a sustained effort at working together for a more just world."

The first of the three 1991 festivals was held at Stowe, Vermont, in conjunction with our annual shareholders' meeting. In addition to a full lineup of music, which ranged from Toots and the Maytals to NRBQ, the free, two-day festival featured opportunities for social activism. For twenty-five cents you could buy a stamped postcard with which you could write your congressperson and tell him or her whatever was on your mind. Completed cards could be turned in for free ice cream cones.

There were "new games" such as "Human Bowling" and the "Tug of Love"; a multiscreen slide-and-sound show by Patrick Giantonio entitled "Footsteps into Change," which documented his four-year walk across the African continent; and a huge truck that dumped a billion seeds of grass in an attempt to help people conceive how much money we were spending on the military.

The festival was organized by Evie Dworetzky, the company's self-described "special events logistics freak." Almost all three hundred of our employees worked at the festival, doing everything from coordinating traffic in the parking lots to scooping ice cream. It was an incredible team effort, and just about everyone came away incredibly pumped up that we had been able to pull off a party for 22,000 people without a hitch, on the weekend before the Fourth of July and the ice cream industry's busiest week. Later in the summer and that fall, the event was repeated on the Navy Pier in Chicago and in Golden Gate Park in San Francisco.

To increase our reach beyond those who could visit our factory or attend one of the three festivals, the company purchased a bus to transport a three-member troupe of "new vaudevillians" on a cross-country tour. The vehicle was completely retrofitted, equipped with a stage that pulled out from underneath, and solar panels on the roof that ran the freezers and sound system. The bus drove from town to town, putting on shows that were either free or raised money for a local cause, at which we could also give away ice cream. Sampling was a major component of our marketing strategy. We were convinced that if we could get our ice cream and yogurt into people's mouths, they'd be inclined to buy it.

There was an indirect benefit that went beyond those who had a firsthand experience with any of the above-mentioned marketing events. The offbeat nature of the promotions, combined with the fact that most had either a tangible social benefit or helped articulate the values of the company, helped to feed what Chuck described as the "word-of-mouth network." As a result, they generated both tremendous goodwill among our customers and attention in the media that multiplied their impact many times over.

The years 1990, 1991, and 1992 were also notable for our progress in clarifying and bringing focus to the company's social mission. At board meetings, the debate was no longer over whether it was appropriate for the company to attempt various initiatives, but was instead a discussion on how best to implement them. We began to think of the social mission in terms of three distinct components: how we did business; what stands we took on issues; and how we chose focus areas for our public agenda.

The first component referred to our workplace and business practices, and recognized that we had to demonstrate socially responsible behavior within the company for us to have any credibility when we spoke out on national or global issues. It was our intent to be an excellent employer and to make sure, whenever possible, that our actions as a business took into consideration more than just the financial bottom line.

One example of the above was our efforts to find additional alternative suppliers like Greyston, from which we had bought over $830,000 worth of brownies in 1991. In 1990 we produced Wild Maine Blueberry as a seasonal flavor, purchasing the fruit from the Passamaquoddy Indians in northeastern Maine. We weren't aware of it at the time, but the 2,700-member Passamaquoddy tribe had won a

$40-million land-claim suit in 1980, and had managed their money so effectively that it had become a case study at the Harvard Business School. Ben & Jerry's $330,000 blueberry purchase was just a small part of the tribe's successful economic development efforts.

The company also found a cookie to substitute for the Oreos we'd been using, following through on a commitment we'd made at a shareholders' meeting a few years earlier no longer to do business with a company that marketed cigarettes.

In 1991 the company also reaffirmed its support for the Vermont dairy farmers whose cows supplied our company with the basic ingredients of our ice cream and yogurt. After federal support programs were cut, which resulted in a 25-percent decline in milk prices, we announced our intent to pay the farmers who supplied us a premium that was based upon the average price for milk between 1986 and 1990. "We would not expect any of our other suppliers to sell to us at prices below their cost of production," Ben said, in announcing the board's decision, "and we don't expect it of our dairy suppliers, either." The roughly half-million dollars was going to come out of "our profits, where it doesn't belong, and into farmers' pockets, where it does belong."

Other actions that fit into this component of the social mission included committing the company's excess cash to investment vehicles designed to blend financial growth with social purpose, and operating the company in a way that minimized our impact on the environment. In 1992, Ben & Jerry's publicly codified that commitment when it became what was to date the largest company to sign the CERES principles, a set of environmental guidelines for businesses that were promulgated by a coalition of environmental groups in response to the *Exxon Valdez* oil spill off the coast of Alaska.

The second component of the social mission was taking a stand on issues. In 1990, following up on Ben and Chuck's participation at the anti-Seabrook rally, we placed a billboard in opposition to the licensing of the nuclear power plant that read, "Stop Seabrook, Keep Our Customers Alive and Licking."

Also in 1990, the company started working with other progressive, socially responsible businesses by creating an organization called ACT NOW. The group's first action was an attempt to build support for passage of the Bryan bill, which would have increased the fuel-efficiency standards for the auto industry. Reducing the country's dependence on foreign oil was a particularly relevant issue at the time, given the events that were unfolding in the Persian Gulf.

As a follow-up to ACT NOW's initial efforts, eighteen businesses took out a full-page ad in *The New York Times* on Christmas Eve, 1990. Under the headline "An Unnecessary War," the ad called for the President and members of Congress to give the economic sanctions against Iraq a chance to work. It also urged that the country begin work immediately on a national energy policy based on conservation and development of alternative energy sources. "The price of gasoline," it concluded, "should never be a reason to send our sons and daughters off to die in a foreign war." According to Milton Moskowitz, a pioneering writer in the field of corporate social responsibility, it was the first time that actual business logos were used in conjunction with a stand against war.

The company also took a stand in 1991 against James Bay II, the second phase of the largest hydroelectric power complex in the world. Given the highly visible position we had taken on preservation of the Brazilian rain forests, we were challenged by several employees in the Waterbury factory to pay comparable attention to the indigenous people of Québec, who were living almost literally in our backyard.

Prior to taking a position, the company sent a group of seven rank-and-file employees to tour the first phase of the project and spend a week living with the Cree Indians whose land would be lost to the dammed rivers. A statement that was drafted by the employees upon their return, which called into question the social and environmental justification for flooding an area the size of Lake Erie, was printed by the company in the *Burlington Free Press* as a full-page ad.

The final component of the social mission was to take a single focus area and integrate it into the company's marketing and promotions. It was an attempt to get away from the "cause of the month" mentality that led many in the company to conclude that some of our early efforts were too scattered and not of enough substance to have a measurable impact other than to generate favorable publicity. Any previous attempts to focus the social mission had resulted in five or six categories that were so broad (i.e., economic disparity, world peace) they eliminated only a handful of possibilities. At the end of 1991 we decided to pick just one cause and put all the resources of the company behind it. After soliciting input from throughout the company, the area the board chose to focus on for the next two years was children.

A key aspect of the effort would be working to promote the Children's Defense Fund's "Leave No Child Behind" campaign.

We also decided in 1991 to create a senior executive position to head up the social mission, and hired Liz Bankowski, a member of our board of directors, to work for us full time. Her job was to coordinate our actions and make sure that we were holding ourselves accountable to objective goals. It was our intention to achieve quantifiable results from our efforts, and to treat the social mission no differently from any other area of the business. Since 1988, a review of our social performance that was compiled and/or verified by an independent auditor had been included in our annual shareholders' report, along with the company's financial statements.

As we continued to actualize the social mission of the company in increasingly nontraditional ways, the donations of both cash and product that the company made became a smaller component of how we defined what a socially responsible business could be. Still, they were substantial and increasing in size every year.

Allocations to the Ben & Jerry's Foundation, which represented 7.5 percent of our pre-tax profits, were $528,000 in 1991 and now totaled more than $1.5 million for the seven years since it had been created. Another $61,000, half of the revenues from the factory tours, was given out by a committee of employees that made grants mostly to local organizations in the communities in Vermont in which we operated retail and manufacturing facilities. Through yet another program, over $200,000, which represented a percentage of sales of our factory-second pints, was earmarked annually for local causes throughout the state. It was also still the company's policy to try to accommodate every Vermont-based nonprofit and community group's request for ice cream donations.

Ultimately the social mission and, in particular, its most radical elements were what came to define the company in our customers' minds. Although some people were offended by specific positions that the company took, a substantial and growing core group of consumers were more inclined to buy our products because of the values of the company that had produced them.

When the board had first talked about the social mission back in 1988, we had debated what impact it would have on the profitability of the company. By the end of 1991 we had our answer. Sales for the year were up another 26 percent, to $97 million, a tenfold increase from 1985. Profits were up 43 percent from the previous year, to $3.7

million. In 1992, sales jumped another 36 percent, to $132 million, while profits increased a whopping 79 percent, to $6.7 million.

In a letter to our shareholders in early 1992, Ben wrote,

> The most amazing thing is that our social values—that part of our company mission statement that calls us to use our power as a business to improve the quality of life in our local, national and international communities—have actually helped us to become a stable, profitable, high-growth company. This is especially interesting because it flies in the face of those business theorists who state that publicly held corporations cannot make a profit and help the community at the same time, and moreover that such companies have no business trying to do so. The issues here are heart, soul, love and spirituality. Corporations which exist solely to maximize profit become disconnected from their soul—the spiritual interconnectedness of humanity. Like individuals, businesses can conduct themselves with the knowledge that the hearts, souls and spirits of all people are interconnected; so that as we help others, we cannot help helping ourselves.

Indeed, Ben felt so good about the way things were going at the start of 1992 that he decided to take a six-month sabbatical. Given that he had come and gone more than once, there was some unfounded public speculation about whether he'd return. A short piece in the March 30 issue of *Forbes*, which broke the story, said that Ben had quit as CEO after coming down "with a bad case of the guilties" over the company's financial success. The article claimed he had traded in his Saab for a pickup truck and gone on a rice-and-beans diet as a gesture of solidarity with the masses of the Third World. The day the magazine hit the streets our stock dropped four points, losing 10 percent of its value.

Overall, however, the company's financial performance had earned the respect of Wall Street. Even *Forbes*, when forced to discount politics and evaluate the company based strictly on its five-year average return on equity, had to agree. In November 1992 the company was named to the magazine's list of "The 200 Best Small Companies in America" for the third straight year.

The one thing *Forbes* did get right was Ben's change of vehicles. He was intending to spend his sabbatical doing some sculptural things

225

involving welding, and had gotten the truck so he could pick up scrap metal at the junkyard.

"It appears that the financial community overreacted to Ben's announcement in February that he was taking a six-month sabbatical," Chuck stated in the press release that went out with our next earnings report. "In addition to a strong increase in sales and profits, we are pleased to announce that Ben's most recent sabbatical activity was a successful welding of ferrous and nonferrous metals while making a new mailbox for Jerry. The mailbox should be complete by the end of the second quarter."

Epilogue
July 1993

If Those Idiots Ben and Jerry Can Do It, Why Can't We?

"The nineties are the sixties standing on your head."
—Wavy Gravy

In 1992 the company broke ground in St. Albans, Vermont, on what will be our third manufacturing plant. When it comes on line, sometime in 1994, it will enable the company to end its co-packing arrangement and return 100 percent of the company's production to Vermont, as was always intended.

Chocolate Chip Cookie Dough became a national phenomenon and was selected as one of *Fortune* magazine's "Products of the Year" for 1992, along with Apple's Powerbook computer and Ross Perot! It's people eating Cookie Dough, Ross, not NAFTA, that's making that giant sucking sound.

The success of Cookie Dough didn't go unnoticed within the industry, and by the end of year virtually every ice cream manufacturer had introduced a variation of the flavor—even Häagen-Dazs. Our formerly staid competitor, which is now owned by Grand Metropolitan PLC, a British conglomerate, introduced a complete line of chunked and funky flavors, called Exträas, which were targeted right at our market niche.

With the emergence of frozen yogurt, we reconfigured the market data we were accumulating to include all the superpremium frozen desserts in a single category. At the end of 1992 our market share was 35 percent, compared with Häagen-Dazs's 47 percent. Frusen Glädjé

227

had less than 1 percent of the market. Steve's volume was almost nil. The number-three brand in the category was Columbo Yogurt, which had a 5-percent share.

One notable market entry in 1990 was Simple Pleasures, an imitation ice cream made with Simplesse, a fake fat that was being marketed by NutraSweet. It was Robert B. Shapiro, the company's then chairman and CEO, who reportedly asked the rhetorical question from which this section of the book derives it's title, while dining with executives of Ogilvy & Mather, NutraSweet's advertising agency. Simple Pleasures ended the year with a rapidly eroding 3-percent share, and was being written off by most people within the industry.

Maintaining sales growth at the huge rates that Ben & Jerry's posted in 1991 and 1992 will be difficult. The superpremium category is not growing at the same rate as it was when frozen yogurt was being added to the category in 1991 and 1992, and with most of the weaker players already reduced in size, future increases in market share will be harder to achieve. There may still be debates at future board meetings about growth, but it's possible those debates will be about there not being enough growth as opposed to too much.

Recognizing that the company needs to continue to innovate in order to maintain its edge, it introduced its newest flavor, Wavy Gravy, in July 1993. The flavor is named after the announcer at Woodstock, and it's the first food product to be packaged in a tie-dyed container. The story of the development of Wavy is a book in itself. Over two years in the making, its final(?) formulation is rumored to be cashew and Brazil-nut ice cream with almonds, caramel, and a chocolate-hazelnut swirl.

The transition of leadership from me to Chuck went well, and a follow-up employee survey given in 1992, two years after the original questionnaire, showed even more promising results than the first time around. Ninety-three percent of the employees said they liked working for Ben & Jerry's; 84 percent thought the social mission was important to the company's success.

The general consensus, though, is that we've backslid some since then. The incredible sales growth in the past two years and the increase in the number of facilities and employees have re-created many of the same organizational problems the company faced in 1987. We've begun to realize that the struggle to continue to actualize the social mission in increasingly innovative and powerful ways, and at the same time run a growing business profitably, presents ongoing challenges that the company will always face.

In some ways, the external reputation of the company still exceeds the internal reality—something that Chuck, Ben, and Jerry are well aware of. "We do not represent ourselves to be the most environmentally sensitive, socially conscious, well-run company in the country," Ben wrote in his letter to shareholders in the 1992 annual report. "We discover daily that we can learn from other companies about concerns such as environmental awareness, company and community team building, development of minority-owned supplier relationships, employee ownership, and grassroots global activism."

What does make the company unique, however, is its willingness to acknowledge its shortcomings publicly, going so far as to print them as part of the social assessment in its annual report to shareholders. For all of its successes and failures, both perceived and real, the leadership of the company remains committed to improving the quality of the organization continuously.

Some aspects of the culture were bound to change with the transition from my leadership to Chuck's. Though his management style is more reserved than mine, Chuck did dress up in a pink tutu on Halloween. Chuck has what he once described to his managers as "inner enthusiasm." "When you go through life over six foot eight, you spend most of your time trying not to stand out," he says.

Chuck's ascent to the presidency was celebrated by the *Daily Plant*, which, in the tradition of the Disfigure Fred's Head contest, encouraged our employees to "Displacy Lacy's Facey." Unrelated to the above, in 1993 the *Plant* was replaced by *The Rolling Cone*, a semimonthly newspaper with a slightly more serious news bent.

The company's famous five-to-one salary ratio was increased by the board to seven-to-one at the end of 1990, after two years of debate, but the compensation policies of the company remain a divisive issue at the board level that is still unresolved as of this writing.

Adding to the debate on compensation and the goal of linking the prosperity of employees throughout the organization to the company's performance are the comments of Paul Hawken, who did the 1992 independent assessment of our social performance that's printed in our annual report. Despite an across-the-board grant in 1986, by which all our employees received the equivalent of 10 percent of their salary in stock as a one-time bonus, and an ongoing plan that enables employees to purchase stock at 85 percent of market value, Paul pointed out that, not including Ben, Jerry, and a few other senior managers, less than half of one percent of the company is owned by employees. Between 1990 and 1992 the company's market value increased substantially, but for the most part our employees weren't the beneficiaries of that increased wealth. Belatedly, the board is trying to address the issue.

Many of the managers who participated in the organizational development work with Phil Mirvis are no longer with the company. Dave Barash stepped aside as the head of human resources, and now works with Liz Bankowski on the social mission. Jim Miller, the head of manufacturing, resigned in 1993. Rick Brown, the boisterous director of sales, left at the end of 1990 and, for a time, worked for Richie Smith.

Phil's only ongoing involvement with the company has been to administer the biannual employee survey. He's living on a farm outside of Washington, D.C., writing, and consulting with other businesses.

Jerry is more involved in the management of the business than at any time since he left for Arizona in 1982. His responsibilities have included filling in as the director of sales, and along with Chuck and Ben, Jerry is now actively involved in setting the strategic direction for the business. He and Elizabeth were married in 1977 and have a son.

Ben did return to work in September 1992, after his sabbatical. He enjoyed the time off, but didn't do as much welding as he would have liked. Despite the bold prediction that went out with our earnings report, Jerry's mailbox has yet to be completed.

Chuck's relationship with Ben has been a positive one. When the new office space was being designed, Chuck put his, Jerry's, and Ben's offices all in a row, with sliding glass doors in between, literally aligning the three of them. Ben, refusing the corner office, wound up in the middle.

Ben's role still comes up regularly at board meetings. He remains interested in being less active, yet at the same time immerses himself in the operational details of whatever projects are of interest to him. In short, Ben is still Ben.

Discussions on compensation policies aside, board meetings are much more civil than in years past. In 1992, Frederick A. Miller, an African American who is the president of the Kaleel Jamison Consulting Group, joined the board. In a reversal of roles, I now find myself as an outside director whose job it is to hold Chuck, Ben, and Jerry accountable for the performance of the company. Yes, Virginia, there is a Santa Claus.

The end of the Cold War hastened the demise of 1% For Peace. It changed its name to Business Partnership for Peace, and, in 1993, was merged into Businesses for Social Responsibility, which also absorbed ACT NOW. BSR, which counts such *Fortune* 500 companies as Reebok and Stride-Rite among its members, grew out of a Social Venture Network meeting and is intended to be a voice for progressive businesses in the media and legislature. The legacy of 1% For Peace, perhaps, is that it showed that businesses can play a role in trying to address the basic issues confronting society. Consistent with our decision to focus the social mission on a single issue, the copy on the package for the Peace Pops now describes the Children's Defense Fund's "Leave No Child Behind" campaign.

The gas station where the business began was home to two more entrepreneurial ventures after Ben & Jerry's moved out in 1981—Pops Tropi-Grill and the Slippery Banana produce stand. Neither endured, and in January 1984, the structure was torn down and converted into a parking lot for an adjacent office building. The aluminum skin of the gas station was saved during the demolition, and each piece was photographed and numbered. It currently resides in a warehouse and the old gas station may be resurrected by the company one day, perhaps in Waterbury as part of the factory tours.

Lyn Severance, the freelance artist who created Ben & Jerry's graphic image, stopped doing work for the company in 1982, but became the head of our art department in 1987.

Don Rose still works at the IBM plant in Essex Junction, Vermont, and plays piano in the Burlington area on the side. He continues to put his membership in the Ice Cream for Life Club to good use.

Lanny Watts still refuses to advertise his plumbing services in the Yellow Pages, and continues to regret his decision to cash in his membership in the club, so many potential ice cream cones ago.[1]

With great—some would say atypical—foresight, I conferred membership in the club on myself, prior to stepping down as CEO.

Jeff Furman also joined the club. Despite living and working in Ithaca, Jeff had at one time shared almost equally with Ben and me in the management of the company, albeit from a distance. He had been

---

1. If you live in the Burlington area and you need a good plumber, call Lanny at 862-3392.

instrumental in all of the company's fund-raising, and in many ways had been responsible for our balance sheet, in the same way I was responsible for the income statement. With the emergence of the management team, Jeff's role diminished, and after spending most of his time in 1988 through 1990 on social mission initiatives, he too resigned. He remains a member of the company's board of directors, and oversees certain projects for the business from time to time.

Two of Jeff's most significant undertakings came to fruition in 1992. After multiple trips to the Soviet Union, Jeff and Ben finally found joint-venture partners for a scoop shop in Russia to be located in Petrozavodsk, a city two hundred miles from the Arctic circle, up around the Finnish border. The city was chosen because it's in Karelia, the region of Russia with which Vermont has a sister-state relationship. Dave Morse, a shift supervisor in the Waterbury plant, spent a summer learning Russian and was then sent to Petrozavodsk with his wife, Katie, and two kids, under instructions not to come back home until the shop was up and running. Overcoming incredible adversity, some of which was created by the breakup of the Soviet Union, Dave somehow got the store built. In July 1992, I tagged along with Ben and Jeff on a trip to Russia for the store's grand opening, an event that was blessed by a black-robed Russian Orthodox priest. The store manufactures all of its ice cream and, since they aren't otherwise available, also bakes its cones on the premises. The first-year traffic counts matched any in our franchise system, and the store is actually making rubles.

One week after the Russian store started serving ice cream, our latest Partnershop, modeled after the first one Jeff had started in Ithaca, opened on 125th Street in Harlem. The store is run by Joe Holland, an African American who graduated from Harvard Law School. Seventy-five percent of the profits of the store will go toward a nearby drug-counseling center and homeless shelter that Holland helped found eight years ago. Residents of the shelter are employed at the store, giving them an opportunity, as at the Greyston Bakery, to break the cycle of homelessness and return to normal life.

The Greyston Bakery made $1.5 million worth of brownies for the company in 1992.

In 1993 the company started buying apple pies for an Apple Pie yogurt, from LaSoul Bakery in Red Bank, New Jersey. LaSoul has its roots in the ministry of Reverend James W. Carter, who started to offer counseling and guidance to recovering alcohol and drug addicts in 1985.

Most of my time since leaving Ben & Jerry's has been spent writing this book or traveling with my wife, Yvette. Less than forty-eight hours after my last day at work, we left on a three-month trip to Europe and Africa. Toward the end of our travels, we found ourselves confined at the airport in Nairobi, Kenya, with a ten-hour layover before our connecting flight that night onto Zurich.

There were no international flights scheduled until the evening, and the terminal was deserted. Yvette took off to walk through the duty-free shops, and I sat down in a molded plastic chair in front of a TV that was permanently tuned to CNN.

After thirty minutes or so, an upcoming feature story titled "Having Fun at Work" was previewed by the announcer. "Maybe they'll mention us," I thought, and sure enough, after describing the antics of Herb Kelleher, the CEO of Southwest Airlines, they started to describe the Joy Gang at Ben & Jerry's. I watched the screen in disbelief. There I was, along with three other employees, all of us dressed like Elvis, singing "Hound Dog."

Instinctively, I turned to nudge the person next to me, ready to say something like "Hey, that's me," only there wasn't anybody else around. I looked back up at the TV, but the reporter was already talking about some other company, and a minute later CNN was back to the post–Gulf War news that still dominated its coverage.

So I sat there, halfway around the world from Vermont, contemplating the past eight years and what I'd just seen on TV, and I wondered to myself, "Now did that really happen, or did I just imagine it?"

Acknowledgments

any people, some of whom are only mentioned briefly in the book, and others who aren't mentioned at all, deserve a great deal of credit for the success that Ben & Jerry's has enjoyed. Included in this list are past and current employees, distributors, retailers, and the owners of our franchised scoop shops. To single out any risks offending others by their exclusion, but I'd be remiss if I didn't personally thank and acknowledge Jim Miller, Dave Barash, Rick Brown, Diane Shea, and my assistants, Cindy Balser-Eaton and Gail Mayville.

Despite having firsthand knowledge of most of the company's history, I conducted extensive interviews while researching the book. Ben, Jerry, Jeff Furman, and I spent two weeks in a tropical climate, during which we collectively reconstructed the past with what I hope is reasonable accuracy. Ben's recollections, although somewhat fuzzy at times, were extremely clear when the subject was food ("Remember the chowder at the Steuben Athletic Club when we met with Ken Cartledge?"). Jerry graciously suggested that I make up whatever I had to. "Who's gonna know?" he asked.

During two days of interviews, Phil Mirvis provided a third-party perspective to the events covered in the second half of the book. His insights, editorial comments on early drafts, encouragement, friendship, and support were invaluable.

Fred Thaler, Jeff Durstewitz, Darrell Mullis, Lanny Watts, Lyn Severance, Don Rose, Mark Mumford, Caryl Stewart, and Don Miller filled in details on Ben and Jerry's youth and the early days at the gas station. Research that Curtis Ingham had done previously for another project also helped re-create the events of that time period.

ACKNOWLEDGMENTS

Diane Shea, Bob Wood, Wendy Yoder, Paul Stephens, Cia Rochford, Martha Perry, Sut Marshall, Jim O'Donnell, Frank Stracuzza, Chuck Green, and Wayne Bernard told me stories about the start of the wholesale business. Steve Cooperman sat for two days of extensive interviews during which he gave me a richly detailed history of the ice cream business in New York.

Interviews were also conducted with Harry Lantz, Allen Martin, Kim Reidinger, Jill Broderick, Ken Cartledge, Howie Fuguet, Phil Snyder, Dan Cox, Peter Lind, Alice Blachly, Chuck Lacy, Liz Bankowski, Rick Brown, Merritt Chandler, and Henry Morgan.

The project would not have been possible without the support of Ben & Jerry's, in particular, its board of directors, all of whom have been previously mentioned except for Fred Miller. Lee Holden, Rob Michalak, Maureen Martin, Sean Greenwood, Nancy Eames, Peter Kennedy, and Arnold Carbone helped me pull together photos and reference material from the company's files. I also want to thank Kayne, who's been holding my calls for two years, Norma for getting me my mail, and Lester for keeping my feet warm.

I'm also deeply indebted to Peter Ginna at Crown, whose editing kept the story focused on its most compelling aspects. His feedback consistently improved the manuscript, and he deserves a great deal of credit for whatever success the book enjoys.

I would also like to thank everyone at Crown who helped with the production and marketing of the book, and my agent, Jane Dystel.

Finally, my heartfelt thanks to my family, including my parents, Bernice and Ralph, my sister, Anita, my stepfather, Milton, and most of all, my wife, Yvette, without whose love and support neither this book, nor the events described in it, would have been possible.

Index

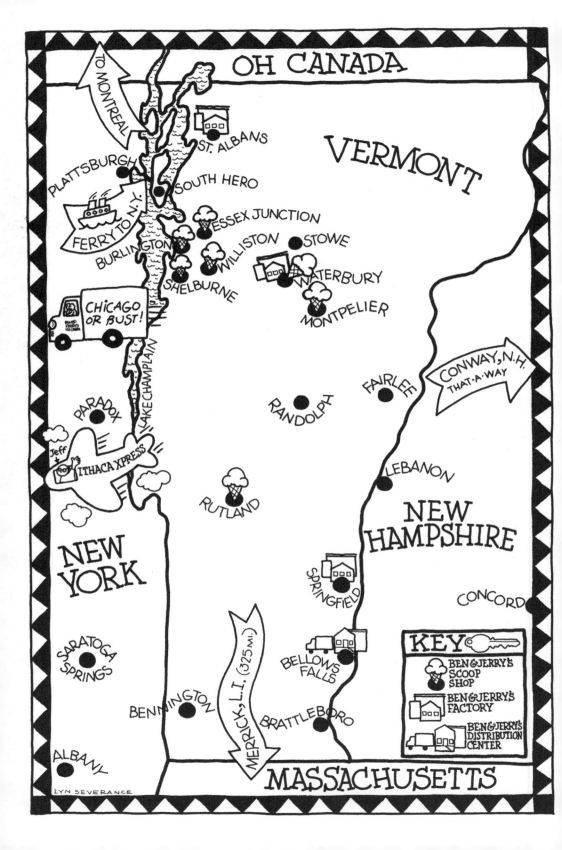